Hike of the Week

A Year of Hikes in the New York Metro Area

D0067734

Hike of the Week

A Year of Hikes in the New York Metro Area

Daniel Chazin

2013

NEW YORK-NEW JERSEY TRAIL CONFERENCE

Library of Congress Cataloging-in-Publication Data

Chazin, Daniel D.
Hike of the week : a year of hikes in the New York metro area / Daniel Chazin.
    pages cm
    Includes index.
    ISBN 978-1-880775-78-3 (pbk.)
    1. Hiking--New York Metropolitan Area--Guidebooks. 2. New York Metropolitan
Area--Guidebooks. I. New York-New Jersey Trail Conference. II. Title.
    GV199.42.N652N482 2013
    917.47'1--dc23

Published by
New York-New Jersey Trail Conference
156 Ramapo Valley Road
Mahwah, New Jersey 07430-1199

Book and cover design: Sara Abad
Cover photo: *A hiker taking in the view from the Hawk Watch in the Mohonk Preserve*
by Daniel Chazin

Table of Contents

Fall

Winter

Preface

This book had its genesis in February 2002, when Ed Goodell, Executive Director of the Trail Conference, received a phone call from Marc Schwarz of *The Record*. The newspaper – the largest newspaper of general circulation in Bergen County, New Jersey – was starting a new section on Thursdays that would be called "*Get Set!*" The theme of the section would be outdoor recreation, and they wanted to publish a hike each week. Marc proposed that they use trail descriptions that appeared in the *New Jersey Walk Book*, and he proposed to start with the description of a particular trail in the Ramapo Valley County Reservation. Ed asked me what I thought of the idea.

I very much liked the idea of a "Hike of the Week," but I pointed out that merely copying a trail description from the *New Jersey Walk Book* was not the way to do it. A *hike* description is quite different from a *trail* description, as most loop hikes incorporate more than one trail. I offered to write a sample loop hike in the Ramapo Reservation, and my offer was accepted. The hike was favorably received, and I was asked to submit another hike for the following week. This continued for the next year and a half, during which I submitted about 75 hikes for publication in the *Get Set!* section.

The *Get Set!* section was discontinued by *The Record* in October 2003, but my hiking column has continued without interruption and has remained consistently popular with its readers. Over the years, my column has appeared in various sections of the newspaper; its frequency has varied between weekly and biweekly.

This book is a selection of 52 hikes taken from the approximately 225 hikes that I wrote for publication in *The Record* between February 2002 and July 2008. The hikes are grouped by season, with the "season" representing the month in which the hike originally appeared in *The Record*. Of course, most of the hikes can be done in any season. Hikes of every level of difficulty have been included, and an effort has been made to include a selection of hikes that is geographically representative of the various areas covered by my hikes in *The Record*. I made sure to include some of my favorite hikes, such as Millbrook Mountain in Mohonk Preserve (Hike 34), the Giant Stairs of the Palisades (Hike 38) and Bearfort Ridge (Hike 51).

Every hike in the book has been field-checked by a team of volunteers, and I personally have rechecked many hikes, especially when the field-checker indicated that a number of changes were required. While I have updated all of the hikes so that the hike description is accurate as of the date of publication of the book, I have tried in each instance to retain the basic route of the hike as originally published in *The Record*. I have modified the route of the hike only when required by changed conditions. Occasionally, as in Hike 45, Westchester Wilderness Walk, I have incorporated a newly established trail to avoid retracing one's steps.

To enhance the reader's experience, this book contains two important features that were not included with the hikes published in *The Record* but have been created especially for this book. First, a map has been prepared for each hike, showing the route followed by the hike, as well as other trails in the area and road access. These maps do not include contour lines. For most hikes, reference is also made to the maps (which do include contour lines) published and offered for sale by the New York-New Jersey Trail Conference. These maps may be purchased at outdoor stores throughout the New York metropolitan area or ordered online at www.nynjtc.org. In addition, for some hikes, reference is made to maps available online or at trailhead kiosks.

Second, a sidebar has been created for every hike. Each sidebar is a short essay that focuses on some interesting aspect of the hike – history, geology, wildlife, etc. These sidebars are designed to increase one's enjoyment of the hike, and they provide interesting information relating to the hike that many hikers may not be aware of. I have written many of the sidebars; some were written by other volunteers, in which case a credit appears at the end of the sidebar.

Each hike is accompanied by at least one photo, and an effort has been made to include, wherever possible, "season-appropriate" photos for each hike. Whenever a photo was taken by someone other than the author, a photo credit appears on the right side of the photo.

Within each season, the hikes are arranged by level of difficulty – starting with the easiest hikes and ending with the most strenuous ones. It goes without saying that the degree of difficulty is subjective – what might be an "easy" hike for an athlete in top shape could be considered "strenuous" by a person who is not as fit. But the ratings indicate the comparative difficulty of the various hikes. The "time" of the hike is intended to allow for a hiker of ordinary experience to complete the hike without rushing, allowing for stops at scenic overlooks and other features of interest. Some hikers will be able to complete the hikes in far less time, while others may take more time.

In most cases, the directions to the trailhead are those that accompanied the hike when printed in *The Record*. They were primarily designed for use by residents of Bergen County, New Jersey, and those coming from elsewhere may wish to approach some of the hikes by another route.

Unless indicated otherwise in the hike description, dogs are permitted on all hikes in the book, provided they are leashed.

Nearly all of the hikes in the book are loop hikes. Loop hikes permit one to experience all of the features of the hike without retracing one's steps to any significant degree. Hike 40 (Old Croton Aqueduct) is a one-way hike, but the return is by Metro-North train, so the hiker need not retrace his steps.

I hope that the readers of this book will enjoy these 52 hikes as much as I have enjoyed them. Happy Trails!

-Daniel Chazin
June 2013

Acknowledgments

This book would not have been possible without the dedicated efforts of Charlotte Fahn, who coordinated all stages of production and made many helpful suggestions. Charlotte's special interest is the Old Croton Aqueduct, and she particularly enhanced Hike 40, which describes a pleasant hike along this engineering landmark.

The attractive layout and design of the book is the result of the tireless work of Sara Abad, another dedicated and skilled volunteer. She spent many hours designing this guidebook, and I am grateful that she enabled us to produce such a beautiful book.

The maps that accompany each hike were designed by Jeremy Apgar, the Trail Conference's cartographer. Most were taken from the Tyvek maps published by the Trail Conference, but some cover areas not included on Trail Conference maps. In each case, Jeremy expertly designed a map that clearly shows the route of each hike, as well as all important features that the hiker will encounter along the way.

I also want to thank Nora Porter, a talented graphic designer, for providing her expert advice and reviewing various aspects of the book.

The sidebar that accompanies each hike is a special and unique feature of the book. I personally wrote 20 sidebars, but the remaining 32 sidebars were composed by other volunteers – Dan Case, Jane Daniels, Charlotte Fahn, John Magerlein, George Petty, Ruth Rosenthal, Jim Simpson and Jim Wright. I particularly want to thank Jim Simpson, a talented writer with extraordinary skills in research, who wrote 14 sidebars, many of which offer unusual insights. I also want to specially thank George Petty,

Charlotte Fahn, Ruth Rosenthal and Dan Case, all of whom wrote more than one sidebar.

Although most of the photos in the book are my own, I am grateful that Dan Balogh, Jason Harcsztark, Karen Peterson, Benedicte Scheiby and Jim Simpson have contributed one or more photos to accompany hikes in the book. The book has also been enhanced by the inclusion of several historical photos and illustrations. I wish to thank Joe Macasek for contributing the historical photos of the Mount Hope Mines (Hike 14), Pat McKnight of the Steamtown National Historic Site for the historical photo of the Delaware Water Gap (Hike 25), the Friends of the Old Croton Aqueduct for the magnificent illustration of a stone-arch bridge along the Aqueduct (Hike 40), and the Rockefeller Archive Center for the photo of the Rockwood Hall mansion (Hike 43).

Each hike in the book was carefully field-checked by one or more volunteers. I would like to thank Laurette Bachert, Pete Beck, Hanna Abolitz Benesch, Andy Benesch, Gail Brown, Jim Brown, Dan Case, Jocelyn Coalter, Chris Connolly, Ann Cowan, Merilee Croft, Katherine de Vries, Charlotte Fahn, Bob Fuller, Suzan Gordon, Conrad Gosset, Ari Greenberg, Michele Hammond, Jonathan Hammond, Gerard Hazel, Art Horst, Mary Horst, Lucas Kane, Seth Kutikoff, Theresa Lahr, Luz Lee, Todd Lotcpeich, Bob Maher, Jules Papp, Thom Patton, Joseph Pettorino, Joseph Principe, Dale Ramsey, Sarah Schindler, Houston Slatton, Laine Slatton, Bill Taggart, Linda Taggart, Pete Tilgner and Kathleen Whysner, who volunteered their time to check out hikes for the book. Special thanks are due to Bill and Linda Taggart, who field-checked seven hikes, and to Theresa Lahr, Pete Beck, Luz Lee and Jules Papp, each of whom field-checked several hikes.

Last but not least, I would like to express my appreciation to my friends Adam Belson, Aaron Bierstein, Adiel Brown, Shimron Brown, Sam Chasan, Dan Crane, Ben Friedman, Kenny Harcsztark, Jason Harcsztark, Ben Hutt, Garrett Kroner, Valerie Miller, Chris Piccoli, Justin Robbins, Avi Rosenfeld, Benzy Sanders, Gabe Schoenberg, Joel Shuart, Daniel Vun Kannon and Jonathan Weinstein – all of whom accompanied me on various hikes that appear in this book and are included in one or more photos in the book.

Legend for Hike Maps

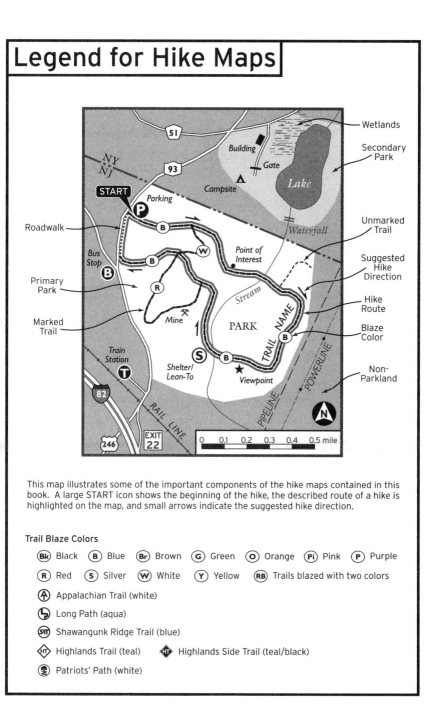

This map illustrates some of the important components of the hike maps contained in this book. A large START icon shows the beginning of the hike, the described route of a hike is highlighted on the map, and small arrows indicate the suggested hike direction.

Trail Blaze Colors

- (Bk) Black (B) Blue (Br) Brown (G) Green (O) Orange (Pi) Pink (P) Purple
- (R) Red (S) Silver (W) White (Y) Yellow (RB) Trails blazed with two colors
- (A) Appalachian Trail (white)
- (L) Long Path (aqua)
- (SRT) Shawangunk Ridge Trail (blue)
- (HT) Highlands Trail (teal)   (HT) Highlands Side Trail (teal/black)
- (P) Patriots' Path (white)

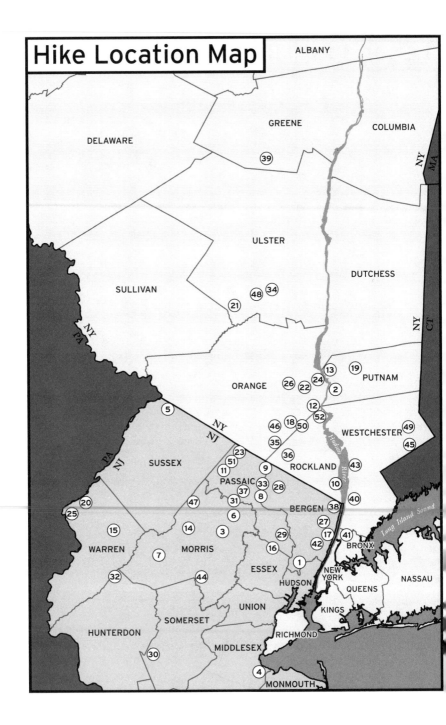

List of Hikes by Region

New Jersey

New York

Spring

Richard W. DeKorte Park | Arden Point and Glenclyffe | Tourne County Park | Cheesequake State Park | High Point State Park | Pyramid Mountain Natural Historic Area | Black River County Park | Ramapo Mountain State Forest | Ringwood State Park | Long Path/Old Erie Railroad Bed | Wawayanda State Park | Harriman State Park | Hudson Highlands State Park

1 Richard W. DeKorte Park
Lyndhurst, N.J.

This loop hike traverses boardwalks and dikes through salt marsh wetlands and climbs a landscaped hill – a former landfill – with views over the New York City skyline.

Difficulty: Easy

Length and Time: About 1.3 miles; about one hour.

Map: Richard W. DeKorte Park Trail Guide (available at the Environment Center or online at www.njmeadowlands.gov).

Directions: Take the New Jersey Turnpike to Exit 16W and proceed west on N.J. Route 3. Take the exit for N.J. 17 South. At the traffic light at the end of the ramp, turn left onto Polito Avenue and follow it to its end at Valley Brook Road. Turn left onto Valley Brook Road and continue for 1.5 miles to a railroad crossing. Bear left just past the railroad crossing and enter Richard W. DeKorte Park.

Along the Marsh Discovery Trail

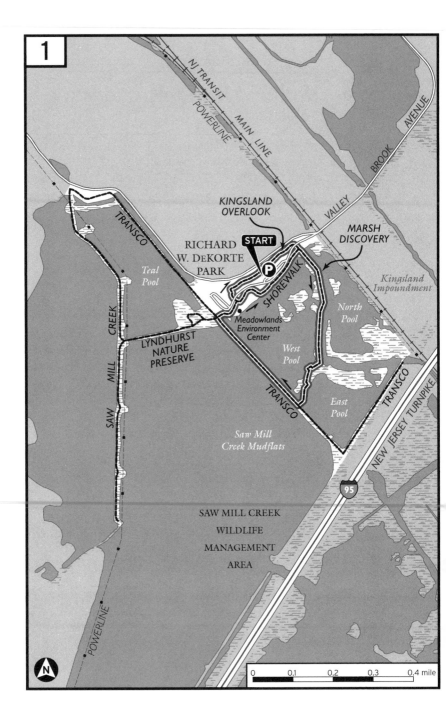

Begin the hike by visiting the Meadowlands Environment Center, just south of the parking area, where you can view informative exhibits and obtain a copy of the trail guide.

From the Environment Center, follow the brick-paved Shorewalk north along the shore of the Kingsland Impoundment, with the parking lot on your left. In a quarter mile, the Marsh Discovery Trail begins to the right (a short distance north of the security booth at the entrance). The trail follows a boardwalk which links a series of dredge-spoil islands – formed by dumping sediment from dredging operations along Kingsland Creek.

Since the park is situated along the Atlantic Flyway, many species of birds and waterfowl can be observed along the trail. Benches and wildlife observation blinds provide opportunities to linger for a while and observe the natural surroundings. Phragmites marsh reeds line the trail, and you can see the New York City skyline in the distance.

A wildlife observation blind along the Marsh Discovery Trail

Birds in Richard W. DeKorte Park

Richard W. DeKorte Park is a bird-watchers' paradise year-round. According to *Birder's World* magazine, it is one of the "premier urban wildlife spots in the country." This is not surprising, as some 280 species of birds have been observed in the one-square-mile park, including more than half of New Jersey's threatened and endangered bird species.

One reason for the multitude of birds is the park's location. Not only is it on the mid-Atlantic Flyway – the I-95 for migratory birds – but it is also within the southern range for wintering birds from Canada. That means a cavalcade of warblers in the spring and fall, plenty of shorebirds in the summer, and lots of ducks and some awesome rarities from north of the border in winter.

In fact, DeKorte Park is visited by so many kinds of ducks each winter that the New Jersey Meadowlands Commission annually publishes a "duck map" that includes the locations where one is most likely to find 12 species of ducks. Common winter ducks include canvasbacks by the hundred, pintails and shovelers by the dozen, as well as green-winged teal and mergansers.

Another reason why the park is frequented by so many species of birds is the wonderful variety of habitat in the park – including uplands, woodlands, wetlands and tidal impoundments that become vast mudflats at low tide every day. A variety of habitat results in a variety of birds.

In summer and early fall, you are likely to observe ospreys, ruddy ducks, snowy egrets, great blue herons, yellowlegs and terns – many visible from the benches or paths along the water just inside the park's main entrance. The floating Marsh Discovery Trail allows for a better view of the Shorebird Pool, where (if you are lucky) you can see black skimmers in late spring. These graceful, silent birds fly so low that their beaks skim the water's surface as they scoop up fish. Rare species that have been sighted at DeKorte Park include northern wheatear, northern shrike, American avocet, common moorhen, Virginia rail and least bittern.

-Jim Wright, New Jersey Meadowlands Commission

In about half a mile, the Marsh Discovery Trail ends at a junction with the Transco Trail. Turn right and follow the Transco Trail along a dike constructed in 1950 for a buried gas pipeline. The dike separates the waters of the Kingsland Tidal Impoundment – to your right – from the Saw Mill Creek Wildlife Management Area – to your left. Many native species have been planted along the trail, and several former truck turnarounds to the right of the trail have been converted to scenic overlooks.

Just past a gate at the end of the trail, you will reach a four-way junction. Turn right and follow a dirt path, which passes a memorial to the tragic events of September 11, 2001. Two wooden piers symbolize the shadows of the fallen towers, and a steel silhouette suggests the view of the pre-9/11 Manhattan skyline. Continue on a brick-paved path, passing in front of the Administration Building of the New Jersey Meadowlands Commission. In 400 feet – near the end of the building – turn left, cross the paved road, then turn right and continue up a hill.

Along the Kingsland Overlook Trail

You are now on the Kingsland Overlook Trail, which climbs an artificial mound, created by a landfill for household waste. This former eyesore has been capped by a waterproof plastic substance, covered with topsoil, and planted with attractive shrubs and trees. Walking along this beautiful trail, it is hard to imagine that it was once the site of a garbage dump! The trail provides views of the Kingsland Tidal Impoundment below, and the New York City skyline may be seen in the distance (although the views are partially obscured by the vegetation planted to reclaim the area). The Kingsland Overlook Trail ends opposite the start of the Marsh Discovery Trail. Turn right to reach the parking area, where the hike began.

2 Arden Point and Glenclyffe
Garrison, N.Y.

This hike passes several panoramic viewpoints over the Hudson River and follows an historic road used by Benedict Arnold to escape during the Revolutionary War.

Difficulty: Easy
Length and Time: About 3.7 miles; about two and one-half hours.
Map: New York-New Jersey Trail Conference East Hudson Trails Map #101.
Directions: From the east end of the Bear Mountain Bridge, proceed north on N.Y. Route 9D for 4.5 miles to an intersection with N.Y. Route 403. Turn left at this intersection onto Lower Station Road and follow it downhill to the Metro-North Garrison station. Park in the station parking lot (free on weekends; a fee is charged on weekdays).

The hike may be reached by public transportation – Metro-North Hudson Line trains from Grand Central Terminal in New York City to Garrison.

Just south of the southern entrance to the station, you'll notice two stone pillars and a sign for "Arden Point – Hudson Highlands State Park." This is the trailhead of a blue-blazed woods road which heads south. Follow this woods road, soon passing ruins of brick buildings on the right and crossing a wooden footbridge over a stream.

In about half a mile, you'll come to a sign for "Marcia's Mile." To the right, a one-lane steel truss bridge goes over the railroad tracks. Turn right and cross the bridge, which leads to Arden Point. Immediately after crossing the bridge, follow the blue-blazed trail as it turns right onto a footpath, passing through a mixed forest of deciduous trees and white pines.

Near the north end of Arden Point, the blue-blazed trail ends at an intersection with a red-blazed trail. Bear right onto the red-blazed trail and follow it past an old stone wall and down to the water's edge, where

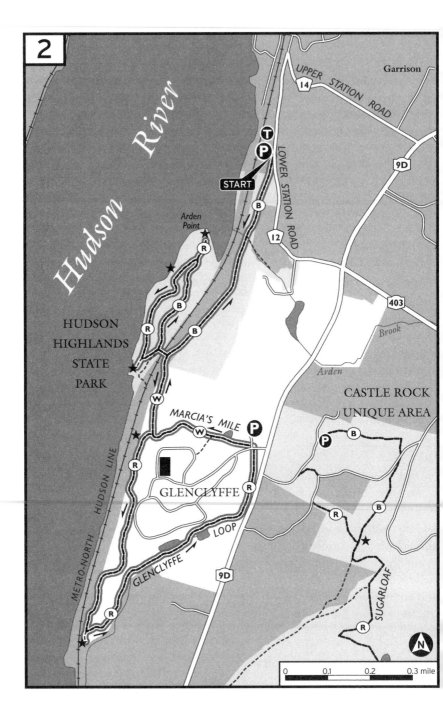

there is a broad view north up the Hudson River, with West Point visible to the left, on the west shore, and Bull Hill (Mt. Taurus) of the East Hudson Highlands in the background.

West Point from the viewpoint at the northern tip of Arden Point

After enjoying the view, retrace your steps to the intersection with the blue-blazed trail and bear right, continuing to follow the red-blazed trail. Soon, a short side trail on the right leads to a west-facing viewpoint over the Hudson River. The large red-brick building directly across the river is the Hotel Thayer at West Point. Running along the west bank of the river is the West Shore Railroad, built in 1883 between Weehawken, N.J. and Buffalo, N.Y. to compete with the New York Central, whose line followed the east bank (now operated by Metro-North). Passenger service on the West Shore line was discontinued in 1959, but the line is now operated by CSX for freight service, and you may see a mile-long freight train snake its way along the river.

When you're ready to continue, return to the red-blazed trail and turn right, heading south. Near the southern tip of the point, the red-blazed trail makes a sharp left turn. Bear right and continue ahead on a wide path to a rock outcrop at the very end of the point, which affords a panoramic south-facing view, with the Bear Mountain Bridge in the distance. The yellow brick buildings on the west side of the river are occupied by the West Point Museum and Visitor Center, established in 1989 on the site of the former Ladycliff College.

After taking some time to enjoy this view (a bench has been placed here), retrace your steps up the hill to the red-blazed trail and bear right,

Benedict Arnold's Escape

September 25, 1780 would be a tumultuous day for the commander at West Point – and not just because George Washington, the commander-in-chief, was coming for a visit.

Benedict Arnold had recently been appointed commander of the strategic Hudson River defenses at West Point, the loss of which would allow the British to control the Hudson and split the colonies. He was known for his courage, and he still limped severely from a wound he had received at the Battle of Saratoga.

But only days earlier, Arnold had met secretly with a British officer, Major John André, and sold the plans to West Point – as well as his cooperation in its capture by the British – in return for money and a commission in the British army. Unknown to him, however, Major André was arrested trying to make his way back to British lines. Suspicious papers found on André that implicated Arnold were sent by messenger to General Washington.

At his headquarters in Garrison, Arnold had just received members of Washington's staff, who told him that the commander-in-chief would be there shortly. As he sat down to breakfast, a courier handed him a note informing him that André had been arrested and his papers sent to General Washington. Arnold, realizing that his treachery was about to be revealed, called for his horse and sent a servant to his barge to ready the crew for departure. Claiming he had to prepare a reception for Washington across the river, he limped out to his horse and raced down the trail to Beverly Dock, where his barge awaited.

He first ordered his crew to take him to Stony Point, but then redirected them to the *Vulture*, a British sloop further down the river. When they hesitated, he assured them that he was on a special mission and that he would give them a bonus of rum when done. Instead, when they arrived – in another act of betrayal – he had them taken prisoner. Perhaps just as surprised were the British crew, for they were expecting Major André, not Arnold.

Arnold joined the British troops, taking part in raids in Virginia and Connecticut. After the war was over, he moved to London, where he died in 1801. Once called "bravest of the brave," today his name is synonymous with "treason" or "betrayal."

-*Jim Simpson*

The south-facing view from the southern tip of Arden Point

now heading north on the trail, which ends at the bridge over the tracks. Bear right, recross the bridge, and turn right (south) onto the white-blazed Marcia's Mile, which follows a woods road, bordered for part of the way by low stone walls.

In about a quarter of a mile, you'll reach a junction, marked by a wooden sign on the left. Turn right and head uphill on stone steps, now following a trail marked by the red blazes of the Open Space Institute (OSI). This is the start of the Glenclyffe Loop, which circles the Glenclyffe property of OSI. Just ahead, you'll reach a large gazebo, with a view over the river.

The trail passes to the left of the gazebo and heads south, parallel to the river. The large brick building on the left was built in the 1920s as a friary by the Capuchin Franciscan order and acquired in 2001 by OSI, which has preserved the property as publicly accessible open space. This building has been conveyed to the Garrison Institute, which operates it as a spiritual retreat center (the buildings on the Glenclyffe property are not open to hikers). The trail passes to the left of a stone patio with benches overlooking the river, descends concrete steps, and bears right to reenter the woods.

After crossing a rock outcrop, the trail turns left, then bears right and continues to parallel the river. It goes by a water treatment facility and bears right at a bamboo thicket. (The red brick building on the left, built in the 1860s, was once the home of Hamilton Fish, governor of New York.)

Soon, the trail comes out at the top of a ravine. It bears right and descends into the ravine, then turns left and continues to parallel the river. At a sign pointing to the "Historic Overlook," the red-blazed trail turns sharply left, but you should continue ahead on a short side trail (also blazed red) that leads south to a wooden viewing platform. The platform overlooks the site of Beverly Dock, used in 1780 by Benedict Arnold to escape when his treason was discovered. Bear Mountain Bridge is visible to the south, with Sugarloaf Hill towering to the east.

Retrace your steps to the junction and bear right, continuing on the red-blazed trail, which descends to a ravine, where it begins to follow an old woods road. Known as the Beverly Dock Road, this road was used by Benedict Arnold to flee. The trail crosses a stream on a large metal culvert and climbs gently, with the stream to the left. After bearing right at a small dam and bamboo thicket, the trail passes to the right of a small pond. Near the end of the pond, a kiosk relates the story of the escape of Benedict Arnold along this road during the Revolutionary War.

Just beyond, the trail turns left, recrossing the stream on another culvert and passing a cinder-block building. It immediately turns right, passing to the left of a second pond. As the trail approaches Route 9D, it bears left, climbs a rise and emerges onto a broad grassy expanse. The trail follows a line of trees parallel to the road, with Castle Rock visible on the hilltop to the east.

At a sign for the Garrison Institute, turn left onto the paved entrance road. To the left of a large trail map, you'll see a white blaze that marks the start of Marcia's Mile. Follow the white blazes down a grassy knoll and along a woods road, passing a small pond on the right. The trail skirts the left side of a meadow, reenters the woods, and passes a concrete foundation on the left. It then turns left at a T-intersection and descends on a footpath.

At the base of the descent, turn right onto the woods road on which you began the hike earlier, still following the white blazes of Marcia's Mile. When you reach the bridge over the railroad (do not cross it), continue ahead on the blue-blazed woods road which leads back to the Garrison station, where the hike began.

3   Tourne County Park

This hike climbs to the top of the Tourne, with panoramic views.

Difficulty: Easy

Length and Time: About 2.0 miles; about one and one-half hours.

Map: New York-New Jersey Trail Conference Jersey Highlands Trails (Central North Region) Map #125; Morris County Park Commission map (available online at www.morrisparks.net or from kiosk at trailhead).

Directions: Take I-80 to Exit 43 (Mahwah/Morristown/I-287), then take Exit 43B onto I-287 North. Take the first exit, Exit 43 (Intervale Road), and turn left at the top of the ramp. Cross over I-287 and turn right at the traffic light onto Fanny Road. At a stop sign, reached in 0.9 mile, continue ahead, following the sign to "West Main Street," then bear left at the next fork, following the sign for County Route 618. In 0.2 mile, turn left onto McCaffrey Lane and proceed for 0.3 mile to a large parking area for Tourne County Park on the right side of the road.

The 547-acre Tourne County Park is the largest remaining undeveloped fragment of the Great Boonton Tract, purchased by David Ogden, Colonial Attorney-General of New Jersey, in 1739. The highlight of the park is the 897-foot-high Tourne, which is reached by the DeCamp Trail, a wide gravel road built over a century ago by Clarence Addington DeCamp, who owned much of the land now preserved as a park. Although the hike gains 300 feet in elevation in 0.6 mile, the grades are moderate (about 10% on average), and there are no steep climbs. It's a great destination for a short hike with the entire family.

You can pick up a trail map from the kiosk at the end of the parking area. Continue downhill along the paved McCaffrey Lane for about 500

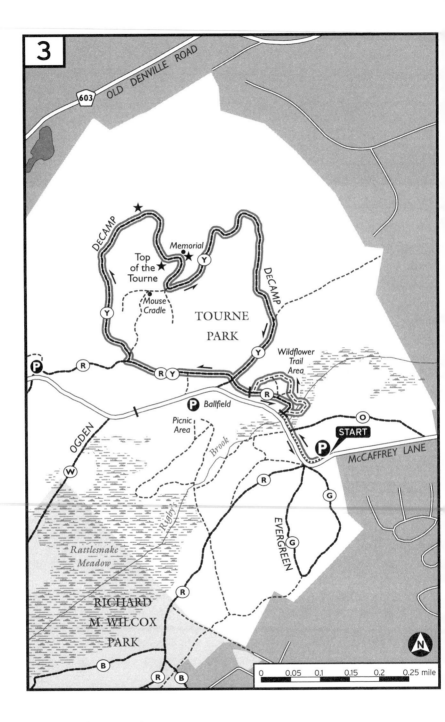

3

OLD DENVILLE ROAD

603

DECAMP

★

Memorial ★

Top
of the
Tourne ★

Y

DECAMP

Y

Mouse
Cradle

TOURNE
PARK

Wildflower
Trail
Area

Y

P

R

R Y

R

P Ballfield

Picnic
Area

Brook

OGDEN

START

O

P

McCAFFREY LANE

W

R

G

Rigby's

EVERGREEN

G

Rattlesnake
Meadow

RICHARD
M WILCOX
PARK

R

N

0   0.05   0.1   0.15   0.2   0.25 mile

B

R B

16 Hike of the Week

feet. Just beyond a bridge over a stream, you'll notice a four-space parking area on the right side of the road. (You could actually drive to this point, but the very small parking area is often full). Turn right onto the Red Trail (marked by a triple-red blaze on a tree). You may wish to obtain a green self-guided trail booklet from a kiosk to the left.

The trail immediately passes through a gate in a chain-link fence (erected to protect the wildflowers from deer) and enters the Wildflower Trail area, maintained by volunteers from the Rockaway Valley Garden Club and the Garden Club of Mountain Lakes. Just beyond the gate, leave the Red Trail and turn right onto the Brookside Trail, which crosses Tourne Brook on a wooden bridge, parallels it for a short distance, then recrosses it on another bridge. Numbers on posts along the trail refer to descriptions in the self-guided trail booklet, and small signs identify many of the wildflowers and other plants and trees.

At a Y-intersection with the Fern Walk, bear right onto the Swamp Trail. Soon, you'll pass Denture Rock (marked as #7) – a rock with "teeth" formed of large quartz crystals – to the left. At the next intersection, turn right onto the Trillium Trail, bear right again at the junction with the Hepatica Loop, and climb to a junction with the Overlook Trail – a wide gravel road which is also the route of the Red Trail.

Turn right onto the gravel road, soon exiting the Wildflower Trail area via a gate in the fence. Just beyond, you'll reach a four-way junction.

Denture Rock

Ogden Ironworks

McCaffrey Lane and the section of the DeCamp Trail on the northeast shoulder of the Tourne follow a Colonial-era road that linked the iron mines of Hibernia to the extensive Ogden Ironworks in the Town of Boonton (which was originally called Boone-Towne). During the middle of the nineteenth century, New Jersey was the nation's third largest producer of iron. According to Boonton historian Jean Ricker, pack horses carried ore from the mines that were located in Hibernia (now known as the Wildcat Ridge Wildlife Management Area) through the Rockaway Valley, across the Rockaway River, around the peak of the Tourne, and down to the Ogden furnaces and forges in Boonton. The forges, powered by the great falls of the Rockaway at Boonton, hammered iron ingots into sheets and rods and, during wartime, forged cannon and rifle barrels. There were also nearby stone furnaces for smelting iron ore at Charlottesburg, at the south end of present-day Clinton Reservoir, and at Split Rock Pond. The remains of both of these furnaces can still be seen today. The eighteenth century industrial complex in the Town of Boonton, so vital to the early years of our country, is now immersed under the waters of Jersey City's Boonton Reservoir.   -*George Petty*

Rock outcrop along the DeCamp Trail

West-facing view over Rockaway Valley and Green Pond Mountain

The road to the right will be your return route but, for now, continue ahead, still following the red blazes along the gravel road, which begins a moderate climb. Soon, a path leads downhill to the left, but you should continue ahead on the gravel road, passing interesting boulders on the hillside to the right.

At the next intersection, the Red Trail continues ahead, but you should bear right, following a sign to "Top of the Tourne." You're now on the unmarked DeCamp Trail, which continues to climb on a moderate grade, with many rock outcrops to the right.

Near the top of the climb, there is a view to the west over the Rockaway Valley, with Green Pond Mountain beyond. A bench has been placed here so you can rest from the climb and enjoy the view. The trail continues ahead and soon levels off.

A grassy clearing with picnic tables to the right (with a huge, nearly flat rock outcrop beyond) marks the high point of the Tourne. To the left is a viewpoint over the Town of Boonton. Continue ahead on the gravel road, which descends slightly to reach a panoramic viewpoint to the east, with the New York City skyline visible in the distance on a clear day. To the left, you'll notice a memorial to the tragic 9/11/01 terrorist attack on the World Trade Center, which was visible from this point.

After taking in the view, continue ahead on the wide gravel road, which now begins a steady descent. Follow the road downhill for about half a mile to a four-way junction at the base of the descent, where you should turn left onto the Red Trail (following the sign for the Wildflower Trail). You are now briefly retracing your steps. Go through the gate in the fence and enter the Wildflower Trail area, but when you reach junctions with the Trillium Trail and Hepatica Loop, which begin to the left, continue ahead on the wide Overlook Trail. After exiting the Wildflower Trail area, you'll come to the four-space parking area with the kiosk. If you've parked in the main parking area on the top of the hill, turn left and follow the paved road back to your car.

4 Cheesequake State Park

This loop hike passes through diverse habitats, including upland hardwoods, pine barrens, fresh-water swamps and an Atlantic white cedar swamp.

Difficulty: Easy to moderate

Length and Time: About 2.9 miles; about two hours.

Map: Cheesequake State Park map (available at the park office and at the Interpretive Center or online at www.njparksandforests.org).

Directions: Take the Garden State Parkway to Exit 120 (be sure to stay in the local lanes south of the Raritan Toll Plaza). Turn right at the end of the ramp and continue to the first traffic light. Turn right at the light onto Morristown Road, then turn right again at the next traffic light onto Gordon Road. Follow Gordon Road as it turns sharply left and continue ahead, past residential subdivisions on the left, into the park. You will pass a toll booth (an entrance fee is charged from Memorial Day weekend to Labor Day weekend) and the park office. Continue for 0.1 mile beyond the toll booth, and park in the trailhead parking area on the left side of the road. GPS address: 300 Gordon Road, Matawan, NJ 07747.

The park – located in a transitional zone between New Jersey's southern and northern vegetational types – has four marked hiking trails, blazed in yellow, green, blue and red, respectively. This hike will follow the Green Trail, which is the longest and most interesting of the park's trails, proceeding for most of its route through a protected natural area. The Green Trail is sparsely blazed for much of the way, but there are green blazes at all intersections and important turns in the trail. In addition, green blazes on brown wands indicate each tenth of a mile along the way.

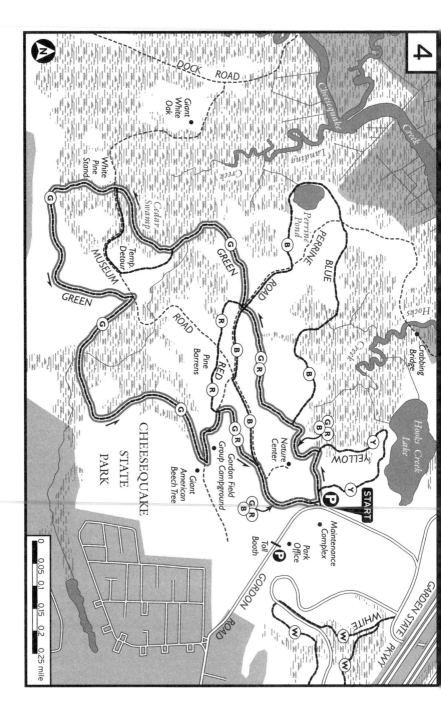

All four trails begin at the large trail map at the southern end of the parking area. Soon after the start, the trails fork. Bear left and follow the blazes downhill along a wooden boardwalk with many long steps. At the next intersection, the Yellow Trail continues straight ahead, but you should turn left, following the green, blue and red blazes. After crossing the first of many wooden bridges you'll encounter on this hike, the trail heads uphill to the park's Nature Center. You will want to stop here to view the informative exhibits and obtain a trail map.

A wooden boardwalk with many long steps along the Green Trail

Continue ahead along the trail through the hardwood forest. You will soon reach a spot with a view through the trees over the Cheesequake Salt Marsh to the right of the trail (the view is obscured by vegetation in the late spring and summer). Continue downhill on wooden steps and a boardwalk, then climb a long flight of wooden steps. Just beyond the top of the steps, the Blue Trail leaves to the right, but you should bear left, following the green and red blazes.

After paralleling a ravine on the left, the trail descends wooden steps to cross a bridge over the ravine. Soon, the trail climbs some more wooden

Cheesequake — Land of Many Uses

Visitors have been exploring the grounds of Cheesequake State Park since its opening in June 1940. But there is evidence of human presence in the area for over 5,000 years. It is even possible that the crew of Hendrik Hudson's *Half Moon* may have stopped there in 1609 while exploring Raritan Bay before heading into what is now New York Harbor and the Hudson River in their quest for a Northwest Passage.

The proximity to Raritan Bay and the navigability of Cheesequake Creek made the area ideal for settlement. At first, the settlers farmed the uplands above the creek. Subsequently, the area became a center of ceramic, brick and terra cotta manufacture, using the rich alluvial clay found in the region. The clay was deposited in strata between 60 and 140 million years ago and was easily extracted. Although ceramics were in great demand in the late 1800s and early 1900s, changing architectural styles and the Great Depression resulted in the demise of the industry.

But the Great Depression led to a new role for Cheesequake. In 1938, the state purchased 250 acres of farmland for $30 an acre, and over the next two years, it purchased adjoining properties to expand the park to its present size of 1,274 acres. Many of the facilities in the park were built by the Civilian Conservation Corps (CCC), the federal work relief program of the New Deal that provided conservation work for young men of impoverished families, as well as veterans. Another New Deal program, the Works Progress Administration (WPA), built roads in the park. The WPA also built roads throughout Monmouth County that made the park more accessible.

Dairy farming played an important role in the county's history, but the park's name is not a reference to a joggling dairy confection. It has a more venerable etymology: it is a transliteration of the Lenni Lenape name for "land that has been cleared." The Lenape, or Delawares, were a Native American tribe who populated parts of the eastern United States and Canada. Their own name translates as the "original people."

-Jim Simpson

steps, levels off, and crosses a sandy road known as Perrine Road. Just beyond the road, the Red Trail leaves to the left, but you should bear right to continue along the Green Trail.

After another level stretch, the trail climbs a little, then bears left at a fork and descends rather steeply, passing a beautiful stand of tall phragmites (swamp grass) on the right. Next, it descends wooden steps to cross a fresh-water swamp on a long boardwalk, the end of which has been built around several large red maple trees.

At the end of the swamp, the trail climbs wooden steps and bears right. Soon, it goes down to cross another boardwalk which passes through an Atlantic white cedar swamp, with dense thickets of sweetbay magnolia. Here, a layer of clay beneath the surface traps the water and prevents it from draining off. After crossing this interesting and unusual swamp, the trail continues through deciduous woods, crossing a boardwalk over a wet area. It climbs over a ridge and descends to cross Museum Road, another sandy road.

The boardwalk through the Atlantic white cedar swamp

The same boardwalk after the devastating Hurricane Sandy, which struck the park on October 29, 2012

NOTE: Due to severe damage that the boardwalk over the Atlantic white cedar swamp sustained during Hurricane Sandy in October 2012, the trail section across the swamp has been closed and is expected to remain closed at least until late 2014. In the interim, the Green Trail has been rerouted. After climbing the steps at the end of the fresh-water swamp, the Green Trail bears left and follows a relatively level footpath to Museum Road. It turns right and follows the road for about 0.2 mile, then turns left at a sign and gateway for the Green Trail, reenters the woods, and continues as described below.

After crossing the road, look for several large 150-year-old white pine trees on the right side of the trail. After another level stretch, the trail climbs over exposed tree roots, ascends wooden steps, and bears left at the top of the rise. It descends gradually, turns right to cross a ravine on a wooden bridge, then turns left to cross a smaller ravine on another bridge and continues ahead on a level path.

After descending on an eroded path through a shallow ravine, the sandy Museum Road is visible straight ahead. Here, the Green Trail bears right, as an unmarked trail joins from the left. Just beyond, you will notice a depressed area to the left of the trail. This is the site of the former park museum, built in the 1950s but never used. The building – after which Museum Road is named – was demolished soon after it was constructed.

The trail bears right to skirt a low-lying area with deciduous trees on the left, often flooded during periods of heavy rain. Just beyond a huge fallen oak tree, the trail turns left and proceeds across the low-lying area on a long boardwalk. After crossing a stream on a bridge, the trail bears left and continues to skirt the low-lying area. Soon, it curves to the right and crosses a short boardwalk, with a viewing platform that overlooks a grassy, wet area on the left. The dead trees in this area were killed by siltation from development outside the park that settled into this low area.

The trail now turns left and crosses another boardwalk. It then bears right, climbs over a small hill, and continues along a level footpath. After descending into a ravine and crossing a wooden bridge, the trail climbs to Perrine Road, opposite a restroom building at Gordon Field, a group camping area.

Turn left and continue along the paved road for about 900 feet, passing another restroom building. About 150 feet beyond this building, follow the Green Trail as it turns right at a wooden arch and – along with the Red Trail – follows a footpath into the woods. It skirts to the left of the field, then bears left and descends to Museum Road. Turn right on this road and follow it, past a turnoff to the Nature Center, back to the parking area where the hike began.

5 High Point State Park

This loop hike traverses two ridges of Kittatinny Mountain, with panoramic views to the east and west, and runs along the shore of Lake Marcia.

Difficulty: Easy to moderate
Length and Time: About 3.5 miles; about two and one-half hours.
Map: New York-New Jersey Trail Conference Kittatinny Trails Map #123.
Directions: Take N.J. Route 208 to I-287 South. Follow I-287 to Exit 52B (N.J. Route 23 North), and continue north on Route 23 for about 35 miles to High Point State Park. Turn right and follow the park entrance road for about 1.5 miles, past Lake Marcia, to its end at the parking area for the High Point Monument. Park at the northern end of the parking area. (Between Memorial Day and Labor Day, a parking fee is charged.)

At the end of the parking area, you will notice, at a break in the guard-rail, a brown sign marking the start of the Monument Trail. You will be following this trail, marked with red-square-over-green-square blazes (on a white background), for the entire hike. The first part of the hike is also marked with the aqua blazes of the Shawangunk Ridge Trail, which is co-aligned with the Monument Trail. Proceed north along this trail, which follows a relatively level footpath along the easternmost ridge of Kittatinny Mountain, passing through a mixed forest of pitch pines and deciduous trees. The trail was built by the Civilian Conservation Corps in the 1930s, and you may see large stone blocks along the left side of the trail, placed there to provide a stable surface for the trail. Soon, views appear through the trees to the right.

In about half a mile, a short side trail to the left leads to a west-facing viewpoint over the Delaware River, Port Jervis, N.Y., and Matamoras, Pa.

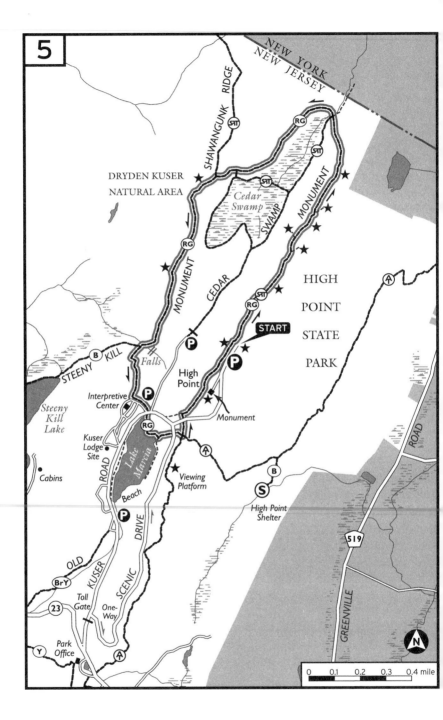

(You can see three states – New Jersey, New York and Pennsylvania – from here.) A short distance beyond, a short side trail to the right leads to a panoramic southeast-facing viewpoint from a rock ledge over the wide expanse of the Great Valley. After passing another viewpoint to the right, the Monument Trail begins a steady descent.

About a mile from the start, at the base of the descent, the Monument Trail crosses a grassy woods road. The Shawangunk Ridge Trail and the Cedar Swamp Trail turn left here, but you should continue ahead, now following only the Monument Trail.

The trail immediately crosses a wooden bridge over the outlet of Cedar Swamp, curves to the left, and soon begins a gentle climb of the next ridge of Kittatinny Mountain. The blazes along this section of the trail are rather sparse, but the footpath is clear and obvious. In another half a mile, the aqua-blazed Shawangunk Ridge Trail joins from the left and runs concurrently with the Monument Trail for about 500 feet. After a short climb, the Shawangunk Ridge Trail leaves to the right, but you should continue ahead on the Monument Trail. A short distance beyond this intersection, you'll reach a broad west-facing viewpoint from a rock ledge to the right of the trail. Here, amid pitch pines and scrub oak, you can see the Delaware River, Port Jervis, N.Y., and Matamoras, Pa.

West-facing view over Port Jervis and the Delaware River from the Monument Trail

Lake Marcia

After passing another viewpoint, the trail levels off. It soon begins another gentle climb, reaching a more limited viewpoint at the crest of the ridge, then descends steadily. At the base of the descent, the trail crosses a wooden bridge over a stream. Just beyond, the blue-blazed Steeny Kill Trail (which leads for about one mile to a parking area on Route 23 near Steeny Kill Lake) leaves to the right.

The Monument Trail now begins a steady climb, utilizing stone steps built in the 1930s by the Civilian Conservation Corps for part of the way. It finally emerges on a paved road, with a stone building – the park's Interpretive Center – just ahead. Follow the trail as it turns left, descends on the paved road, and crosses the park entrance road to reach the northern end of Lake Marcia.

The trail follows a gravel road along the shore of this beautiful lake (during the summer, swimming is permitted at a beach at the southern end of the lake). After about 500 feet, the trail turns sharply left, leaving the lakeshore, and climbs on a rocky footpath to cross another paved road. A short distance beyond, you'll reach a junction with the white-blazed

High Point State Park

As early as 1855, the public used the Lake Marcia/High Point area for picnics and outings. In 1890, Charles St. John, a Port Jervis newspaper publisher, built the High Point Inn, which operated until 1908. Much of the estate was purchased in 1910 by John Fairfield Dryden, founder of the Prudential Life Insurance Company. When Dryden died the following year, the property was inherited by his daughter, Susie Dryden Kuser, and her husband, Colonel Anthony Kuser – a New Jersey industrialist, philanthropist and conservationist. The Kusers renovated the inn to serve as their summer residence but rarely used it. In 1923, they donated the 11,000-acre property to the State of New Jersey, and it became the state's first state park. The Kusers' residence was renamed The Lodge and once again opened to the public for lodging, but after many years of neglect, it closed in 1977 and was subsequently demolished.

In 1927, Colonel Kuser hired architects to design a monument to be erected on the highest point in New Jersey, 1,803 feet above sea level. This memorial – built of New Hampshire granite and modeled after the Bunker Hill Tower – was dedicated in 1930 as a lasting tribute to the "glory and honor and eternal memory of New Jersey's heroes by land, sea, and air in all wars of our country."

Soon after High Point State Park was established, the park engaged the Olmsted Brothers – a prominent landscape architecture firm – to design both a general development plan and specific features. Their design reflected the American romantic style of landscape architecture, with an emphasis on natural scenery, use of native raw materials, and curvilinear roads.

In 1933, a Civilian Conservation Corps camp was established at High Point. Men stationed at Camp Kuser worked under the direction of the National Park Service to expand and improve the park. Among the trails built by the CCC was the Monument Trail, followed by this hike. Today, High Point State Park includes 15,278 acres.

Appalachian Trail, which proceeds straight ahead and to the right. Follow the Monument Trail, which turns sharply left, traverses a very rocky area, and once again crosses the park entrance road.

Just beyond the crossing of the paved road, the trail turns right on a wide gravel road and climbs rather steeply to reach the base of the High Point Monument. Built in 1930 on the highest point in New Jersey (1,803 feet), this 220-foot monument offers panoramic views in all directions, but the same views can be had from the wide platform at its base.

After taking in the views, return to the Monument Trail, turn right, and continue parallel to the paved road leading up to the monument. (If you wish, you may choose instead to go down along the paved road.) After passing concession and restroom buildings, the trail follows the western edge of the parking area to its terminus at the northern end of the parking area, where the hike began.

High Point Monument

6 Pyramid Mountain Natural Historic Area

This loop hike passes two unusual glacial erratics – Tripod Rock and Bear Rock – and climbs to several panoramic viewpoints.

Difficulty: Moderate
Length and Time: About 5.0 miles; about three hours.
Map: New York-New Jersey Trail Conference Jersey Highlands Trails (Central North Region) Map #125; Morris County Park Commission map (available from kiosk at trailhead or online at www.morrisparks.net).
Directions: Take I-287 South to Exit 47 (Montville/Lincoln Park) and turn left at the bottom of the ramp onto Main Road (U.S. Route 202). (If coming north on I-287, take Exit 47 and turn right at the bottom of the ramp.) In 0.7 mile, just before reaching a fire station, turn right onto Taylortown Road and continue for 1.8 miles to Boonton Avenue (County Route 511). Turn right and continue for 0.7 mile to the entrance to the Pyramid Mountain County Park Natural Historic Area, on the left, opposite Mars Park.

From the southern end of the parking area, follow the access trail, which starts just north of a large bulletin board and immediately passes a memorial plaque for Stephen Klein, Jr. In 400 feet, you'll reach a junction with the blue-blazed Mennen Trail (part of the Butler-Montville Trail). Continue ahead on the blue-blazed trail, which soon crosses Stony Brook on a wooden footbridge. In another 125 feet, the Yellow Trail begins on the right. Turn right and follow the Yellow Trail, which crosses under power lines and heads north along a nearly constant contour, with huge boulders above on the left and a camp recreation area (with a grassy ball-field, a picnic area and a small pond) below on the right.

In a quarter of a mile, the Orange Trail leaves to the right at a large cairn. Continue along the Yellow Trail, which soon bears left and begins

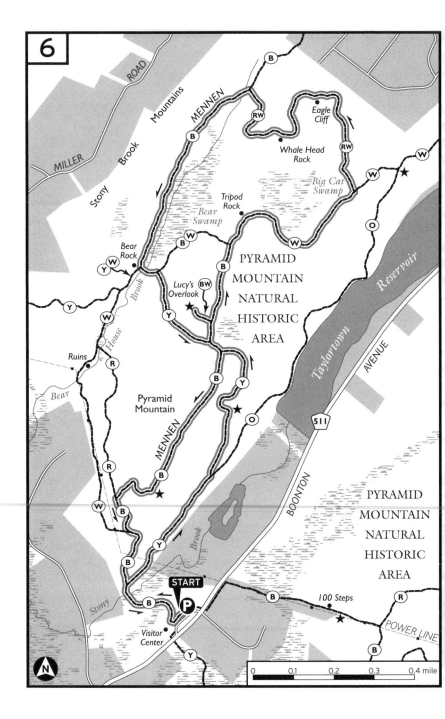

34 Hike of the Week

to climb rather steeply. At the top of the climb, there is a view through the trees over Turkey Mountain to the east. The trail now heads back into the woods, bears right and descends slightly.

Almost a mile from the start, you will again reach the blue-blazed Mennen Trail. Turn right here and follow the joint blue and yellow trails through deep stands of mountain laurel. After a short distance, the Yellow Trail leaves to the left. Keep to the right here, and continue along the blue-blazed trail. In 250 feet, a blue-and-white side trail goes off to the left. Follow this trail, which leads in a short distance to Lucy's Overlook, a west-facing viewpoint from open rocks, named for Lucy Meyer, the leader of the fight to save this mountain.

After enjoying the view, return to the blue trail and turn left. In less than a quarter of a mile, you will arrive at a junction with the white-blazed Kinnelon-Boonton Trail. Continue straight ahead (north) here, leaving the blue trail, and now following white markers. In about 500 feet, you will come to Tripod Rock – a huge boulder, perched on three smaller stones. Geologists explain that this boulder was deposited here by glacial action, although some believe that it may be a Native American calendar site. This unusual feature helped galvanize public support to preserve the mountain when it was threatened by development. This is a good place to take a break. When you're ready to continue, follow the white trail north for 0.4 mile to a junction with a red-blazed trail with white stripes.

Turn left onto this trail, which goes through interesting, remote and rugged mountain scenery. In about a third of a mile, you will see a house

View from Lucy's Overlook

Tripod Rock

directly ahead. Here the trail turns sharply left and climbs to the top of Eagle Cliff. After passing a huge balanced rock on the left – a glacial erratic known as Whale Head Rock – the trail bears left and begins a steep, rocky descent through mountain laurel thickets.

At the base of the descent, the trail turns right and heads north for about 0.2 mile. It then bears left, crosses a branch of Bear House Brook and reaches a junction with the blue-blazed Mennen Trail. Turn left onto the blue trail, following the sign for "Visitors Center," and cross Bear House Brook on a wooden bridge. The blue trail continues south, paralleling Bear House Brook, which runs through the valley below to the left and eventually widens to form Bear Swamp.

In another half mile you'll reach the huge Bear Rock. This massive glacial erratic, which can be said to resemble a giant bear, has been a local landmark for centuries. It was probably used as a shelter by Native Americans, and today it marks the boundary between Kinnelon Borough and Montville Township.

From Bear Rock, turn left and follow the yellow, blue and white trails across Bear House Brook on a wooden footbridge. A short distance beyond, at a fork, the blue and white trails bear left, but you should bear right, following the Yellow Trail. At first, the trail is level, but it soon bears left and climbs rather steeply up to the ridge, where it meets the blue-blazed Mennen Trail.

A Mountain for a Ballfield

Hiking trails have criss-crossed Pyramid Mountain at least as far back as 1923, when the first edition of the *New York Walk Book* described a route that traversed the valley between Stony Brook Mountain and a "pyramidal hill" and passed by Bear Rock. At the time, the mountain was privately owned, although the landowners did not object to hikers traversing their property.

By the 1970s, though, developers began to construct houses on surrounding parcels. Local residents, including Lucy Meyer and her husband Karl, became alarmed that development might encroach upon the unique features of Pyramid Mountain. They began to inventory the special natural features of the area and compile a statement of reasons why the mountain should be protected.

In the mid-1980s, development pressures increased, and several landowners prepared plans for housing developments on the mountain. The Meyers alerted others, and the Committee to Save Pyramid Mountain was formed. Among those who championed the cause were Ken Lloyd and Bruce Scofield of the Trail Conference. But funds were needed to finance the purchase of the mountain by public entities.

Around 1986, a breakthrough came from an unlikely source. The Mennen Corporation had previously donated to Morris County a 32-acre parcel adjacent to their headquarters in Morris Township. A sports arena was built on 14.5 acres, and a ballfield on the remaining 17.5 acres. Now, the corporation wanted the 17.5-acre tract back for possible future expansion. New Jersey Green Acres regulations did not permit the sale of parkland. But they did allow parkland to be exchanged for other land that would be devoted to park purposes.

The New Jersey Conservation Foundation came up with an ingenious solution. They acquired an 11-acre parcel at the base of Pyramid Mountain (which included Bear Rock and a portion of Bear Swamp) for $15,000 and promptly sold it to Mennen (subject to a conservation easement) for twice that amount. Then, Mennen exchanged that parcel for the far more valuable 17.5-acre tract adjacent to their headquarters. To make up the difference in value, Mennen paid the County $2.5 million, which the County in turn used to purchase 180 acres on Pyramid Mountain, including Tripod Rock.

Subsequently, additional properties were acquired with Green Acres funds, and today Pyramid Mountain Natural Historic Area includes over 1,300 acres.

Hikers at Bear Rock

Turn right at this T-intersection, briefly retracing your steps along the joint yellow/blue trail. A short distance beyond, the Yellow Trail leaves to the left, but you should continue ahead on the blue-blazed trail, which gradually climbs to the highest elevation on the Pyramid Mountain ridge (934 feet). Here, a sign indicates that the trail turns right, but first bear left and head to an east-facing overlook from open rocks, with the New York City skyline visible on the horizon.

After taking in the view, return to the blue trail and follow it as it gradually descends the southwest face of the mountain on switchbacks. At the base of the descent, a large cairn marks the start of the Red Trail on the right, but you should continue ahead on the blue trail, which bears left, climbs a little, then continues to descend gradually, passing another large cairn that marks the start of the white-blazed Kinnelon-Boonton Trail. Proceed ahead along the blue trail, which continues to descend on a switchback and soon crosses under the power lines. At the next intersection, where the Yellow Trail begins on the left, bear right, continuing along the blue trail, which crosses a footbridge over Stony Brook and proceeds ahead to the access trail that leads to the parking area where the hike began.

7 Black River County Park
Chester, N.J.

For much of the route, this "lollipop" loop hike runs along the scenic Black River, following an abandoned railroad grade for part of the way and passing through a spectacular rocky gorge.

Difficulty: Moderate
Length and Time: About 6.4 miles; about four hours.
Map: Morris County Park Commission map (available at www.morrisparks.net).
Directions: Take I-80 West to Exit 27A and continue south on U.S. Route 206 for 8.0 miles. Turn right onto County Route 513 and follow it for 1.2 miles to the entrance to Cooper Mill Park, on the left side of the road.

Cooper Mill

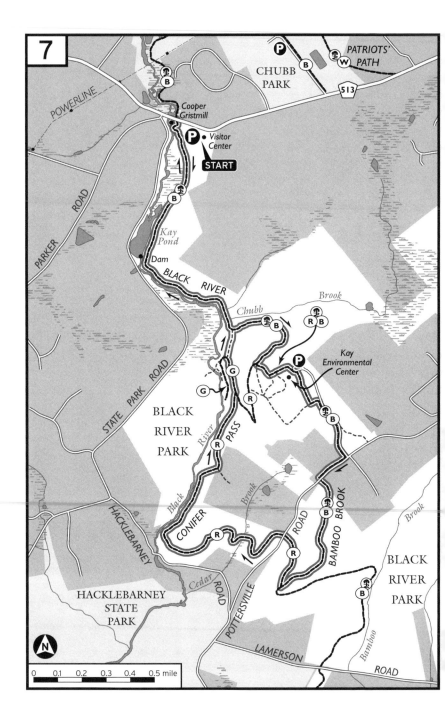

From the northwest corner of the parking area, proceed south to the stone Cooper Mill. The mill, built in 1826, is open for tours in the summer. Descend the stairs alongside the mill and continue south on the blue-blazed Black River Trail, part of the Patriots' Path system (also blazed with the path-and-tree logo), which crosses several tributary streams on wooden bridges. About a third of a mile from the start, the trail turns left onto an abandoned railroad grade – the former route of the Hacklebarney Branch of the Central Railroad of New Jersey, built in 1873 to carry iron ore from mines along the river and abandoned in 1900. The trail follows this railroad grade for the next mile.

Half a mile from the start, you'll pass Kay Pond (formerly known as Hacklebarney Pond) on the right. Here, the railroad had to be blasted through a rock cut, and the drill marks from the blasting may still be seen in the rock. The small building at the south end of Kay Pond was once used to store ice cut from the pond in the winter.

After passing the stone dam at the end of the pond, the trail goes by a fenced-in area to the left. This is the site of the former Hacklebarney Mine, where a considerable amount of iron ore was mined in the last quarter of the nineteenth century. Just beyond, the trail reaches a bridge over the river and turns left, continuing to follow along the river. Soon, the railroad grade ends and the trail continues on a slightly rougher footpath parallel to the river.

The dam at the south end of Kay Pond

About 1.2 miles from the start, after crossing two wooden footbridges over tributary streams, the trail reaches abandoned concrete abutments in the river – the remnants of a former bridge. Here, the trail bears left and begins to head uphill. It bears left at the next fork and soon begins to parallel a tributary stream. The trail now curves right and continues to climb, passing a stone wall on the right and continuing through former fields, now overgrown with dense vegetation.

Soon, the trail reaches a junction in a clearing, marked by a signpost. Turn left, now following both blue and red blazes, then turn left again at the next intersection. Just ahead, you'll come to a parking area, with the Kay Environmental Center to the right.

Just past the environmental center, the blue-blazed Bamboo Brook Trail begins on the right. Continue along this trail, which follows a wide path through overgrown fields, turns left onto a dirt road, then joins the paved entrance road. It continues along the road for a quarter mile, then turns right onto Pottersville Road. After following Pottersville Road for 750 feet, the trail turns left and reenters the woods.

The rocky gorge of the Black River

The Hacklebarney Mine and the Hacklebarney Branch Railroad

The Hacklebarney Branch of the Central Railroad of New Jersey was constructed in 1873 to serve the Hacklebarney Mine, from which iron ore had been mined for over a century. It was built as a short spur from the Chester Branch of the Central Railroad, but that branch was not completed until 1876. Thus, for the three years before its own line to Chester was finished, the Central Railroad had to ship ore from the Hacklebarney Mine via a competitor, the Delaware, Lackawanna and Western Railroad.

Although the main purpose of the Hacklebarney Branch was to transport ore from the mines along the river, it also was used to carry ice from Hacklebarney Pond. No scheduled passenger service was ever operated on this branch, which was said to have the steepest grade of any railroad in the state.

The Hacklebarney Mine included not only the fenced-in mine pits on the east side of the Black River which the hike passes by, but also several pits on the opposite side of the river. In 1884, an ore roaster was built on the west side of the river to purify the ore. The ore was then brought across the river and loaded into rail cars on the Hacklebarney Branch.

In the early 1880s, the Hacklebarney Mine produced over 20,000 tons of ore a year. But various factors caused production to decline, and the mine was closed in 1889. It was reopened in 1890, but closed again in 1893. It reopened briefly in 1899, but closed for good a year later. It has been estimated that the Hacklebarney Mine yielded a total of about 250,000 tons of ore during the period of 1867 to 1900, making it the most productive of all the mines in the Chester area.

The tracks of the Hacklebarney Branch were pulled up in 1901, with a nearby school dismissed for the day so that the students could watch the last train come up the branch, removing the tracks behind it. But over a century later, the railroad grade remains in remarkably good condition, providing an enjoyable trail route along the river for hikers.

The trail continues along a relatively level footpath, then bears right at a fork and begins to climb the rocky hillside. After reaching the top of the hill, the trail descends to reach a junction with the red-blazed Conifer Pass Trail (marked by a signpost). Turn right and follow the red-blazed trail as it descends to recross Pottersville Road.

On the other side of the road, the trail enters a beautiful pine forest and descends past old stone walls to cross Cedar Brook on rocks. It ascends on switchbacks through a grove of fir trees, continues through a deciduous forest to the crest of the rise, and descends once again to the Black River, passing two mine pits on the right along the way.

The red-blazed trail now heads north through the rocky gorge of the Black River, running directly along the river for part of the way. This wild and spectacular section of the river is an interesting contrast to the relatively placid section that you followed at the start of the hike. After about a quarter of a mile, the trail begins to climb out of the gorge. At the top of the climb, it turns right at a T-intersection, bears sharply left in 100 feet, then bears left again at a Y-intersection.

The trail continues high above the river, with views of the river below through the trees. In another 0.4 mile, you'll reach a T-intersection with a wide dirt road. The red blazes turn right, but you should turn left and follow a green-blazed trail that heads downhill along the woods road. In another 750 feet, you'll reach a Y-intersection. Here, the green blazes bear left, but you should bear right and continue ahead on the woods road, now unmarked, which heads north, parallel to the river. Continue along the road for another 600 feet to its end at the blue-blazed Black River Trail. Turn left and follow the Black River Trail north along the Black River for 1.2 miles, retracing your steps to the Cooper Mill parking area where the hike began.

8 Ramapo Mountain State Forest
Castle Point Short Loop

This loop hike runs along the shore of scenic Ramapo Lake and climbs to the ruins of an old stone mansion and tower, with panoramic views.

Difficulty: Moderate
Length and Time: About 3.0 miles; about two and one-half hours.
Map: New York-New Jersey Trail Conference North Jersey Trails Map #115.
Directions: Take I-287 to Exit 57 (Skyline Drive). Proceed north on Skyline Drive for about one mile to the upper parking area for Ramapo Mountain State Forest on the left side of the road, just beyond milepost 1.4 (opposite the entrance to Camp Tamarack).

At the northwest end of the parking area, opposite the entrance to Camp Tamarack, you will see a yellow blaze of the Hoeferlin Memorial Trail, as well as a triple red/white blaze, which marks the terminus of the Skyline Connector Trail. You will be returning to the parking area on the Skyline Connector Trail, but the Hoeferlin Trail will be your route for the first part of the hike.

Head into the woods and turn left, following the yellow blazes, then bear right onto a footpath parallel to a gravel road. After passing a small pond to the right, follow the yellow blazes as they briefly turn right onto the road (this portion of the road is paved), then turn left onto another woods road. After passing an interesting rock outcrop on the right, you'll come to a Y-intersection, where the yellow-blazed trail bears right and begins to descend.

Soon, the gravel road briefly reappears to the right, but bear left to stay on the yellow-blazed trail. Eventually, the yellow blazes turn right, leaving the road, and follow a footpath over undulating terrain. After crossing a stream and once again briefly approaching the paved road, the Hoeferlin

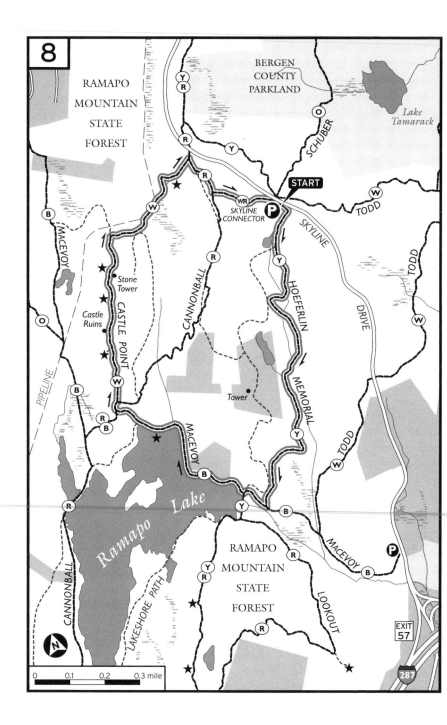

Foxcroft

Towards the end of the nineteenth century, Jacob Rogers, the son of the founder of the Rogers Locomotive Works in Paterson, N.J., assembled a three-square-mile tract of land around Ramapo Lake and increased the size of the lake by building a stone dam across its outlet. When Rogers died in 1901, he bequeathed the property to the Metropolitan Museum of Art, which sold it several years later. In 1909, the property was purchased by William Porter, a stockbroker, who hoped to develop it into an exclusive community like Tuxedo Park. That plan was never realized but, in 1910, Porter built himself a large home, which he called "Foxcroft," overlooking the lake. Unfortunately, in May 1911, Porter died from injuries he sustained in an automobile accident while heading back to Manhattan from Foxcroft, and the mansion was inherited by his wife, Ruth.

In 1913, Ruth married Warren C. Van Slyke, an attorney who served as Assistant Chief of Naval Intelligence in World War I, and later represented claimants in lawsuits against the German government resulting from the sinking of the *Lusitania*. They lived in New York City and used Foxcroft as a weekend and summer home. After Van Slyke's death in 1925, his widow lived at Foxcroft until she died in 1940 at the age of 63. Foxcroft was sold by her estate in 1942. In the early 1950s, the property became entangled in a bitter divorce dispute and was abandoned. Vandals soon broke in, and they set fire to the mansion in 1959. The property was acquired by the State in 1976.

Trail descends to a woods road – the route of the blue-blazed MacEvoy Trail. Turn right, now following both yellow and blue blazes. Soon, the trail bears left and descends a short pitch to a paved road.

Turn left along the road and head down to Ramapo Lake. At the lakeshore, the yellow-blazed Hoeferlin Memorial Trail continues ahead, crossing the dam, but you should turn right onto North Shore Drive, the route of the blue-blazed MacEvoy Trail. The MacEvoy Trail follows this gravel road along the northeast shore of the lake, passing a private home on the right and crossing a small stream on a stone-arch bridge, with an attractive cascade to the right.

A short distance beyond, you'll come to a rock ledge on the left that overlooks the lake. This is a good place to take a break. Once known as

View of Ramapo Lake from a rock ledge along the Castle Point Trail

Rotten Pond, and later as Lake LeGrande, Ramapo Lake is the centerpiece of Ramapo Mountain State Forest. It was formerly surrounded by private property, but most of the land around the lake was acquired by the state in the 1970s.

Just beyond, the trail reaches the northern tip of Ramapo Lake. Bear right at the fork in the road and pass between two concrete pillars. A short distance ahead, the blue-blazed MacEvoy Trail leaves to the left, and a triple-white blaze indicates the start of the Castle Point Trail. You should continue ahead on the road, now following the white blazes of the Castle Point Trail. Just beyond, as the road curves sharply to the right, turn left, leaving the road, and follow the white-blazed trail as it climbs steadily and rather steeply.

As you approach the top of the climb, bear left onto a rock ledge that offers a spectacular view. Directly below you is Ramapo Lake, with the Wanaque Reservoir to the right (west). On a clear day, you can see the New York City skyline on the horizon to the left. You'll want to pause here to rest from the steep climb and enjoy the view.

When you're ready to continue, follow the white trail uphill. After climbing over a stone wall, you'll reach the ruins of a mansion. Known as Foxcroft, it was built around 1910 by William Porter, a stockbroker. His widow occupied it until her death in 1940, and it fell into ruin in the late 1950s. Use caution if you wish to explore the remains of this once-elegant stone structure.

The trail continues to the north, passing the remains of a concrete swimming pool. A short distance beyond, an unmarked side trail to the

The ruins of Foxcroft

left leads to an unobstructed west-facing viewpoint over the Wanaque Reservoir and the Wyanokie Mountains. Continue on the white trail, which soon climbs to reach a stone tower. Contrary to what one might think at first glance, this was not a lookout tower; rather, it held a cistern that supplied water to the mansion (note the rusted pipes adjacent to the tower). Just beyond, there is another view from an open rock ledge to the left of the trail over the Wanaque Reservoir to the west. The trail now begins to descend.

Watch carefully as the Castle Point Trail turns right, just before reaching the route of a gas pipeline. It briefly joins a woods road, turns left onto a footpath before reaching a wide gravel road, then again turns left onto the woods road. It turns right and follows the gas pipeline for 350 feet, then turns right again, leaving the pipeline, and crosses a stream. The trail now climbs, first gradually, then rather steeply through mountain laurel, to a rock ledge, which provides a view of the stone tower you passed about half a mile back.

A short distance beyond, the Castle Point Trail reaches a paved road, with Skyline Drive just to the left. Here, the Castle Point Trail ends, and you turn right to continue along the Cannonball Trail (white-"C"-on-red blazes). The trail follows the road for 200 feet, then turns left onto a footpath through the woods. Soon, you'll reach a junction where the red/white-blazed Skyline Connector Trail begins to the left. Turn left and follow this red/white trail along a footpath roughly parallel to Skyline Drive until you reach the parking area where the hike began.

Stone water tower on the Castle Point Trail

9   Ringwood State Park

This loop hike climbs to the summit of Mt. Defiance, with panoramic views, and passes several scenic ponds.

Difficulty: Moderate
Length and Time: About 7.0 miles; about four and one-half hours.
Map: New York-New Jersey Trail Conference North Jersey Trails Map #115.
Directions: Take Skyline Drive to its northwestern terminus at Greenwood Lake Turnpike (County Route 511). Turn right, continue for 1.5 miles, and turn right onto Sloatsburg Road. Continue for 2.1 miles and turn right onto Morris Road. In 1.3 miles, just before the entrance to the Skylands section of Ringwood State Park, turn left onto Shepherd Lake Road and proceed for 0.8 mile to Shepherd Lake. Past the entrance booth, bear left and park in the designated parking area (a parking fee is charged from Memorial Day to Labor Day). NOTE: Shepherd Lake is a popular destination on summer weekends, and the parking area can fill up early in the day.

This hike follows a combination of footpaths, carriage roads (built for the estates that once dominated this area) and a mountain bike trail. Created primarily for bicyclists, the mountain bike trail – part of which is a narrow, "single-track" route – is also open to hikers. However, hikers should be alert for bicycles and, although park rules provide that bicyclists must yield to hikers, hikers may choose to step off the trail and allow bicyclists to pass.

From the parking area, follow the paved path down to the beach on Shepherd Lake. Continue through the boat launch parking area and past the boat house, with the lake to your left. You will notice the red-on-white blazes of the Ringwood-Ramapo Trail, which you will follow for the first part of the hike.

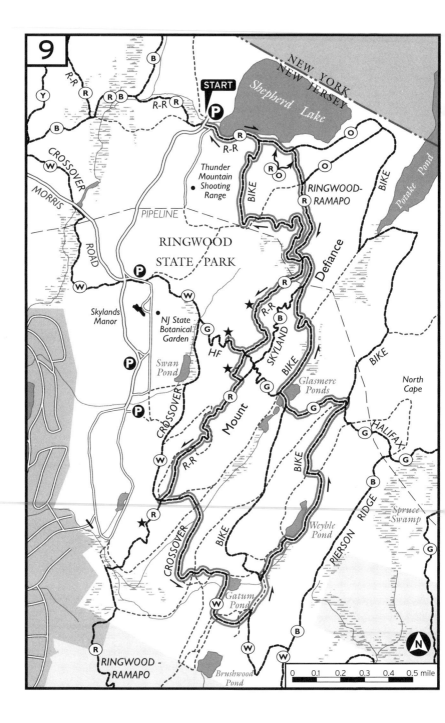

Shepherd Lake from the Ringwood-Ramapo Trail

After passing a kiosk, where an orange-blazed trail begins, continue on a gravel road along the lake, following both red-on-white and orange blazes. In about a third of a mile, both trails turn right, leaving the road. Continue to follow the blazed trails, which head uphill on a footpath. At an intersection with a woods road, the orange-blazed trail turns left, but you should continue ahead, now following only the red-and-white blazes of the Ringwood-Ramapo Trail.

The trail climbs to the top of a rise, then descends to cross a mountain bike trail. This will be your return route, but for now, continue ahead on the red-on-white-blazed trail, which passes an old stone foundation to the left. After crossing a gas pipeline, the trail begins to climb the northern shoulder of Mt. Defiance, first gradually, then more steeply. Just below the 1,040-foot summit, there is a limited view to the west over Ringwood Manor and the Cupsaw Lake area.

After a short but steep descent, the trail follows the crest of the ridge, paralleling impressive cliffs on the right and passing an interesting split boulder. Soon, you'll reach a junction with the green-on-white-blazed Halifax Trail. You will be continuing ahead on the Ringwood-Ramapo Trail, but for now, turn right on the Halifax Trail.

Skylands Manor and its Ponds

The ponds along the route of this hike are not natural gouges left by an ice-age glacier in retreat. Their shape came from a subtler hand: the designs of one of the leading landscape architects at the turn of the twentieth century.

The hike traverses what once was an 1,100-acre estate, assembled in the early 1890s from several farms by Francis Lynde Stetson, a prominent and influential lawyer. Stetson represented several railroads and the U.S. Steel Corporation and was the personal attorney to J.P. Morgan. At one time, he had Grover Cleveland as a law partner.

To design the landscaping for his estate, Stetson brought in Samuel Parsons, Jr., a protégé of Frederick Law Olmsted and Calvert Vaux, the designers of New York City's Central Park. Parsons had designed several parks and squares in New York City, as well as Balboa Park in San Diego. He would subsequently serve as New York City's Commissioner of Parks and was a founding member of the American Society of Landscape Architects.

Parsons' design for Stetson's estate included the construction of several dams to create spring-fed ponds that would provide a water supply for the farm and estate grounds. A map dated 1911 shows the final plan, with the ponds including Weyble, Gatun, Grasmere (four ponds) and Brushwood. Grasmere (now known as Glasmere) was named after the lake and village in England that had been home to William Wordsworth, the poet. Gatun was named after the lake and eastern set of locks for the Panama Canal, then under construction.

After Stetson's death in 1920, the estate was purchased by Clarence McKenzie Lewis, an investment banker and trustee of the New York Botanical Garden. Lewis tore down the manor house and built a new one (the present Skylands Manor) and extensively expanded the plantings and gardens.

The property served as a college campus in the 1950s, and it was purchased by the state as parkland during the following decade. In 1984, 96 acres of the property around the manor house were designated as the state's official botanical garden.

Today, Skylands Manor and the other park buildings are connected to the municipal water system, but the grounds of the botanical garden are still irrigated by water from Weyble and Gatun Ponds.

-*Jim Simpson*

In about 500 feet, as the trail bears left and begins a steady descent, you'll notice an unmarked trail to the right. Follow this trail, which heads slightly uphill to a panoramic west-facing viewpoint. Skylands Manor may be seen directly below, surrounded by the exotic trees of the New Jersey State Botanical Garden, and the Wanaque Reservoir is visible to the left (south).

The west-facing view from the viewpoint on the Halifax Trail

After taking in the view, return to the Ringwood-Ramapo Trail and turn right. In about 350 feet, there is another west-facing viewpoint from a rock outcrop to the right. The view of Skylands Manor is largely obscured by trees, but you get a better view of the Wanaque Reservoir.

Continue south on the Ringwood-Ramapo Trail, which descends gradually on a winding footpath, then turns left onto a wide gravel carriage road. It climbs a little, then descends gradually to reach another wide carriage road – the route of the white-blazed Crossover Trail.

Turn left onto the Crossover Trail, which continues to descend. After crossing another woods road, the trail levels off. About half a mile from the Ringwood-Ramapo Trail, watch for a double white blaze and follow the Crossover Trail as it leaves the carriage road and enters the woods on a footpath. The trail crosses another road, climbs gradually, then turns left onto yet another carriage road.

After following this road only briefly, the Crossover Trail turns right onto a footpath and reaches Gatun Pond, where it turns right, rejoining the carriage road. At a clearing to the left, stone steps lead down to the water's edge (a remnant of a former swimming area). This tranquil, pleasant setting is a good spot for a break.

Gatun Pond

Continue ahead on the Crossover Trail along the carriage road. Soon, the trail parallels an old cable fence to the right, with Brushwood Pond visible in the distance, beyond an open field. At the next Y-intersection, bear left, continuing to follow the white blazes. But at the following intersection, where the white-blazed trail turns sharply right, you should continue straight ahead on an unmarked carriage road.

Soon, you'll pass small ponds on each side of the road (note the rusty fire hydrant on the left). A narrower road branches off to the left, but you should continue to follow the wider road straight ahead. A short distance beyond, a path – marked only by a brown wand to the left, with "hiker" and "bike" symbols – crosses. Here, you should turn right and follow this path, which is part of the mountain bike trail shown on Trail Conference Map #115 and is more pleasant than the road that it parallels.

The path rejoins the road just south of Weyble Pond. Turn right and follow along the east side of the pond. At the next intersection (north of the pond), turn left, but when you reach the following intersection, turn right, following the arrow on the brown wand.

In another third of a mile, the green-on-white-blazed Halifax Trail crosses. Turn left onto the Halifax Trail, which almost immediately crosses another carriage road and continues to descend on a footpath. At the base of the descent, turn right onto a road which passes between the two Glasmere Ponds.

Just beyond, you'll reach a T-intersection. Here, the Halifax Trail turns left, but you should turn right, now once again following the mountain bike trail. The carriage road that you are following soon goes by an old frame building on the left and passes between two abandoned stone buildings (originally, the gate house for the estate).

About a quarter of a mile beyond, you'll notice a clearing on the left, with an arrow on a brown wand. Here, the mountain bike trail leaves the road, and you should turn left and follow the "single-track" mountain bike trail, which will take you back to Shepherd Lake. Although not

This abandoned stone building was built as the gate house for the estate

marked (except with occasional brown wands at intersections), the trail is well-defined and easy to follow. It climbs on switchbacks to cross the gas pipeline and the Ringwood-Ramapo Trail, then descends gradually, crosses a woods road, and finally ends at the Ringwood-Ramapo Trail at the shore of Shepherd Lake. Turn left and follow the Ringwood-Ramapo Trail back to the parking area at the southwest corner of the lake, where the hike began.

10 Long Path/Old Erie Railroad Bed
Piermont to Nyack, N.Y.

This loop hike traverses historic Rockland Cemetery, goes through the remains of a pre-World War I rifle range and returns via a rail-trail with views over the Hudson River.

Difficulty: Moderate to strenuous
Length and Time: About 10.0 miles; about six hours.
Map: New York-New Jersey Trail Conference Hudson Palisades Map #109.
Directions: Take the Palisades Interstate Parkway to Exit 4. Continue on U.S. Route 9W north for 2.3 miles and turn left, following the signs for N.Y. Route 340. Bear right at the bottom of the hill and turn right, at the next intersection, onto Ferdon Avenue. In 0.7 mile, the road turns sharply left, crosses a stream and becomes Piermont Avenue beyond the next intersection. At the following intersection, bear right onto Gair Street, and park in the municipal parking lot on the right.

Piermont railroad station

Walk back to 450 Piermont Avenue (the building with a large mural painted on it) and turn right onto Tate Avenue, a narrow street which heads uphill, soon curving to the right. You will notice the aqua blazes of the Long Path, which you will follow for the next six miles. When you reach a flight of stairs on the left, climb the stairs, and continue uphill along a footpath that leads

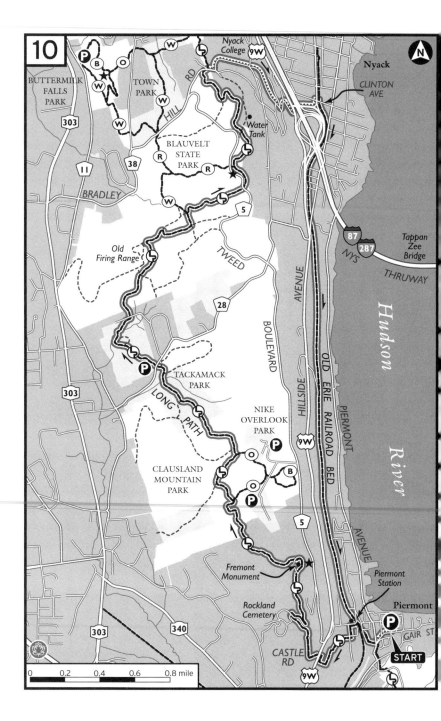

to Ash Street across from the former Piermont railroad station. Turn left here and follow Ash Street uphill as it curves to the right. At the next intersection, turn left onto Piermont Place, then turn right onto Crescent Road, which soon curves to the left. When the driveable road ends, continue ahead, then turn right at a double blaze just beyond a house with a wooden fence, and reach U.S. Route 9W.

Follow the Long Path as it turns right, briefly following Route 9W. Almost immediately, it turns left onto Castle Road, which soon curves to the right. When the paving ends, the Long Path turns right and continues through the woods. It soon rejoins the road, which leads into Rockland Cemetery. At the next intersection, turn sharply right and follow the paved cemetery road as it climbs to the crest of the Palisades, making a sharp switchback to the left on the way. After about half a mile, the road reaches the upper section of the cemetery. Bear right at the fork in the road, then bear left at the next intersection. You will pass the monuments marking the graves of Henry Honeychurch Gorringe, who brought Cleopatra's Needle from Egypt, and of General John Charles Fremont, the first Republican candidate for President of the United States (he lost the election to James Buchanan in 1856).

General Fremont's grave in the Rockland Cemetery

As the road curves left, you will notice a sign setting forth the cemetery's rules. Here the Long Path turns right, leaving the cemetery, and

The Old Erie Railroad Bed

Like the imprint of a fossil on stone, the right-of-way of the old Northern Railroad line leaves a long, level footprint on the topography of a stretch above the Hudson River running from Piermont to Nyack.

In 1841, the river town of Piermont became the eastern terminus of what was, for a brief time, the world's longest railroad line. It extended to Dunkirk, near Buffalo on Lake Erie, which opened it to Detroit, Chicago and other western markets. The town, originally called Tappan Landing, was renamed to reflect two prominent features, one of them railroad related: Tallman Mountain, and the huge man-made Erie Railroad pier stretching out into the Hudson River, built for transshipping of goods and passengers down to New York City. However, by 1850, the Erie had moved its terminus to Jersey City, just across the Hudson from Manhattan.

In 1859, the Northern Railroad of New Jersey completed its line between Piermont and Jersey City, and in 1870 an extension stretching three miles north to Nyack was opened. By then, the railroad had been leased to the Erie. At the ceremonial launch, a train loaded with a brass band and officials who included the infamous James Fisk, made the first run. Mr. Fisk, along with his partner Jay Gould, had recently battled for control of the Erie with Cornelius Vanderbilt in a stock war that reportedly involved the bribing of the state legislature in Albany.

For passengers, the ride from Nyack to Jersey City, where ferry service to New York City awaited them, took about an hour. By 1940, patronage had declined significantly, and passenger service was reduced to three rush hour trains in each direction. The Erie Railroad acquired the line in 1942, and from then on it was known as the Northern Branch. In 1958, the southern terminus for the line's passenger trains was moved to the former Lackawanna Terminal in Hoboken. Passenger service finally ended in 1966, and the line north of Piermont was abandoned (although freight service to Piermont continued into the 1970s).

The ribbons of steel rail are gone, but what remains today are a beautifully restored Victorian-era station in Piermont and a level trail where strollers, joggers and bicyclists can glimpse stunning river scenery, including views of another transportation icon from a later era — the Tappan Zee Bridge.   *-Jim Simpson*

reenters the woods, soon entering Clausland Mountain County Park. In another 0.7 mile, the Long Path turns sharply left, as an orange-blazed woods road continues straight ahead uphill. This orange trail leads in 0.3 mile to a parking area on Nike Lane and rejoins the Long Path in 0.6 mile. Follow the Long Path as it descends to cross a stream and then climbs to its second junction with the orange-blazed trail. Here, the Long Path turns left and begins a steady descent. At the base of the descent, it crosses a stream on a wooden bridge and ascends rather steeply to reach Clausland Mountain Road, 3.3 miles from the start of the hike.

The Long Path crosses the road and goes through a parking area for Tackamac Town Park, from where it descends on a series of woods roads. Pay careful attention to the blazes here. It reaches a water impoundment by an old dam and turns right, following a stream, then turns left and crosses the stream on a wooden bridge. After crossing paved Marsico Court in a residential area, the trail enters Blauvelt State Park, passing through several stands of evergreens that were devasted by Hurricane Sandy.

In another half a mile, the Long Path climbs over an embankment, descends a short set of wooden steps, and turns right on a woods road. This embankment is the site of the rifle range of Camp Bluefield, a pre-World War I National Guard training camp. It was abandoned after only three years because bullets often landed in the Village of Grand View, on the eastern side of the ridge! At the end of the embankment, you will note the entrance to a long concrete tunnel that served as a safe passage between the target wall and the firing line. The tunnel can be entered, but extreme caution must be exercised.

The Long Path turns right at a T-intersection, swings left, then turns left at a four-way intersection (where the blazes may be hard to find). It descends to a T-intersection, where it turns right to cross a stream, then climbs steadily to Tweed Boulevard. It crosses the road and continues uphill to an expansive southwestern-facing viewpoint over the Hackensack River valley. The Tappan Zee is to the left, and in the distance, both New York City (to the left) and Newark may be seen on a clear day. You've now gone 5.3 miles from the start, and this is a good place to take a break.

The trail continues along the ridge, with some ups and downs. To the right, there are seasonal views through the trees of the Tappan Zee Bridge and Nyack. In another half a mile, it begins a steady descent, finally emerging onto Bradley Hill Road. You will now leave the route of the Long Path and follow a series of roads downhill to reach the Village of South Nyack. Turn right onto Bradley Hill Road, then left at the next intersection. Continue downhill, past the athletic fields of Nyack College. At the following intersection, continue straight ahead onto Terrace Drive, then turn sharply left onto Lowland Drive, which switchbacks to the right and ends at Hillside Avenue (Route 9W). Turn left and, in about 200 feet, turn right and cross over the New York Thruway. Bear left at the fork in the road, and make the first right onto Clinton Avenue.

View of the Tappan Zee Bridge from the Old Erie Railroad Bed

You will immediately come to the Old Erie Railroad Bed. This is the route of the Nyack spur of the Northern Railroad of New Jersey, later the Erie Railroad, which provided passenger service to Jersey City. Built in 1870, the line was abandoned in the late 1960s and has been converted into a rail-trail. Turn right and follow this delightful, nearly level trail for three miles back to Piermont, with intermittent views to the left over the Tappan Zee Bridge and the river. You will notice old telegraph poles along the right-of-way and, near Piermont, you may spot a concrete marker on the left with the inscription "JC 25" – indicating the distance to Jersey City. When you reach the old Piermont station, cross the street and follow the footpath down to Tate Avenue, then turn right and continue to Piermont Avenue, the start of the hike.

11 Wawayanda State Park
Terrace Pond

This loop hike climbs over puddingstone rock outcrops to reach beautiful Terrace Pond and several panoramic viewpoints.

Difficulty: Moderate to strenuous
Length and Time: About 5.2 miles; about three and one-half hours.
Map: New York-New Jersey Trail Conference North Jersey Trails Map #116.
Directions: Take I-287 to Exit 57 (Skyline Drive) and continue on Skyline Drive to its western terminus at Greenwood Lake Turnpike (County Route 511). Turn right and proceed north on Greenwood Lake Turnpike. When you reach a fork at 8.4 miles, bear right to continue on Warwick Turnpike (still County Route 511). Proceed for another 2.3 miles and turn left onto Clinton Road. Continue on Clinton Road for 1.7 miles to a large parking area (designated as P-7) on the right side of the road, about 0.2 mile south of a gas pipeline crossing (and just north of the entrance to the Wildcat Mountain Wilderness Site – Project U.S.E.).

From the parking area, cross the road and enter the woods at a trailhead with a triple-blue blaze and a triple-yellow blaze. These mark the start, respectively, of the Terrace Pond North Trail and the Terrace Pond South Trail. Follow the yellow blazes, which almost immediately bear right (the blue trail, which goes off to the left, will be your return route.) You will soon find yourself in deep woods, following a rocky trail through mountain laurel, hemlock and white pine, and crossing several wet areas on plank puncheons.

In about half a mile, the trail goes through a magnificent rhododendron grove, with the large rhododendrons forming an arch over the trail in places. As you leave the rhododendron grove, the laurel and evergreens end, and you proceed through a second-growth forest of deciduous trees.

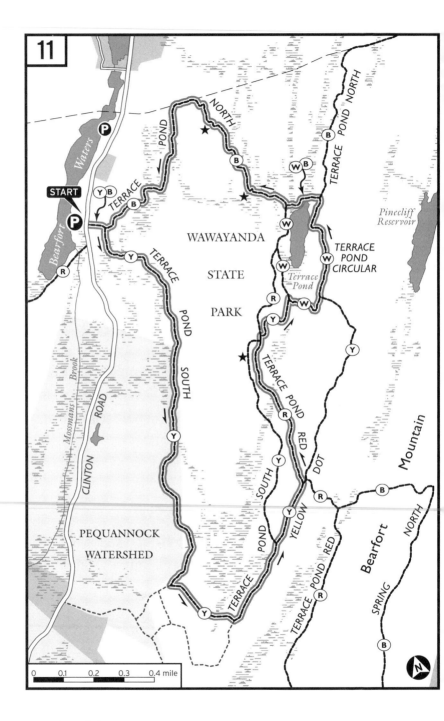

Rhododendrons arching over the Terrace Pond South Trail

After following an interesting whaleback rock and crossing two low stone walls, the yellow trail turns left onto a woods road. You'll be following woods roads, with gentle grades, for the next 1.3 miles.

Soon, the yellow markers bear left again onto another woods road lined with barberry bushes – indicating that this area was once farmed. Then, after half a mile, take care to follow the yellow markers as they bear very sharply left at a junction of woods roads. Soon, the yellow trail passes a swamp on the left, with many dead trees. A quarter of a mile beyond the sharp turn, the yellow trail bears left at the top of a rise, with another woods road going off to the right.

The trail once again begins to run along the interesting swamp on the left. Towards the end of the swamp, the yellow markers twice bear right, bypassing flooded sections of the woods road, and crossing the outlet of the swamp on rocks. Between the two detours, the trail crosses a large concrete pipe, with much beaver activity visible in the swamp. A short distance beyond, you'll reach a junction with the Yellow Dot Trail,

A Jetport that Never Took Off

Terrace Pond on Bearfort Mountain is one of the state's most pristine and serene glacial lakes. But in the 1960s, Bearfort Mountain (along with Bowling Green Mountain in Morris County) was considered by the Port of New York Authority as the site for a major jetport to serve the New York metropolitan area. It was stated by the proponents of the jetport that "public opposition to the proposed sites is unlikely... because of the sparse population in these areas."

Incredibly, one proposal called for the use of hydrogen bombs to level the mountaintop for the jetport. As far-fetched as that might seem to us, in the early 1960s, a program called "Project Plowshare" proposed various peaceful uses for nuclear explosions – including the construction of another canal in Central America to link the Atlantic and Pacific Oceans.

Fortunately, the plan for thermonuclear excavation of Bearfort Mountain was rejected by a consultant on the ground that it was "impractical and would cause too many adverse side effects," such as the necessity "to evacuate an area with a radius of 15 miles during blasting and for the necessary contamination period." It was also stated that the effects on the watersheds of the metropolitan area "would represent an unknown."

Despite the predictions of its proponents, the jetport proposal was strongly opposed by environmentalists and local residents. Among those who voiced their opposition to the plan was Fred Ferber, who had purchased the 6,800-acre tract surrounding Terrace Pond several years earlier, with the intent of developing "a wilderness nature center... as well as campsites, bicycle and hiking trails, and other recreational programs." He characterized the jetport plan as "sheer insanity," stating that it would destroy a "priceless natural asset unique on the east coast."

By the end of 1964, the Port Authority had rejected the Bearfort Mountain site, despite its proximity to Interstate Route 80, which would have made it easily accessible to New York City. But by 1971, Mr. Ferber owed about $1.5 million in back taxes and mortgage payments, and the creditors threatened to foreclose on the property. Finally, in June 1973, the State of New Jersey purchased the tract for $2.8 million, using Green Acres funds. It was designated as the Bearfort Mountain Natural Area in 1978, recognizing its unique natural features and ensuring protection of its ecosystem.   *-Jim Simpson and Daniel Chazin*

narked with yellow-on-white blazes. Bear right here, leaving the yellow
rail, and continue ahead on the Yellow Dot Trail, which follows a pleasant
voods road.

Beaver activity is visible in this swamp along the Terrace Pond South Trail

In another quarter of a mile, after passing cliffs to the left, you'll reach
a junction with the red-blazed Terrace Pond Red Trail (marked by a sign).
Turn left and follow the red trail. The hike now becomes more rugged.
After a steep climb up a ridge, the trail follows the ridge to the north,
continuing to ascend gradually. It then descends to a valley, crosses an
intermittent stream, and continues across several low ridges.

A huge rock outcrop soon appears directly ahead. The trail turns right,
parallels the outcrop, then climbs to its top and continues along it. The
outcrop is composed of reddish-purple "puddingstone" conglomerate
rock, with quartz pebbles embedded in the rock. You'll have to look carefully to find the red blazes painted on the rock.

After following the outcrop for some distance, the trail descends to the
right and soon reaches a junction with the yellow-blazed Terrace Pond
South Trail (the same trail that you followed for the first two miles of the
hike). The two trails run jointly for a short distance. When they again
divide, turn right and follow the yellow blazes.

A "puddingstone" conglomerate outcrop along the Terrace Pond Red Trail

The yellow trail now climbs steeply up a rock outcrop and descends to a valley. After continuing over rugged, rocky terrain, it ends at a junction with the white-blazed Terrace Pond Circular Trail. Turn right onto the white trail, which soon climbs to a rock outcrop with pitch pines. Here, a triple-blaze marks the end of the Yellow Dot Trail, but you should continue along the white trail, which follows the long rock outcrop for some distance before reentering the woods.

After passing a huge glacial erratic to the left, the white trail comes out onto another rock outcrop, from which it descends steeply. At the base of the descent, you'll come to a fork. Here, you should turn left onto a short unmarked side trail which leads to a rock outcrop, with fine views over

Terrace Pond. This is a great spot to take a break and enjoy the beauty of his secluded glacial pond.

When you're ready to continue, bear left at the fork and continue along he white trail, parallel to the pond. After passing another viewpoint over he pond, you'll come to a T-intersection, where the blue-blazed Terrace Pond North Trail joins from the right. Turn left, now following both white and blue blazes.

Terrace Pond

Just beyond, the trail descends very steeply. You'll need to use both your hands and your feet to make your way down the steep rock faces. At the base of the descent, the trail crosses the outlet of the pond on logs. This crossing can be extremely difficult in wet periods. The trail now climbs, steeply in places, over rock ledges and outcrops, soon reaching another junction, marked by a triple white blaze (indicating that the Terrace Pond Circular Trail technically begins and ends here).

Bear right and continue to follow the blue blazes of the Terrace Pond North Trail, which crosses several wet areas on planks, logs and rocks. After a short climb, you'll emerge onto a large open rock outcrop. Just to the left of the trail, there are panoramic west-facing views from the top of a rounded peak of conglomerate rock. This is another good spot for a break.

The rounded peak of conglomerate rock along the Terrace Pond North Trail

Continue along the blue trail, with level stretches interrupted by several short, steep descents (and a few short climbs). At one point (just before beginning one of the descents), you'll notice a steep rock outcrop immediately to your left. Climb this outcrop for another panoramic view to the west and northwest.

Soon afterwards, you'll come out onto a wide cut for a gas line. Bear left here and follow along the left side of the steep and eroded gas line for about 450 feet to the bottom of the hill. Here, the blue trail re-enters the woods on the left and leads in about half a mile, over relatively level terrain, back to the trailhead, crossing several wet areas on rocks.

12 Harriman State Park
Bald Mountain/Doodletown Loop

This loop hike steeply climbs to a panoramic viewpoint atop Bald Mountain and descends on old woods roads through the historic former settlement of Doodletown.

Difficulty: Strenuous

Length and Time: About 5.0 miles; about three and one-half hours (allow additional time if you wish to explore the many former homesites in Doodletown).

Map: New York-New Jersey Trail Conference Harriman-Bear Mountain Trails Map #119.

Directions: From the south, take the Palisades Interstate Parkway to its terminus at the Bear Mountain Circle. From the east, cross the Bear Mountain Bridge and reach the Bear Mountain Circle. From the circle, head south on U.S. Route 9W for 1.3 miles to a small hikers' trailhead parking area on the left side of the road, just past a concrete bridge over a stream.

Cross Route 9W (use caution when crossing this very busy highway) and enter the woods on the south side of the stream, following the blue blazes of the Cornell Mine Trail. The trail heads uphill on a footpath, climbing steeply, then levels off. It soon begins to climb again, with cascades visible in the stream below to the right. After bearing left, away from the stream, the trail levels off. For the next half mile, the trail is generally uphill, with a few minor dips and level sections.

After about half an hour of hiking, you'll notice the huge, massive Bald Mountain directly ahead of you. The summit of this mountain is your destination. A short, level stretch follows, but the trail soon begins a steep, unrelenting climb up the mountain. To ease the grade somewhat, the trail follows switchbacks for the first part of the climb and an old woods road

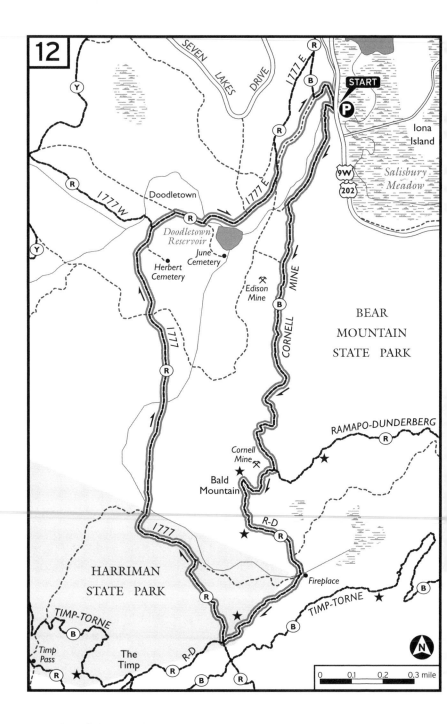

or the latter part, but you'll be climbing a vertical distance of 500 feet in ess than half a mile.

Near the top, the Cornell Mine Trail ends at a junction with the red-dot-on-white-blazed Ramapo-Dunderberg Trail. The small pit at the junction is a remnant of the Cornell Mine. Turn right onto the Ramapo-Dunderberg Trail and continue climbing, now somewhat more gently. After passing another mine pit, you'll reach the summit of Bald Mountain (elevation 1,080 feet), where the trail bends sharply left. You've climbed more than 1,000 vertical feet from the start of the hike, and this is a fine place to take a well-deserved break.

The summit affords fine views over the entire area, but the best views are from the open rocks straight ahead (just north of the actual summit). The wide panorama includes Iona Island, Anthony's Nose and the Bear Mountain Bridge to the northeast, Bear Mountain (with the Perkins Memorial Tower on its summit) to the northwest, and West Mountain to the west.

Bear Mountain Bridge, Anthony's Nose and Iona Island (in foreground on right) from the summit of Bald Mountain

When you're ready to continue, return to the red-dot-on-white trail and bear right, now heading south. (Make sure you don't retrace your steps, as the trail routes leading to and from the summit closely parallel each other!) After reaching a south-facing viewpoint, the trail begins a

Iona Island

Iona Island, visible from the summit of Bald Mountain, has an interesting history. The Native Americans called the island "Manakawaghkin"; in Revolutionary War times it was known as Salisbury Island and later was called Weygant's Island. The island was first settled by the Dutch in 1683. It became known as Iona Island after it was bought in 1849 by John Beveridge, who sold a part-interest to his son-in-law, Dr. C.W. Grant. Dr. Grant planted 20 acres to Iona grapes, imported from the Hebrides, as well as several thousand fruit trees. His attempt to produce wine that could compete against French imports was unsuccessful, and in 1868, the island was taken over by his creditor, the Bowery Savings Bank. When the West Shore Railroad was built in 1882, the island became more accessible, and an amusement park, hotel and picnic grounds were constructed.

In 1900, the U.S. Navy bought the island for $160,000 for use as a naval ammunition depot, and it proceeded to erect nearly 150 buildings on the island. In November 1903, an ammunition explosion killed six workers and broke windows as far away as Peekskill. During World War I, over two million pounds of ordnance was stored on the island – enough to supply the U.S. and British fleets in the Atlantic Ocean. In 1958, the Navy decommissioned the island, and in 1965, the Palisades Interstate Park Commission acquired the island for $290,000. Plans were drawn up to develop the island as a recreation area, but the proposed development never took place. The Park demolished nearly all the buildings on Iona Island, with the few remaining buildings currently used for storage.

Iona Island, as well as its surrounding marsh, have been designated a National Natural Landmark as well as a Significant Coastal Fish and Wildlife Habitat Area. Iona Island and Doodletown have been designated as an Important Bird Area, with over 165 species of birds having been observed there.

---

steady descent. It then climbs briefly through dense mountain laurel and descends to reach an old stone fireplace along a stream.

Proceed ahead, following the red-dot-on-white blazes, which cross the stream and continue over two low hills. At the top of the second hill, there is a north-facing view from a rock outcrop that looks back over Bald

Mountain. The trail now descends to a grassy woods road, the route of the 1777 Trail (which marks the route followed by British troops under Sir Henry Clinton on October 6, 1777, on their way to attack Forts Clinton and Montgomery). The 1777 Trail is marked with white circular blazes with a red "1777."

Turn right and follow the 1777 Trail, which proceeds steadily downhill, but on a much gentler grade than the Cornell Mine Trail, which you followed up to the summit. After a while, the woods road followed by the trail becomes rather eroded. To the right, through the trees, you can see Bald Mountain, which you just climbed.

After about half a mile, the trail levels off and crosses a stream. To the right, stone foundations and a trail shelter may be seen. These are the remnants of a camp once operated by Riverside Church of New York City. Continue ahead on the woods road, now proceeding through the former settlement of Doodletown, which thrived for two centuries until it was acquired by the park about 1960. Soon you'll notice several white markers that show the locations of former homes. From here on, the road is paved, although the paving is beginning to disintegrate, as the road has been closed to traffic for nearly half a century.

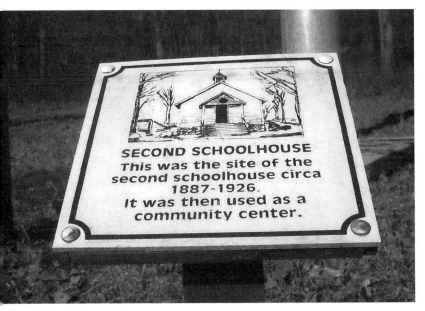

SECOND SCHOOLHOUSE
This was the site of the second schoolhouse circa 1887-1926.
It was then used as a community center.

Historical marker in Doodletown

Continue following the 1777 Trail along the road, known as Pleasant Valley Road, passing the remnants of many homes and other features of interest, which are commemorated by markers. For a detailed history of each of these sites, you may wish to consult *Doodletown: Hiking Through History in a Vanished Hamlet on the Hudson*, by Elizabeth "Perk" Stalter, a former resident of the village, or *Harriman Trails: A Guide and History*, by William J. Myles and Daniel Chazin (available from the Trail Conference). After about a mile, the 1777 Trail divides into the 1777W Trail, which leaves to the left, and the 1777E Trail, which continues ahead on the road. Proceed ahead, now following the 1777E blazes.

Soon you'll reach a T-intersection, where Pleasant Valley Road ends. Turn right, now following Doodletown Road. Bear left at the next intersection and go around the Doodletown Reservoir (built in 1957). Continue ahead at the following intersection, where Lemmon Road leaves to the left. A short distance beyond, you'll notice a marker to the right, where a path leads down to a waterfall in the stream. Just ahead, the 1777E Trail leaves to the left, but you should continue along the road (now unmarked), which begins a steady descent.

When you reach a dirt-and-rock barrier across the road, climb over it, and continue ahead as the road makes a sharp turn to the right, with the blue-blazed Cornell Mine Trail joining from the left. The road ends at Route 9W, just north of the parking area where the hike began.

13 Hudson Highlands State Park

This loop hike steeply climbs Bull Hill (Mt. Taurus), with many spectacular views over the Hudson River, and descends past the ruins of the Cornish estate.

Difficulty: Strenuous

Length and Time: About 5.0 miles; about four hours.

Map: New York-New Jersey Trail Conference East Hudson Trails Map #102.

Directions: From the east end of the Bear Mountain Bridge, proceed north on N.Y. Route 9D for about 8.5 miles to its intersection with N.Y. Route 301 (Main Street) in the Village of Cold Spring. Continue ahead on Route 9D for another 0.7 mile past the intersection with Route 301 to a parking area on the right side of the road, opposite the entrance to Little Stony Point.

From the northern end of the parking area, proceed north on the white-blazed Washburn Trail. In 100 feet, you'll reach a junction with the blue-blazed Cornish Trail, which continues straight ahead. The Cornish Trail will be your return route, but for now, bear right and continue to follow the Washburn Trail uphill along an old road, once used to access a quarry.

In about half a mile, you'll reach the site of the quarry, opened in 1931 by the Hudson River Stone Corporation and abandoned in 1967. The quarry site is now overgrown with trees, although the scars in the rock are plainly visible on the left. Here, the trail leaves the road, veers sharply right, and follows the rim of the quarry. You'll notice some rusted pipes and cables along the trail, remnants of former quarrying operations.

The trail soon bears right, leaving the quarry rim, and begins a steep ascent of Bull Hill (also known as Mt. Taurus), with views to the right over the Hudson River. The best viewpoint is from a rock outcrop at the

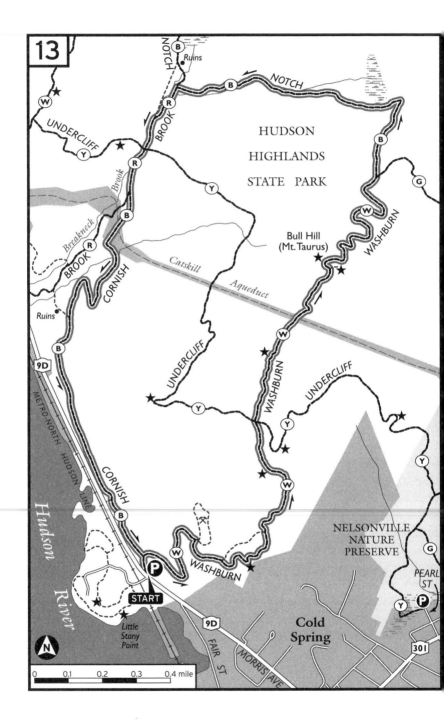

point of a switchback (after a short level stretch), about 30 feet to the right of the trail. Crows Nest Mountain is visible across the river, with Cold Spring directly below and Constitution Island to its south. You'll want to stop here to rest from the steep climb and enjoy the spectacular view.

The abandoned Hudson River Stone Corporation quarry on the Washburn Trail

Past the viewpoint, the trail continues to ascend more gradually. After climbing another 400 vertical feet, it comes out on open rocks, with views over the Hudson River to the west and south. Crows Nest Mountain is directly across the river, and the United States Military Academy at West Point is prominent in the distance to the south. After a short level section, the trail resumes a rather steep climb.

About 1.2 miles from the start, the Washburn Trail crosses the yellow-blazed Undercliff Trail. Continue along the Washburn Trail, which dips slightly and then resumes a steady climb. In another 15 minutes, you'll reach a rock outcrop just to the left of the trail that offers a broad view over the Hudson River. Just north of the sharp bend in the river – of great strategic importance during the Revolutionary War – is Constitution Island, and beyond the bend is the United States Military Academy at West Point. On a clear day, you can see the Bear Mountain Bridge down the river in the distance. You're not quite yet at the summit, but this is another good place to take a break.

Continue ahead, now climbing more gradually, and soon you'll reach the viewless summit of Bull Hill. Here, the trail begins to follow an old carriage road that descends the northeast slope of the mountain. Soon, you'll

The Cornish Estate

The ruins along the Brook and the Notch Trails are the remains o
an estate built in the early 1900s by Sigmund Stern, a diamond mer
chant. In 1917, he sold the estate to Edward Joel Cornish and his wife
Selina Carter Cornish, who called it "Northgate." The 650-acre es
tate included a mansion, swimming pool, gardens, garage and othe
outbuildings. In a stone barn in the northern section of the estate
Cornish raised Jersey dairy cows that, according to local newspape
articles, set records for milk production.

Edward Cornish was Chairman of the Board of the National Leac
Company from 1916 to 1933. Born in 1861, he served on Omaha's
park commission until 1912, made multiple gifts of land to the com
mission, and is known as the father of the Omaha park system. Cor
nish and his wife died within two weeks of each other in May 193£
and, subsequently, the estate was essentially abandoned. A fire in the
fall of 1956 destroyed the interior of the mansion, and its stone walls
are all that remain.

Given the proximity of rock blasting on the other side of Bull Hill
Cornish was probably concerned that his property would be quarriec
after his death. His offer to donate his estate to the State of New York
upon his death was turned down on the grounds that the mountain
ous terrain was not suitable for a public park and that there were
already restrictions against quarrying.

After his death, Cornish's heirs sold the property to the Centra
Hudson Gas and Electric Co., who contemplated building a powe
plant on Breakneck Ridge. This threat to the beauty of the Highlands
was essentially forgotten when, in 1962, Con Edison proposed tc
build a power plant on the side of Storm King Mountain across the
Hudson River. In the midst of that battle, in 1970, New York State es
tablished Hudson Highlands State Park, which included the Cornish
estate – finally protecting the land, as Cornish had wished.

For many years, one could only guess at what the interior of the
mansion must have looked like. But in 2010, a granddaughter o
Edward Cornish's nephew, who had in her possession photographs
of the estate, allowed some photos to be posted on the website
www.hudsonvalleyruins.org/yasinsac/cornish/cornishold.html.

-Jane Daniels

Constitution Island and West Point from the Washburn Trail

reach a T-intersection, where the trail turns sharply left (the path to the right leads to a south-facing viewpoint). Just beyond the intersection, the trail reaches a panoramic viewpoint from a rock outcrop on the left, with the Hudson River visible below to the left. The imposing ridge extending northeast from the river is Breakneck Ridge, with the Newburgh-Beacon Bridge visible through a low point in the ridge. To the right, you can see the fire tower on South Beacon Mountain, the highest point in the East Hudson Highlands. In the distance to the left, the Shawangunk Mountains – and beyond them, the Catskills – may be seen on a clear day.

The Washburn Trail continues to descend, with more views to the left. It follows the carriage road, which switchbacks down the mountain, until it ends at an intersection with the green-blazed Nelsonville Trail and the blue-blazed Notch Trail. Turn left and continue on the blue-blazed Notch Trail.

The Notch Trail descends steadily on a rocky, eroded footpath. After crossing a stream, it levels off and soon crosses a deeply eroded section of a woods road. Here, it turns sharply left, briefly parallels the road, then joins it. The trail continues along the road, which soon resumes a gradual descent, for about three-quarters of a mile, paralleling streams, first on the right, then on the left.

After passing a stone foundation on the left, the Notch Trail reaches Breakneck Brook. Here, the Notch Trail turns right, but you should turn left onto the red-blazed Brook Trail. (You may wish to take a short detour to visit the concrete-and-stone ruins of the Cornish dairy farm, visible on the right through the trees. If so, turn right and continue for a short

The ruins of the stone barn of the Cornish dairy farm

distance on the blue-blazed Notch Trail, which leads to the ruins, then retrace your steps and return to the junction.)

Continue south on the red-blazed Brook Trail, which follows a footpath along Breakneck Brook. In another quarter of a mile, you'll reach an intersection with the yellow-blazed Undercliff Trail, which joins briefly. Just ahead, the Undercliff Trail leaves to the right, crossing a bridge over the brook, but you should continue ahead along the red-blazed Brook Trail, which follows an eroded carriage road along the brook.

After passing a small abandoned concrete building and an old concrete dam on the right, you'll come to a fork. Bear left here onto the blue-blazed Cornish Trail, which follows an old road through the former estate of Edward J. Cornish, who served as Chairman of the Board of the National Lead Company.

The road passes a large cement-and-stone cistern on the right, then curves around two switchbacks and continues with a concrete pavement. Soon, the stone ruins of the Cornish mansion are visible below to the right (a side road leads down to the ruins). The paved road descends steadily towards Route 9D, where it ends at a gate. Just before the gate, the Cornish Trail turns left, crosses a wet area on rocks and stumps, and continues along a footpath parallel to Route 9D for about a quarter of a mile to end just before the parking area where the hike began.

Summer

Mount Hope Historical Park | Jenny Jump State Forest | Mills Reservation | Palisades Interstate Park, New Jersey Section | Harriman State Park | Fahnestock State Park | Delaware Water Gap National Recreation Area | Sam's Point Preserve | Black Rock Forest | Abram S. Hewitt State Forest | Storm King State Park | Worthington State Forest | Schunemunk Mountain

14 Mount Hope Historical Park

This loop hike, through pleasant second-growth woods, follows old woods roads past numerous mine openings of the abandoned Mount Hope Mines.

Difficulty: Easy

Length and Time: About 2.7 miles; about two hours.

Map: New York-New Jersey Trail Conference Jersey Highlands Trails (Central North Region) Map #125; Morris County Park Commission map (available online at www.morrisparks.net or from kiosk at trailhead).

Directions: Take I-80 to Exit 35 (eastbound) or Exit 35B (westbound) and proceed north on Mount Hope Avenue. In 0.5 mile, turn left onto Richard Mine Road. Continue for 0.7 mile and turn right onto Coburn Road (which becomes Teabo Road). The park entrance is 0.7 mile ahead on the left.

Known locally as the Richard Mine, Mount Hope Historical Park was once a booming iron mining and processing site. It forms a part of the original Mount Hope Tract, first developed by John Jacob Faesch in 1772. Over the course of the years, three separate veins of ore – each of which runs in a southwesterly-to-northeasterly direction – were mined on the property. The portion of the property traversed by this hike was divided into three ownerships, which operated the Teabo, Allen, and Richard mines, respectively. During World War II, the eastern end of the site was developed as the New Leonard Mining Complex – a state-of-the-art mining and ore-processing complex that produced 5,600,000 tons of ore by 1950. Mining operations in the area ended in 1959 (they were briefly revived in October 1977, but were abandoned just four months later), and the park was opened in 1997. Second-growth woodlands have reforested the areas that once were cleared for mining operations.

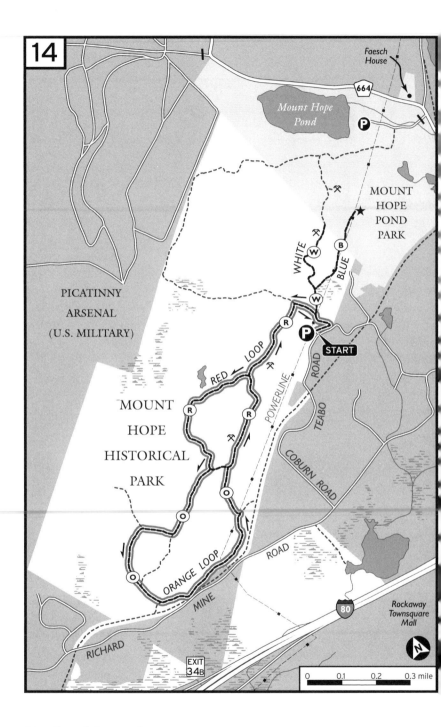

From the trailhead at the east end of the parking area (at a kiosk and a sign for the "Richard Mine"), follow an unmarked trail up a switchback to a trail junction under power lines. Turn left onto the Red Loop Trail, which passes many open mine pits and piles of mine tailings. After crossing a seasonal stream, the pits of the Teabo #2 Mine – opened in the 1850s and abandoned by 1883 – may be seen to the left in about a quarter mile.

About 400 feet beyond the last mine pit, turn sharply right at a double blaze, leaving the mine road, and follow the Red Loop Trail in a counterclockwise direction through second-growth woodlands, with an understory of blueberry bushes. This section of the trail departs from the main ore vein, so no mine pits are visible until a T-intersection is reached in another half a mile. Turn right here onto the Orange Loop Trail, which passes several small mine pits. In a quarter of a mile, follow the Orange Loop Trail as it turns right onto a narrower woods road and soon begins to descend. Then, in 650 feet – with a stream directly ahead – the trail turns left and continues to descend.

About 1.5 miles from the start of the hike, the trail reaches a T-intersection and turns left. Just beyond, the trail passes the remnants of the Richard #6 Mine, opened in 1897. Several mine pits and timbers may be seen to the left of the trail. In another 500 feet, a rail across the trail marks the site of the Richard #2 Mine – one of New Jersey's most productive mines in the 1880s.

The iron bars protruding from this stone foundation anchored machinery used to work the mines

The Sweetser Shaft complex of the Richard Mine, with the Mount Hope Mineral Railroad on the right

After crossing under power lines, follow the Orange Loop Trail as it bears left, leaving the wide woods road it has been following. The trail soon widens to a woods road and passes the stone foundations of several homes. Just beyond, the trail turns right under the power lines, then immediately turns left onto a rocky woods road. After a short climb, the

The head frame (with the wheel at the center) at the top of Inclined Shaft #5 of the Richard Mine. Cables extend across to the engine house on the left

A Mount Hope Travelogue from 1865

In the natural quiet that one experiences walking through the cratered landscape at Mount Hope Historical Park, it's difficult to picture what this area must have looked like when it was a thriving, noisy industrial community. But a glimpse of this past can be had from a newspaper account of a tour of northern New Jersey mining regions after the end of the Civil War – a time when declining demand for industrial products had brought about sharp cuts in wages.

The account appeared in the *New York Times* on September 4, 1865. The correspondent, identified only as "W.W.," began his visit in Boonton, which he reached by "a leisurely creep along the Morris Canal...a mode of traveling recommended by its supreme safety." He noted that "[i]f you make only two and a half knots an hour, you have the proud satisfaction of knowing that at any moment you may leap ashore, and walk three or four."

Among the mines that he visited, he described the Richard Mine (along the route of this hike): "Four openings have been made on a range of about a quarter of a mile," he observed. "One steam engine has geared to it the requisite apparatus for pumping four shafts, some hundred yards apart, and in different directions." He estimated that the 70 to 80 men who worked there extracted from 18,000 to 20,000 tons of iron ore a year. He described the miners as "a very steady set of men" whose houses were "the neatest and most comfortable of any I have seen, renting at between $30 and $40 annually."

At the nearby Mount Hope Mine, he described the village as consisting of "about fifteen double houses, laid out as a street," characterizing the houses as "guiltless of paint as yet, but not untidy in appearance." Of the company store, he said, "[c]omplaint is made, I know not with what justice, that they are in the habit of charging employees extravagantly for groceries, dry goods, etc., which the latter are compelled to purchase." He reported wages at about $1.50 per day, although they had been as high as $2.50 the previous winter.

When questioned about safety, Mount Hope workers claimed there had not been a fatal accident in two years, even though "the boom of a blast going off may be heard every few minutes in some part of the works."

-Jim Simpson

trail passes six shafts of the Allen Mine, first opened in the 1830s (the mine openings are atop a low ridge about 75 feet to the left of the trail).

Just beyond, you'll reach a junction where the Orange Loop Trail ends Continue ahead, now following the Red Loop Trail, which passes several more trenches and mine pits of the Allen Mine to the left. Note the protruding iron bars, which were used to anchor machinery needed to operate the mines. One of the pits, known as the Smoke Stack Shaft, was excavated in the 1850s to provide ventilation for the Allen Tunnel, which extended south to Teabo Road. (The tunnel itself is no longer visible.) As the trail swings to the left, a huge pit of the Allen Mine may be seen to the right of the trail.

Just beyond, you'll reach the start of the Red Loop Trail. Continue ahead, following the Red Loop Trail back to the trail junction under the power lines, then turn right and continue to the parking area where the hike began.

15 Jenny Jump State Forest

This short loop hike climbs to several panoramic viewpoints and passes interesting glacial erratics.

Difficulty: Easy
Length and Time: About 1.4 miles; about one hour.
Map: New Jersey DEP Jenny Jump State Forest map (available from park office).
Directions: Take I-80 West to Exit 12 (Hope/Blairstown). Turn left at the bottom of the ramp and proceed south on County Route 521 for 1.1 miles to the old Moravian village of Hope. Turn left at the blinking light onto County Route 519 (Johnsonburg Road). Continue for 1.1 miles and turn right onto Shiloh Road. In 1.1 miles, turn right onto State Park Road and proceed to the park entrance, 1.0 mile on the left. After entering the park, bear right, continue for 0.1 mile, and park in a small parking area opposite a restroom building.

From the parking area, proceed ahead on the paved road, which curves to the right. You will pass a sign marking the trailhead of the Summit and Swamp Trails, and go by another parking area to the right. Continue beyond this second parking area (where the pavement ends), and in another 200 feet you will see a sign that marks the start of the blue-blazed Spring Trail. Follow this trail, which runs along the base of the south side of the ridge.

After skirting an open area to the left, the Spring Trail passes near the edge of a rocky ravine, with views over the ravine from rock outcrops to the right of the trail. It then swings left and continues along the base of the ridge on a relatively level footpath. At 0.6 mile, after passing cliffs on the left, the trail turns left and makes a short but steep ascent to the ridge, where it reaches a junction with the yellow-blazed Summit Trail.

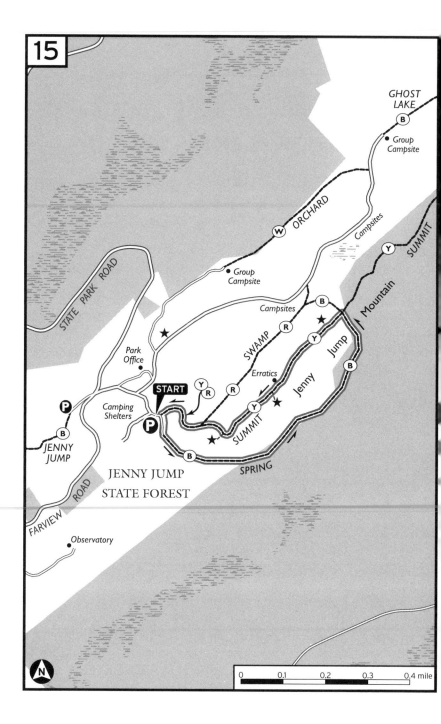

The Geology of Jenny Jump Mountain

Most of the bedrock of Jenny Jump Mountain is the banded crystalline metamorphic gneiss typical of the Jersey Highlands, but the mountain is separated from the main range of the Highlands by a few miles of fertile lowlands known as the Great Meadows. In the 1895 New Jersey Geological Survey, geologist Lewis Westgate noticed this situation and called the mountain an "outlier." Similar detached massive blocks have been found near other mountain ranges, notably in the Alps, where German geologists called them *klippen*, or cliffs. Modern geologists explain that, during continental collisions, enormous force may break off a mass of basement rock from an existing range and thrust it horizontally across newer, softer rocks, sliding like a hockey puck until it comes to rest. The softer rock in between erodes more rapidly and forms a valley, leaving a steep rise, or *klippe*, leading up to the hard ridge of the mountain.

Some of the bedrock at the north end of Jenny Jump Mountain is not gray Highlands gneiss, but rather limestone, formed of calcium from the bodies of aquatic animals in a shallow inland sea. These soft rocks were baked and hardened many miles deep in the earth, and they were pushed down under the weight of the tall mountains that were raised over them. Over hundreds of millions of years, the mountains have eroded, and the limestone is now exposed at the surface. Near the edge of that inland sea, changes in its depth produced sediments alternately of silt and calcareous material, which by heat and pressure were formed into rock. One such boulder, with white layers very different from the gneiss it rests on, has been carried by a glacier onto the ridge, where it may be seen adjacent to the trail.

-George Petty

Turn left, following the yellow blazes, which head southwest along the ridge of Jenny Jump Mountain. According to folklore, the mountain derives its name from Jenny Lee, a young woman living with her aged father on the mountain. While in a remote area on the mountain, she was accosted by (depending on the account) either a spurned suitor or a Native American. After being chased to the edge of the cliff, she chose "death before dishonor" and jumped. (In one account, however, she lived to tell the tale.)

After walking along the summit ridge for about 300 feet, you'll reach a west-facing viewpoint over the Delaware Water Gap from a rock outcrop to the right of the trail. Then, in 0.2 mile, you'll come to two large glacial erratics in an open area. The one on the right is formed of sandstone with calcareous layers, while the one on the left is composed of Precambrian granite gneiss (which forms the underlying bedrock). About 100 feet further along the trail, a side trail leads left to a southeast-facing viewpoint, which includes both forest and the fertile fields of the Great Meadows.

The trail passes between these two glacial erratics — one formed of sandstone with calcareous layers, the other of Highlands gneiss

The yellow trail now widens into a woods road and, in 0.2 mile, turns right and begins a steady descent. Just beyond this turn, at a flat rock along the trail, a side trail leads left to a panoramic viewpoint from a rock outcrop amid cedars. The Pinnacle is directly ahead, with the farmlands of the Great Meadows visible to the left. Glacial striations are clearly visible on the surface of the rock outcrop.

After enjoying the view, return to the main trail and turn left, continuing to descend. Soon, the red-blazed Swamp Trail joins from the right. After skirting Campsite #9, the joint red and yellow trails bear left, pass two cabins, and end at the parking area where the hike began.

16 Mills Reservation
Cedar Grove, N.J.

This loop hike circles this Essex County park and reaches a panoramic overlook.

Difficulty: Easy

Length and Time: About 2.1 miles; about one and one-half hours.

Map: Essex County Parks Department map (available online at www.essex-countynj.org/p/parks/sites/maps/mills.jpg). NOTE: The "trails" shown on this map are woods roads; the hiking trails followed on this hike are not shown on the map.

Directions: Take the Garden State Parkway south to Exit 154 (Clifton). Bear left after the toll booths, following the sign to U.S. Route 46, and continue west on Route 46. In 0.9 mile, take the Valley Road exit. At the bottom of the ramp, bear right onto Valley Road north, but immediately turn left, following the sign for "Montclair," then bear left again at the sign "U-Turn, Montclair." Proceed south along Valley Road for 1.0 mile and turn right onto Normal Avenue. Cross the railroad tracks, continue uphill for another 0.3 mile, and turn left into the parking area for Mills Reservation at the top of the hill, just past the intersection with Granite Drive.

The trailhead can also be reached by public transportation. The park is 0.3 mile (uphill along Normal Avenue) from the Montclair Heights station on the Montclair-Boonton rail line of NJ Transit (service provided only on weekdays), and NJ Transit bus #191/195, which provides limited service on weekdays only, stops at the trailhead.

The 157-acre Mills Reservation, an Essex County park, is a wooded oasis surrounded by suburbia. Situated atop the Watchung mountain range, the park is maintained in its natural state, with a network of woods roads and footpaths. This hike circles the park on footpaths, following the red-blazed Reservoir Trail and the blue-blazed Eastview Trail.

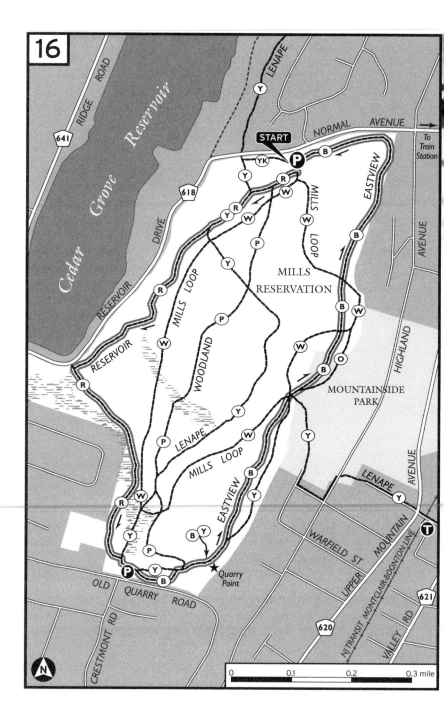

A slab of the basalt rock found in Mills Reservation

Just beyond the southwest corner of the parking area, you will notice a triple-red blaze, which marks the start of the red-blazed Reservoir Trail. Continue ahead along the gravel road for about 125 feet, then turn right opposite a kiosk with map and enter the woods on a footpath, following the red blazes. Soon, a purple-blazed trail begins on the left, but continue ahead on the red trail. A short distance beyond, the yellow-blazed Lenape Trail joins from the right. The yellow and red blazes run jointly for about 500 feet, but when the Lenape Trail branches off to the left, you should continue ahead, following the red blazes.

The trail soon begins to parallel Reservoir Drive, which can be seen and heard to the right (you might be able to catch a glimpse of the Cedar Grove Reservoir behind a fence). In about a third of a mile, as Reservoir Drive curves to the right, the trail bears left, crosses a wooden footbridge, and heads deeper into the woods. Soon, the trail again begins to run close to the park boundary, with the backyards of homes visible to the right of the trail. A green-blazed trail begins on the left, but continue to follow the red trail.

Near the southern end of the reservation, the red trail ends at a woods road. On the right, you'll notice a triple-blue blaze, which marks the start of the Eastview Trail. This will be your route for the rest of the hike. Turn right onto the blue-blazed trail, which is briefly joined by the black-on-

The Quarry below Quarry Point

The abandoned quarry that can be seen from Quarry Point was known as the "Osborne and Marsellis Quarry" or "McDowell's Quarry." Located on the western edge of Edgecliff Road in Upper Montclair, the quarry was worked from about 1890 to 1920. The company that operated the quarry was a supplier of crushed stone, coal, lumber and mason's material, and it built many of Montclair's roads. The company's offices and storage facilities were located south of Bellevue Avenue on Edgecliff Road, just east of the railroad.

The quarrying operation relied on steam power to drill and remove the trap rock from the face of First Mountain. At the base of the cliff, the trap rock was moved to the crusher in horse-drawn wagons, and the broken stone either was delivered directly to a construction site or was placed in the company's storage facility.

When the quarry was closed in the 1920s, Edgecliff Road was extended west to the Cedar Grove border. Subsequently, it was extended into Cedar Grove and given the name "Old Quarry Road."

-Ruth Rosenthal

Circular concrete slab at Quarry Point

View of the City of Newark from Quarry Point

yellow-blazed Lenape Link Trail. Follow the blue blazes as they bear left and climb gradually along a rock outcrop, with a steep drop below to the right. After again curving to the left, the blue trail reaches a junction with the yellow-blazed Lenape Trail. Turn right, now following both blue and yellow blazes.

In another 250 feet, you'll emerge onto an open area, with an abandoned circular concrete slab. You are at Quarry Point, named for the abandoned quarry that once operated directly below. Here, there is a panoramic east-facing viewpoint from a rock outcrop, with the City of Newark visible directly ahead (the best view is from another rock outcrop just to the south). A portion of the New York City skyline may be seen through the trees on the left.

This is a good place to take a break – not only to take in the view, but also to examine the interesting volcanic igneous rock that forms the Watchung mountain range. This rock, known as basalt, was formed when molten lava extruded out onto the earth's surface and cooled rapidly. It is completely different from the metamorphic rock found in the nearby Highlands (and also distinguishable from the igneous rock of the Palisades, known as diabase, which cooled more slowly underground).

When you're ready to continue, head north along a woods road, following both yellow and blue blazes. Just ahead, though, the blue blazes diverge to the left, leaving the woods road. Continue to follow the blue trail, which cuts across several clearings, with occasional blazes painted on the rocks. As the trail begins to descend after the first large clearing, be alert for a sharp left turn where the blue blazes leave the wide route and follow a narrower path.

Soon, you'll arrive at a very complex intersection of woods roads and trails. The yellow-blazed Lenape Trail comes in here and immediately heads off to the right. You should continue to follow the blue trail, which first bears right at a fork of woods roads, then bears left, and almost immediately afterwards diverges to the left, leaving the woods road and continuing on a footpath.

For the rest of the way, the blue trail meanders through the woods, crossing two gravel roads along the way. As the trail bends to head westward, it begins to descend, and it approaches Normal Avenue and begins to parallel it. After crossing a low stone wall, the blue trail ends at the parking area where the hike began.

17 Palisades Interstate Park, New Jersey Section

Huyler's Landing Trail/Dyckman Hill Trail
Loop from Englewood Boat Basin

This hike begins by following the shoreline of the Hudson River and continues along the top of the Palisades cliffs, with many outstanding views.

Difficulty: Moderate
Length and Time: About 8.0 miles; about five hours.
Map: New York-New Jersey Trail Conference Hudson Palisades Trails Map #108.
Directions: Take the Palisades Interstate Parkway to Exit 1 (Palisade Avenue, Englewood). Proceed east on Palisade Avenue and descend on the park entrance road to the Englewood Boat Basin. When you reach the traffic circle at the base of the descent, proceed north, entering the boat basin area (a fee is charged during summer months). Continue to the northern end of the boat basin.

From the northern end of the boat basin, proceed north along the white-blazed Shore Trail. The blazing is rather sparse in places, but the route is unmistakable, as it follows a rocky footpath along the narrow strip between the Palisades cliffs on the left and the Hudson River on the right. The trail goes through an area infested with poison ivy, so be sure to wear long pants and avoid touching this plant, characterized by its three shiny leaves.

Almost immediately, you'll pass the stone ruins of a bathhouse above and to the left. In about half a mile, the trail reaches a beach and briefly runs adjacent to the Henry Hudson Drive, which descends to the river

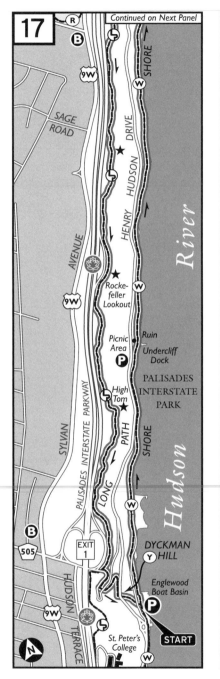

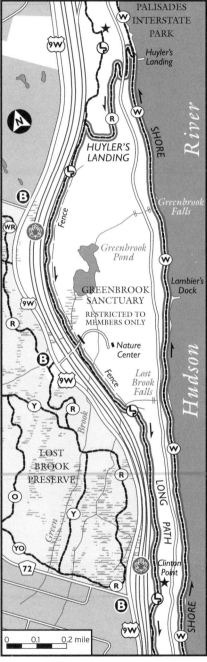

Ruins of the Undercliff Bathhouse

level here. Just beyond, you'll pass the ruins of the Undercliff Bathhouse in an open area.

For the next three miles or so, the trail runs through a secluded area. New York City is across the river, but all is quiet, except for the waves lapping against the shore and the occasional noise from boats in the river, aircraft above, or trains on the other side of the river. You'll pass some old stone picnic tables, and at one point you can look up at the cliffs to the left.

About two miles from the start, you'll cross a wooden bridge and pass a small waterfall, known as Lost Brook Falls. About a third of a mile ahead, you'll notice a beach and a stone jetty to the right. This is the site of the old Lambier's Dock. Then, in another third of a mile, you'll reach Greenbrook Falls, a large waterfall over a rock face to the left of the trail. The trail crosses just below the falls on large boulders.

Half a mile beyond Greenbrook Falls, you'll pass the ruins of a stone jetty to the right, with a beautiful view upriver to the north. Just beyond, a woods road departs to the left. This is the Huyler's Landing Trail, marked with dark red blazes. Bear left here and follow this trail as it switchbacks up a wide woods road, soon reaching the paved Henry Hudson Drive. Turn left and follow the drive for about 250 feet, then turn right, ascend wood-and-concrete steps, and continue to ascend on a narrower path.

Huyler's Landing Trail

The old road that takes you up from the Shore Trail to the Long Path (now known as the Huyler's Landing Trail) was named for George Huyler, a major landowner in Cresskill about 1840. At the time, the road was an important artery that enabled produce grown by Bergen County farmers to be transported to market in New York City. Wagons laden with produce would be driven down the road to the landing, where the produce would be loaded onto boats and ferried across the river. This all changed in 1859, when the Northern Railroad of New Jersey was constructed through the Northern Valley, enabling the produce to be shipped directly to Jersey City – thus avoiding the steep descent of the Palisades.

The road may well have had even greater historical significance. On November 20, 1776, about 5,000 British troops, led by Lt. Gen. Lord Charles, Earl of Cornwallis, landed at Closter Landing on the west bank of the Hudson River and marched up to the top of the cliffs. Their immediate goal was the American-held Fort Lee, which was quickly evacuated by General Nathanael Greene, who marched his troops towards Hackensack. Cornwallis pursued the Continental Army all the way to the Delaware River, which Washington and his troops crossed into Pennsylvania on Christmas Eve 1776.

For many years, it was believed that the "Closter Landing" at which Cornwallis and his troops landed was the area now known as the Alpine Boat Basin, over a mile north of Huyler's Landing. However, in the 1960s, historian John Spring of Cresskill determined that what is now known as Huyler's Landing was originally known as the "Lower Closter Landing." Spring's detailed study of historical records convinced him that Cornwallis and his troops actually set shore at Huyler's Landing, and today, his views are generally accepted as being historically accurate. So when you follow the route of this hike up the Palisades, it is likely that you are retracing the steps of the British soldiers of 1776!

The ascent is steady but moderate. As the trail nears the top of the cliffs, it turns right and climbs wide stone steps. Finally, just before reaching the Palisades Interstate Parkway, the Huyler's Landing Trail ends at a junction with the aqua-blazed Long Path.

Turn left at this junction and follow the Long Path south, parallel to the Parkway. Although the noise of the traffic on the Parkway can constantly be heard, the Parkway itself is often out of sight. At first, the Long Path follows a grassy woods road, with the blazing a little sparse. It soon dips down, climbs back to the level of the Parkway, and begins to parallel the fence of the Greenbrook Sanctuary on the left. A short distance beyond, it dips again to cross a stream. In another half mile, the trail crosses the paved entrance road to the Greenbrook Sanctuary, which is open to members only.

On the other side of the road, the Long Path climbs wooden steps, continues across several wet areas on puncheons (wooden planks), which may be slippery when wet, and crosses the Green Brook on a stone-faced bridge. In three-quarters of a mile, a short side trail on the left leads to Clinton Point – a magnificent viewpoint over the river, with Yonkers visible to the left across the river. There is no fencing here, so use caution and do not approach the edge of the cliffs. In two-thirds of a mile, you'll reach another viewpoint, with the Henry Hudson Parkway bridge across the river to the right. After passing the stone ruins of the former Cadgene estate, you'll soon arrive at the Rockefeller Lookout, with fine views over the river. The George Washington Bridge is visible to the south, with the Manhattan skyline beyond.

View from Clinton Point

Half a mile south of the Rockefeller Lookout, the Long Path swings to the left, away from the Parkway. Just beyond, as the trail curves to the right, you'll notice an unmarked path leaving to the left. Turn left and follow this short side trail, which leads to the High Tom overlook, with outstanding views across the Hudson River and up the river to the north. After enjoying this beautiful spot, return to the main trail, turn left, and proceed south.

You'll soon arrive at Palisade Avenue in Englewood. Turn left and briefly parallel the ramp to the northbound Parkway, then turn left again and follow the sidewalk which descends along the park entrance road. You will notice the yellow blazes of the Dyckman Hill Trail, which begins here. Follow the yellow blazes as they turn left and descend stone-and-concrete steps, passing by a waterfall and then going through an underpass beneath the entrance road. The trail then turns right and continues to descend on stone-paved switchbacks and stone steps. When you again reach the park entrance road, cross the road, turn right, then descend steps to the left. Upon reaching the river level, head north until you reach the northern end of the boat basin area, where you parked your car.

The George Washington Bridge and the Manhattan skyline from the Rockefeller Lookout

18 Harriman State Park
Island Pond/Lemon Squeezer Loop

This loop hike climbs to the summits of Green Pond and Island Pond Mountains, goes through the narrow Lemon Squeezer, and passes the historic Boston Mine.

Difficulty: Moderate to strenuous
Length and Time: About 7.5 miles; about four and one-half hours.
Map: New York-New Jersey Trail Conference Harriman-Bear Mountain Trails Map #119.
Directions: Take N.J. Route 17 north to the New York State Thruway and take the first exit, Exit 15A (Sloatsburg). Turn left at the bottom of the ramp onto N.Y. Route 17 north, and continue through the villages of Tuxedo and Southfields. About two miles north of Southfields, turn right onto Arden Valley Road. Cross the bridge over the New York State Thruway, then make the first right at a sign "Hikers' Trailhead Parking." Park in the dirt parking area to the west of a large meadow, known as the Elk Pen.

From the parking area, follow an unmarked woods road east across the meadow. At the end of the meadow, you will notice three red-triangle-on-white blazes, which mark the start of the Arden-Surebridge (A-SB) Trail. Turn right and follow the A-SB Trail south for about 100 feet, where you will see a wooden sign giving mileages along the Appalachian Trail (A.T.). You will be following the A.T., marked with white blazes, for the next two and one-half miles of the hike. Turn left onto the A.T., which begins a steady ascent of Green Pond Mountain, first moderately, then more steeply. After a climb of over 500 vertical feet, you'll reach the summit of the mountain, where a large boulder to the left of the trail affords limited views to the west. The A.T. now descends the eastern slope of the mountain on switchbacks.

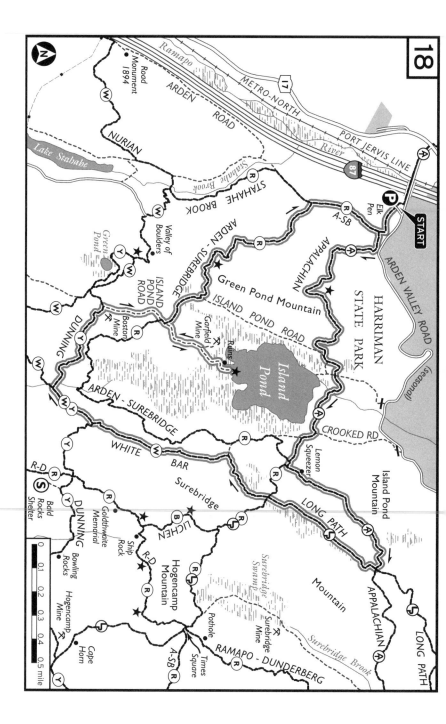

At the base of the descent, follow the A.T. as it turns left onto Island Pond Road, a dirt road built by Edward Harriman (after whom the park is named) about 1905. You'll soon enter a beautiful hemlock grove. After only about 500 feet on Island Pond Road, the A.T. turns right, goes over a small rise, and crosses a gravel road built in the 1960s to provide access for fishermen to Island Pond. The trail descends to cross an outlet of the pond on a small wooden bridge. The stone spillway you see was built by Civilian Conservation Corps workers in the mid-1930s as part of a plan to increase the size of Island Pond by damming it. The work was never completed, though, and the pond remains in its natural state.

The A.T. now ascends to a knoll overlooking beautiful Island Pond. On the way, you will pass a large rusted metal object to the right. This was a rotary gravel sorter, used to separate different sizes of gravel. The trail then descends and turns right on another woods road, known as the Crooked Road. After a short distance, the white blazes leave to the left and climb to a junction with the A-SB Trail, marked with red triangles on a white background. Turn left at the junction and follow the joint A.T./A-SB to the base of a large rock formation, where the two trails split.

Island Pond

The Boston Mine and the West Point Foundry

Just off the Dunning Trail, you can step into a vestige of nineteenth century industrial history. It is the open cut of the Boston Mine, and the dimpled rock face within still bears scars from the hand drills, hammers and blasting powder used by the iron miners who worked it in the mid-1800s.

On the left, past an opening in a rock outcrop, is a cavern that entombs a large shaft leading underground. The depth of this pit is hidden by the murky water that has filled it and continues to seep from the overhanging iron-rich rock, staining it like a rusty wound. You can scramble up the incline opposite the cavern for a panoramic view of the site.

This mine, as well as others in the area, was part of the Greenwood Iron Works – named for the wooded landscape which supplied the charcoal for the smelting of the ore. In time, as the wood was depleted, it was replaced by anthracite coal, which employed a more advanced smelting technology. The Clove Furnace, which used anthracite coal brought by the railroads, was built in 1854, and it was there that the ore from the Boston Mine ore was sent. That furnace, about half a mile north of the trailhead, is now an historic site.

The ironworks were owned by the West Point Foundry in Cold Spring, a principal supplier of artillery and munitions during the Civil War. The foundry produced the Parrott rifled artillery pieces, favored for their accuracy and range.

After the Civil War, the introduction of the Bessemer process and other innovations made steel production less costly, and this stronger, more durable alloy largely replaced the cast and wrought iron produced at the West Point Foundry. These new processes required large capital investment and a larger scale, as well as easy access to vast quantities of raw material. The master craftsmen of the small iron forge gave way to the steel barons of the vertically integrated corporation. Moreover, the large blast furnaces for the production of steel were generally located closer to the sources of coal and more accessible to the huge deposits of iron ore discovered in the Upper Great Lakes Region in the last quarter of the nineteenth century, which were richer and more easily exploited.

With demand for iron products diminishing, the Clove Furnace closed in 1877, and the Boston Mine was last worked about 1880.

-Jim Simpson

A hiker climbing through the Lemon Squeezer

This rock formation, known as the Lemon Squeezer, is one of the most interesting features of the park. Turn left and follow the A.T. as it climbs through a very narrow passage between the rocks and then goes up a steep rock face, where you will need to use both your hands and your feet. Those who are physically able to negotiate these challenges will find them to be a highlight of the hike. But if the climb is too difficult, it is possible to bypass the Lemon Squeezer by following a path to the left.

After reaching the top of the Lemon Squeezer, the A.T. continues on a more moderate grade to the summit of Island Pond Mountain. The stone ruins just north of the summit are the remains of a cabin built by Edward Harriman. This is a good place to stop and take a break.

The A.T. descends from the mountain and enters an attractive hemlock grove. After winding through the hemlocks, you will reach a junction with the aqua-blazed Long Path, marked by a wooden signpost. Turn right, leaving the A.T., and follow the Long Path as it skirts the edge of Dismal Swamp. The ridge visible across the swamp to the east is Surebridge Mountain. A short distance beyond a wet area, crossed on tree roots, you will come to a woods road – the route of the A-SB Trail (now encountered for the third time). Cross the road and bear left, where you will see three horizontal white blazes, marking the start of the White Bar Trail. Continue ahead on the White Bar Trail, which briefly joins a woods road, then turns left on a wider woods road – the continuation of the Crooked Road that you followed earlier in the hike.

Boston Mine

After about a mile on the White Bar Trail, the yellow-blazed Dunning Trail joins from the left. Continue ahead, now following both white and yellow blazes. When the two trails separate a quarter of a mile later, turn right and follow the yellow blazes of the Dunning Trail. After passing a

Ruins of stone ranger station at Island Pond

large cliff to the right, the trail ascends a rise, then descends to the base of the Boston Mine. This iron mine – a large open cut into the hillside, partially filled with water – is reached by a short path to the right. It was last worked around 1880.

After visiting this mine, continue ahead on the yellow-blazed Dunning Trail. In 500 feet, you will reach a wide woods road – the southern extension of Island Pond Road. Turn right, leaving the yellow-blazed trail, and follow unmarked Island Pond Road as it descends through hemlocks and laurels towards Island Pond. When you once again encounter the red-triangle-on-white blazes of the A-SB Trail, continue ahead, bearing right at the fork. At the next Y-intersection, again bear right, and you will soon arrive at the ruins of a stone building, built by the park as a ranger station. Just beyond, a rock ledge affords an expansive view over scenic Island Pond. This is a great spot to rest and take a break.

When you are ready to continue, retrace your steps along the road to the junction with the A-SB Trail. This time, bear right and follow the A-SB as it heads west, crossing a swamp and the southern outlet of Island Pond. A short distance beyond the swamp, turn left, leaving the road, and follow the red-triangle-on-white blazes across the southern end of Green Pond Mountain. You'll pass through an area with many dead trees, where there are good views to the west. Just beyond, the trail begins a steep descent on switchbacks. The grade soon moderates, and after about a mile on the

A-SB, you'll reach a grassy woods road – the Old Arden Road – at the base of the descent. Here, the red-on-white blazed Stahahe Brook Trail begins to the left, but you should turn right and continue to follow this A-SB Trail northward along the road to its terminus, marked by a triple-blaze. Turn left and follow the woods road across the meadow back to the Elk Pen parking area, where the hike began.

19 Fahnestock State Park

This loop hike leads to the remains of an old iron mine, passes an attractive pond, and follows the scenic Appalachian Trail along a forested ridge.

Difficulty: Moderate to strenuous
Length and Time: About 5.0 miles; about four hours.
Map: New York-New Jersey Trail Conference East Hudson Trails Map #103.
Directions: From the Bear Mountain Bridge, proceed north on N.Y. Route 9D for about 8.5 miles to a junction with N.Y. Route 301 in Cold Spring. Turn right and follow Route 301 for 5.0 miles to Dennytown Road, then turn right and follow Dennytown Road south for 1.1 miles to a dirt parking area on the left side of the road.

Proceed to the northeast corner of the parking area (to the right of an old stone building) and follow the blue-blazed Three Lakes Trail, which enters the woods, crosses a stream and bears right to parallel it. After passing a swamp on the right, the trail turns left and begins to climb rather steeply. Near the top of the hill, the trail passes an interesting split rock to the right. Just beyond – at the top of the rise – the remains of the Denny Mine may be seen to the right of the trail. You'll first notice a long, narrow opening, surrounded by piles of tailings (waste rock removed from the mine). If you bushwhack a little further to the northeast, you will reach an even more impressive mine opening – about 100 feet long and 20 feet deep, with the bottom filled with water. Use caution if you wish to explore these mine openings, all of which are to the right (northeast) of the trail.

Return to the trail and head north, descending through mountain laurel into a valley. Here, the trail turns right onto a woods road and soon reaches Sunken Mine Road (also known as Sunk Mine Road), a rough

John Allen Pond

dirt road. Turn right onto Sunken Mine Road and follow it for 0.2 mile, passing the southern end of John Allen Pond on the left. Just beyond, follow the blue blazes as they turn left, leaving the road. The trail crosses the outlet of the pond on rocks just below an old stone dam (now breached) and turns right. After continuing parallel to the lake shore for a short distance, the trail bears right, away from the lake. It reaches an old mine railbed and turns left to parallel it. After crossing a stream on rocks (to the left, the stone abutments of the mine railway are visible, but the bridge is gone), the trail bears left and joins the mine railbed for a short distance. It then turns left, leaving the railbed, and passes the stone foundations of several buildings from John Allen's homestead.

The Three Lakes Trail now climbs to reach a junction with the red-blazed Charcoal Burners Trail, which leaves to the left. Proceed ahead on the blue-blazed trail, which goes through mountain laurel thickets and continues through a grassy area, where it crosses a small stream. Just ahead, the yellow-blazed Old Mine Railroad Trail begins to the left. Continue along the blue-blazed Three Lakes Trail, which bears right at a fork and heads north on a relatively level footpath. Soon, you'll pass Hidden Lake on the left.

The stone abutments of the mine railway

About two and one-half miles from the start, you'll reach a junction (marked by a cairn) with the white-blazed Appalachian Trail (A.T.). Turn sharply right and follow the A.T. as it descends rather steeply to a ravine, then ascends, passing to the right of a cliff. After proceeding through an overgrown field, the trail climbs steeply through hemlocks to the top of a

Hidden Lake

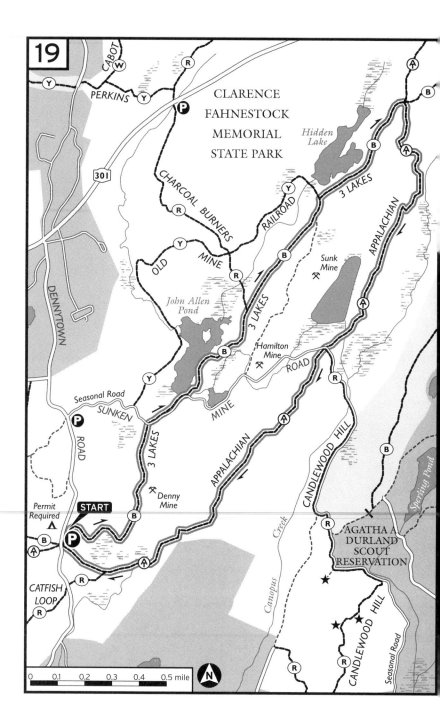

Iron Mining in Putnam County

For much of the 1800s, central Putnam County supported a significant iron mining industry. At first, the iron was used locally, but it was later transported to the West Point Foundry in Cold Spring, which made the Parrott gun – an early rifled cannon which played a major role in the Civil War.

The Denny Mine, just off the trail towards the start of this hike, was opened before 1850. It is named for the Denny family, on whose property it was located. According to the *History of Putnam County, New York* by William S. Pelletreau, published in 1886, "thousands of tons of excellent ore were taken from it." Besides the Denny Mine, there are another half a dozen abandoned iron mines within Fahnestock State Park. The most significant of these were the Sunk Mine and the Canada Mine (now largely covered by Canopus Lake).

During the Civil War, a narrow-gauge mine railroad was constructed to link the Sunk and Canada Mines to a dumping site along present-day Route 301. From there, the ore was transported by horse-drawn wagon to Cold Spring. Sections of the Appalachian Trail, the Three Lakes Trail and the Old Mine Railroad Trail follow the old railbed. Perhaps the most impressive section of the railbed is followed by the Appalachian Trail between Route 301 and the junction with the Three Lakes Trail. The stone bridge abutments seen on this hike along the Three Lakes Trail near John Allen Pond are also noteworthy.

When the mines were abandoned (about 1878), miners and charcoal burners left behind not only the mines, but also the remains of local villages, including Dennytown and Odeltown. The Denny family were the leading citizens of Dennytown, which was centered near the intersection of Dennytown Road and Sunken Mine Road. The much more extensive remains of Odeltown may be found at the north edge of the Durland Scout Reservation, where the White Trail heads north, up Bushy Ridge.

-John Magerlein

---

ridge. It descends a rocky slope and continues along a ridge studded with pine and hemlock, with a steep drop to the right.

After steeply descending from the ridge along a rocky slope covered with pine needles, the A.T. crosses the outlet of a swamp to the right of the trail on rocks, with an attractive cascade below. A short distance beyond, it turns right on Sunken Mine Road, but follows the road for only 60 feet before turning left and ascending on an old woods road, first rather steeply, then more gradually. After passing a split rock on the left, the trail crosses a long, smooth rock and narrows to a footpath. It descends briefly, then continues to climb to a high point, with limited views through the trees to the west.

The A.T. now begins a steady descent. At the base of the descent, it skirts a swamp to the right, crossing its outlet stream on rocks. Soon, it reaches a junction with the red-blazed Catfish Loop Trail, which leaves to the left at a fork. Bear right, continuing on the white-blazed A.T., and in another 0.2 mile you'll reach the grassy field at Dennytown Road where the hike began.

Cascade along the Appalachian Trail

20 Delaware Water Gap National Recreation Area

This loop hike passes an old copper mine, goes through a magnificent gorge, and climbs to the ridge of the Kittatinny Mountains, with several panoramic viewpoints.

Difficulty: Moderate to strenuous
Length and Time: About 7.8 miles; about five hours.
Map: New York-New Jersey Trail Conference Kittatinny Trails Map #120.
Directions: Proceed west on I-80 to the Delaware Water Gap and take Exit 1 (Millbrook/Flatbrookville), the last exit in New Jersey. Bear right at the bottom of the ramp and head north along the Delaware River on Old Mine Road. The road is only one lane wide for about half a mile, and a traffic light has been installed to regulate the two-way traffic. Continue for 7.5 miles to the Copper Mine Parking Area, on the left side of the road (the parking area is 0.5 mile beyond milepost 7 on Old Mine Road). Park here and walk across the road to the trailhead.

From the trailhead, head into the woods on the red-blazed Coppermines Trail. Just past the trailhead, you'll come to a fork. Bear left and follow a branch trail that parallels a cascading stream and leads in 750 feet to the sealed-off entrance of the lower mine – a relic of Dutch explorations for copper in the 1600s.

Retrace your steps to the fork and bear right, soon passing the ruins of a stone building to the left – the remnants of a mill that was built in the early 1900s to process the copper ore from the mines. This mining venture was not commercially successful, and it ceased operations in 1911.

The trail now begins a steady ascent on a woods road. In 0.2 mile, a blue-blazed spur trail that leads to the Kaiser Trail begins on the right, but you should continue ahead on the red-blazed Coppermines Trail. In

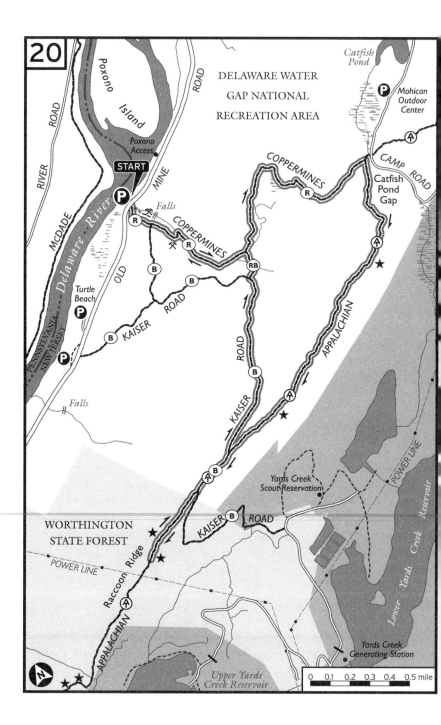

another 400 feet, the barricaded entrance to the upper mine is to the right of the trail. The trail now narrows to a footpath and soon levels off, with a cascading brook in a deep ravine on the left.

After crossing the brook on a wooden bridge below a cascade, the trail begins to climb again. It ascends a switchback and then follows directly along the magnificent gorge, with its series of waterfalls, below on the right. The trail passes attractive stands of rhododendrons, but most of the hemlocks, which once were dominant in the gorge, have been killed by the wooly adelgid.

Footbridge over the gorge below a cascade

Just beyond the end of the gorge, another spur trail on the right leads to the Kaiser Trail. This trail, blazed red/blue, will be your return route, but for now, continue along the red-blazed Coppermines Trail. The Coppermines Trail levels off, twice recrosses the brook, and proceeds through open woods with an understory of blueberry, crossing several seasonally wet areas on puncheons. Soon, the trail resumes a gradual climb, continuing through stands of dense young saplings.

After passing through dense mountain laurel thickets, the Coppermines Trail reaches a rocky area at the crest of the rise, and it descends a short distance to end at the white-blazed Appalachian Trail (A.T.), with Yards Creek and Camp Road visible to the left. You've now gone a little over two miles from the start of the hike. Turn right at this junction, and

Old Mine Road and the Copper Mines

Local history, or legend, asserts that Old Mine Road, the road that leads to the trailhead of this hike, was built around 1650 by Dutch explorers to carry ore from the Pahaquarry copper mine about 100 miles to the Hudson River at Esopus, now Kingston, N.Y. Surveyors sent to the area in 1730 by Thomas Penn reported hearing this story from the grandchildren of the earliest Dutch settlers. They were told that when the English gained control of the area in 1664, the Dutchmen abandoned the mine. A few modern writers enthusiastically publicized the legend, keeping it alive for romantically inclined visitors and hikers.

It is true that a mine shaft was drilled into the mountainside during the Dutch colonization, though just how early is uncertain. A 1659 letter from Dutch officials in Amsterdam asserts that copper ore had been found "in a crystal mountain" between Manhattan and the South River (the Delaware), and directs colonial administrators to "look further into the matter." But the existence of one short exploratory shaft does not support the legend that the Old Mine Road was built to carry large quantities of ore to Kingston.

Geologists and historians have been quite skeptical about the legend of the mines and Old Mine Road. The geologists have found the copper-bearing minerals in the state so diffusely distributed through containing rock, and of such low concentration, that economic exploitation of these minerals has always been impractical. As early as 1840, the New Jersey State Geologist wrote: "In fact, we have no evidence that a regular copper vein, properly so called, has been met with anywhere in the formations of the state."

A 1944 report to the State Geologist suggested that interest in copper mining historically coincided with popular speculative excitement. At the conclusion of a scientific review of all New Jersey copper explorations, the report cautions against further exploitation of the resource, stating: "[T]he potential speculator is [particularly dissuaded] from investing capital in any project relative to these copper mines that does not have actual mining as its primary goal under the direction of a capable and experienced operator." That's about as close as a geologist can come to saying that New Jersey copper mining – including the old Dutch mine – is and always was an economic scam.

-George Petty

View from the Appalachian Trail over Lower Yards Creek Reservoir and Mt. Tammany

climb steadily along the A.T., steeply in places, up the ridge of the Kittatinny Mountains. In about half a mile, you'll reach a limited east-facing viewpoint to the left of the trail. The A.T. now ascends more gradually, then levels off.

In another mile, you'll come to a series of open grassy areas, with panoramic east-facing views. Lower Yards Creek Reservoir is visible directly below, and the northern end of Mt. Tammany may be seen to the south. The A.T. continues south along the ridge, with more views to the left of the trail.

In half a mile, the A.T. descends briefly, then levels off. Here, the blue-on-white-blazed Kaiser Trail joins from the right (the junction is marked with a sign). This trail will be your return route, but for now, continue ahead on the A.T. for another 0.7 mile. When the Kaiser Trail (also designated as Kaiser Road) leaves to the left in a third of a mile, you should continue to follow the A.T., which climbs briefly, descends a little, then begins a steady climb.

Soon, you'll reach a sign marking the boundary between the Delaware Water Gap National Recreation Area and Worthington State Forest. Just beyond, you'll come to a panoramic west-facing viewpoint over the Delaware River, with Poxono Island visible to the north, and Smithfield Beach directly across the river in Pennsylvania. Proceed ahead on the A.T. to the wide-open crest of Mt. Mohican (also known as Raccoon Ridge), marked by a large cairn. From here, there are spectacular views to the west, east and north.

After enjoying the vista, retrace your steps back to the first junction with the Kaiser Trail (now on your left), and follow this blue-blazed trail downhill. For much of the way, the trail is a grassy woods road, but in places it has narrowed to a rocky footpath. After about a mile of relatively easy walking, you'll come to a trail junction at a huge log, with a sign for a spur trail to the Coppermines Trail. Turn right and follow this short red/blue-blazed trail. After crossing two brooks, you'll reach a junction with the red-blazed Coppermines Trail. Make a left here, retracing your steps as you descend through the gorge, and follow the red blazes back to the trailhead, where the hike began.

Hikers at the large cairn at the crest of Mt. Mohican (Raccoon Ridge)

21 Sam's Point Preserve

This hike climbs to Sam's Point, with spectacular views, follows a narrow path through the crevices of the Ice Caves, and continues to Verkeerderkill Falls – the highest waterfall in the Shawangunks.

Difficulty: Moderate to strenuous
Length and Time: About 7.6 miles; about four and one-half hours.
Dogs: Permitted on leash (Ice Caves loop trail may not be suitable for all dogs).
Map: New York-New Jersey Trail Conference Shawangunk Trails Map #104.
Directions: Take N.J. Route 17 north to the New York State Thruway and continue to Exit 16. Proceed west on N.Y. Route 17 to Exit 119, turn right at the end of the ramp, and continue north on N.Y. Route 302 for 9.6 miles to Pine Bush, where Route 302 ends. Turn left onto N.Y. Route 52 and continue for 7.3 miles. Just before the crest of the hill, turn right onto Cragsmoor Road. In 1.3 miles, turn right in front of the Cragsmoor post office, then take the next right onto Sam's Point Road, and follow it for about 1.2 miles to its end at the parking area for the preserve. A parking fee is charged.

From the parking area, walk around the gate and take the right fork of the Loop Road (a gravel road, closed to private vehicles). Follow the road uphill on switchbacks through a deciduous forest. In about half a mile, you'll pass dramatic cliffs of Shawangunk conglomerate on the left, with excellent views from rock outcrops on the right. Just beyond, you'll see a wide dirt road that goes off to the left. Turn left and follow this road, which leads in a short distance to the top of Sam's Point, with even more spectacular views to the south along the Shawangunk Ridge and to the east over the Wallkill Valley. This is a good spot to take a break.

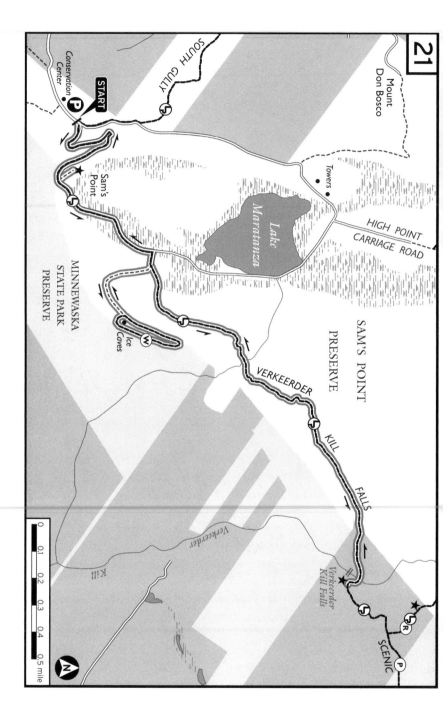

The view from Sam's Point

After taking in the views, return to the Loop Road (now paved) and turn left. The road now levels off, and the vegetation changes dramatically. The deciduous forest that you have encountered up to here is replaced by a ridgetop dwarf pitch pine forest, with a thick understory of blueberries and huckleberries. Most of the pitch pines grow only about three- to six-feet high – not much higher than the blueberries in the understory!

Continue along the road for another half a mile until you reach a junction where a gravel road descends to the right. Turn right, following a sign to Ice Caves Road. In a short distance, you'll notice a sign marking the start of the Verkeerderkill Falls Trail on the left. Continue ahead along the road, but note this turn, as the continuation of the hike will use this trail. As the road descends, it curves to the north, with views ahead over the northern part of the Shawangunk Ridge, including Castle Point and Gertrude's Nose in Minnewaska State Park.

At the end of the road, you'll come to a large open area that formerly was used for parking when the road was open to vehicular traffic. Towards the end of the open area, a sign marks the start of the Ice Caves Loop Trail. Developed as a commercial tourist attraction by a private individual in 1967, the Ice Caves were closed in 1996 when the property was acquired by The Nature Conservancy. In 2002, they reopened, but some artificial features (such as colored lights) have been eliminated.

Sam's Point and the Ice Caves

A scramble through the Ice Caves at the Sam's Point Preserve is geologically, botanically and, quite literally, one of the "coolest" hikes in the region. The "caves" are actually caverns, half a billion years old. Shale formed at the bottom of an ancient ocean and was thrust upward, eventually emerging into the open. The shale ruptured to form faults and crevices. The site, known geologically as the Ellenville Fault, is among the largest known open faults in the country. Because these caverns are located at the base of cliffs, the sheltered location retains the cool air in the summer yet allows snow and ice to accumulate in the winter. The cool temperatures usually preserve the ice and snow in the fissures into mid-summer.

As a result, a microclimate has evolved in the area surrounding the Ice Caves. Alpine flora not usually found at this altitude – including black spruce, mountain ash and creeping snowberry – may be seen here. On the ridgetop, dwarf pitch pines, also unique to these environs, thrive among thickets of blueberries and huckleberries.

The area was known as far back as the French and Indian Wars in the mid-1700s when, legend has it, Samuel Gonsalus gave his name to nearby Sam's Point. An accomplished hunter and scout, he was surprised by a raiding party of Native Americans while out hunting and found himself cut off from open ground. To avoid capture, he leaped from the cliffs and landed, unharmed, in a bough of hemlock.

The Ice Caves and the surrounding property were once owned by the Village of Ellenville. Attempting to cash in on the area's popularity, Ice Caves Mountain, Inc. – a commercial venture that offered tours of the caves – opened in 1967, the same year that the caves were designated a National Natural Landmark. The concessionaire installed colored lights that highlighted various features of the caves. When the Open Space Institute purchased the property in 1996, the commercial operation at the Ice Caves ended, and the caves themselves were closed to the public for several years.

After various improvements were made, the Ice Caves were reopened in 2002 under the management of The Nature Conservancy. The colored lights have been removed, but energy-efficient, solar-powered, motion-sensitive lighting has been installed. Hikers continue to enjoy these unique caves, but are now afforded a more natural experience.   -Jim Simpson

Turn right and descend, steeply in places, on a winding footpath with wooden guardrails. Soon, you'll descend stone steps into a crevice in the rock, passing underneath a rock wedged overhead. The difference in temperature is quite noticeable! After turning left and passing through a narrower crevice, the trail emerges into the open. Follow the white blazes, which cross several wooden bridges and lead along the base of cliffs on the left, passing beneath overhanging rock ledges. At one point, you'll have to climb a short wooden ladder.

A narrow crevice in the Ice Caves

Soon, the trail turns left and continues through a rock crevice deep below the surface. Motion-sensitive lighting has been installed to illuminate your passage through this cool, dark area. When you leave this crevice and again emerge into the open, you'll descend wooden steps, climb stone steps and a wooden ladder, and continue past more dramatic cliffs and under overhanging rock ledges.

A short distance ahead, the trail bears left and goes through another narrow crevice on a raised boardwalk. The Ice Caves are named for this spot, where ice and snow can usually be seen even in late summer!

Leaving this rock crevice, you'll climb a wooden ladder and emerge on an open rock outcrop where a solar panel has been installed to provide power to the lighting in the caves. This marks the end of your spectacular trip through the Ice Caves. Here, the white-blazed trail turns right and returns to the start of the loop. Before following this trail, turn left and proceed a short distance to exposed rock outcrops, with excellent views to the north and east.

After enjoying the views, continue ahead on the white-blazed trail and follow it back to the open area where you started the descent into the Ice Caves.

Now retrace your steps up the gravel road to the junction with the Verkeerderkill Falls Trail (just before you reach the main Loop Road). Turn right and follow this trail, marked with the aqua blazes of the Long Path, which proceeds through a dwarf pitch pine forest, with a thick understory of blueberries. There are good views ahead of the northern Shawangunk Ridge.

Along the trail to Verkeerderkill Falls

After about 20 minutes, you'll cross the outlet stream of Lake Maratanza. Here, the vegetation briefly changes to a deciduous oak-birch forest, with an understory of ferns. Soon, the pitch pines reappear. As the trail begins to descend towards Verkeerderkill Falls, the pitch pines first increase in size, then disappear altogether, with deciduous trees becoming more prevalent.

In about an hour from the beginning of the Verkeerderkill Falls Trail, you'll reach the Verkeerder Kill – a braided stream in an area of hemlock, mountain laurel and rhododendron. Unless the water is very high, the stream can be easily crossed on rocks. The open rock slabs along the stream provide a pleasant setting to take a break, but you'll want to con-

Verkeerderkill Falls

tinue ahead a short distance along the aqua-blazed trail. After passing a sign designating this area as one of the world's "last great places," the trail makes a sharp turn to the left. Bear right here and follow an unmarked path to a rock ledge overlooking the dramatic 180-foot-high Verkeerderkill Falls – the highest waterfall in the Shawangunks. Be careful, as there is a sheer drop from here to the bottom of the falls! You'll want to spend some time at this place of special beauty.

It is possible to make a longer ten-mile loop hike by continuing ahead on the aqua-blazed Long Path for another 0.4 mile, turning left onto the red-blazed High Point Trail (a relatively difficult route, requiring the use of hands as well as feet), then turning left and following the High Point Carriageway back to the Loop Road. However, the most direct return route is to retrace your steps along the Long Path to the Ice Caves Road, turn right for about 200 feet along the road, then turn left and follow the Loop Road back to the parking area where you began the hike.

22 Black Rock Forest

This loop hike parallels a cascading stream and climbs to several panoramic viewpoints.

Difficulty: Moderate to strenuous
Length and Time: About 7.5 miles; about five and one-half hours.
Map: New York-New Jersey Trail Conference West Hudson Trails Map #113; Black Rock Forest map (may be available from kiosk at trailhead).
Directions: Take the Palisades Interstate Parkway to its northern terminus at the Bear Mountain Bridge and continue north on U.S. Route 9W for 8.8 miles. About half a mile after passing a parking area marked with a blue sign, turn right onto Mountain Road. Immediately, turn right again and proceed through a very narrow underpass beneath Route 9W (large vehicles may not fit in this underpass). Continue ahead for 0.2 mile to a parking area on the right side of the road, just before a locked gate.

From the kiosk at the end of the parking area, proceed ahead on the red-blazed Duggan Trail. In about half a mile, the red trail ends at a junction with the blue-blazed Reservoir Trail. Continue ahead on the blue trail, which immediately crosses Ben's Bridge (a wooden footbridge) and climbs along a picturesque stream, with cascades and waterfalls, following an old woods road. When the blue trail ends, bear right and continue ahead on the yellow-blazed Stillman Trail.

Soon, the Stillman Trail reaches the dirt White Oak Road. Here, it is joined by the teal-diamond-blazed Highlands Trail, which comes in from the left. The joint Highlands/Stillman Trails now turns right and follows the road for 100 feet, then turns left and begins a steep climb of Mt. Misery on a footpath. At the top, you'll reach a viewpoint to the west and northwest which is partially obscured by trees. Continue ahead for a short

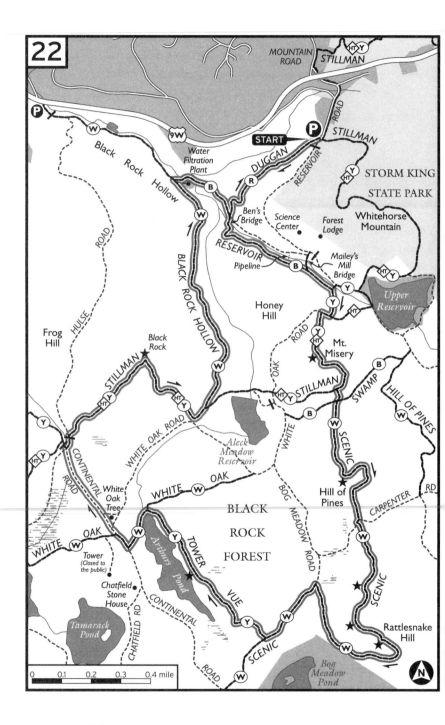

Waterfall along the Reservoir Trail

distance, and you'll come to a much better viewpoint, with Black Rock Mountain visible directly ahead, and Aleck Meadow Reservoir below to the left. You'll want to stop here for a few minutes to savor the view and take a break from your arduous climb (you've climbed nearly 700 feet from Ben's Bridge).

Continue ahead on the yellow/teal diamond trail, which begins its descent of Mt. Misery, first gradually and then more steeply. In a rocky area at the base of the descent, you'll notice a triple white blaze, which marks the start of the Scenic Trail. Turn left and follow the white-blazed

Dr. Stillman's Legacy

The Black Rock Consortium, which administers the 3,800-acre Black Rock Forest, reflects the legacy of Dr. Ernest G. Stillman (1884-1949). In 1928, Dr. Stillman, a physician and major benefactor of Harvard University, his alma mater, created the preserve with the intent of restoring it to health and fostering research in silviculture: the establishment, development and care of forest trees. The property showed the effects of long years of commercial activities. Dr. Stillman employed a small crew to remove weak trees and species considered undesirable – efforts that, with time and enlightened management, achieved substantial improvement to the Forest.

The Stillman family had assembled the parcels comprising Black Rock Forest during the late nineteenth and early twentieth centuries, when land values were declining as the resources supporting the logging and mining activities of the 1800s were depleted. During this period, a few households inhabited the Forest, eking out a meager existence. Earlier still, during the Revolutionary War, the tract's strategic location had aided American forces. The Continental Army moved cross-country on the Continental Road, which bisects the Forest, and used Spy Rock, the Forest's highest point (1,461 feet), to observe British naval movements on the Hudson.

In his will, Dr. Stillman bequeathed the preserve to Harvard, together with a large endowment to support forestry research. However, Black Rock Forest was located a significant distance from Harvard, which had another research forest – the Harvard Forest in Petersham, Massachusetts. In 1981, Harvard proposed to sell Black Rock Forest to William T. Golden, a philanthropist and environmentalist, but to retain Dr. Stillman's endowment to support the Petersham forest. Some members of the Stillman family and the New York State Attorney General's Office questioned the arrangement. After extensive discussions and negotiations, the sale took place in 1989, with Harvard retaining the Stillman endowment but contributing the purchase price for an endowment to support Black Rock Forest.

Golden gathered a group of educational and research institutions to manage the Forest, first placing ownership in a non-profit organization, the Black Rock Forest Preserve, which then leased it to the Black Rock Forest Consortium. The consortium, of which the New York-New Jersey Trail Conference is a member, manages the Forest with a focus on forestry research and education.   -*Charlotte Fahn*

Scenic Trail, which crosses the blue-blazed Swamp Trail at the end of the rocky area and begins a steady climb of the Hill of Pines, passing through attractive mountain laurel and hemlock.

At the top of the climb, the trail comes out on open rocks, with a spectacular west-facing view. Black Rock Mountain may be seen on the right, and the Black Rock Forest fire tower is to its left. (Despite the name "Hill of Pines," there are only two pine trees near the summit, which is mostly covered with oaks). You'll want to spend some time at this magnificent vantage point.

View from the Hill of Pines

The trail climbs a little to the true summit, descends the hill, and soon crosses the dirt Carpenter Road diagonally to the right. It now begins a gradual climb of Rattlesnake Hill. After about ten minutes, you'll reach a viewpoint to the right of the trail (the best view is from a rock ledge adjacent to a large pine tree). The fire tower may be seen straight ahead, and Bog Meadow Pond is to the left. After a short but steep descent and a relatively level stretch, you'll reach a second viewpoint – this one marked by a cairn and a gnarled, nearly horizontal pine tree. Continue ahead through a dense mountain laurel thicket to the third viewpoint on Rattlesnake Hill, which offers a panoramic view from open rocks. Bog Meadow Pond is below on the left, with the rolling hills of Orange County beyond.

Bog Meadow Pond from Rattlesnake Hill

After pausing to enjoy the view, continue ahead on the white trail, which begins to descend, first steeply, then more gradually. The trail briefly runs along the southern boundary of Black Rock Forest, with Bog Meadow Pond visible through the trees to the left. After crossing the inlet stream of the pond, the trail reaches the dirt Bog Meadow Road. Turn left and continue along the road, which is marked with the white blazes of the Scenic Trail.

After about five minutes, you'll reach a junction with the yellow-blazed Tower Vue Trail, marked by a cairn. This junction – which is easily missed – is just before a large rock outcrop. Turn right and follow the Tower Vue Trail over undulating terrain, through mountain laurel with an understory of blueberry. In about a third of a mile, there is a view through the trees of the fire tower from a rock ledge to the left of the trail. The trail now begins to run above Arthurs Pond, with views of the pond through the trees on the left.

When the Tower Vue Trail ends at the northern tip of the pond, by the dam, turn left onto the white-blazed White Oak Trail, cross below the dam, and continue along a gravel road. Soon, the White Oak Trail reaches Continental Road at a T-intersection. Turn right onto the road, continuing to follow the white blazes, but when the white blazes turn left and leave the road, proceed ahead on the road. Just beyond, you'll come to a junction, marked by a huge white oak tree. Here you should continue ahead on Continental Road, as White Oak Road leaves to the right.

In another third of a mile, you'll reach a complex intersection, with a cable barrier straight ahead. Turn right and continue on the yellow-rectangle-blazed Stillman Trail (also the route of the teal-diamond-blazed Highlands Trail). Just ahead, as the woods road bears left, bear right and follow the yellow and teal diamond blazes, which begin a gradual climb of Black Rock Mountain on a footpath.

After a short but very steep climb, you'll reach the summit of the mountain (1,410 feet) amid scrub oak and pitch pines. The panoramic view from the summit includes Schunemunk Mountain and the Metro-North Railroad's Moodna Viaduct to the west, and the Hudson River (crossed by the Newburgh-Beacon Bridge) to the northeast. Again, you'll want to take a break to appreciate the view – the broadest of the entire hike.

View from Black Rock Mountain

The trail turns right and descends gradually. With the wide White Oak Road visible ahead, the trail bears left and joins a woods road. A short distance beyond, the yellow and teal-diamond blazes turn right, but you should continue ahead on the road, now following the white-blazed Black

Rock Hollow Trail. This trail continues to descend along the road, with portions rerouted to bypass very eroded sections of the road.

At the base of the descent, the white-blazed trail ends at a filtration plant. Turn right onto the blue-blazed Reservoir Trail and follow it around the plant and along the brook to a junction with the red-blazed Duggan Trail just before Ben's Bridge. Turn sharply left onto the red-blazed trail and follow it uphill to the parking area where the hike began.

23

Abram S. Hewitt State Forest

State Line Trail/Ernest Walter/A.T. Loop
from State Line Marina

This loop hike traverses the Bearfort Ridge, with its unusual puddingstone conglomerate rock and pitch pines growing out of bedrock, reaches a panoramic viewpoint over Greenwood Lake, goes through a rhododendron tunnel, and passes Surprise Lake and West Pond.

Difficulty: Moderate to strenuous
Length and Time: About 4.1 miles; about four hours.
Map: New York-New Jersey Trail Conference North Jersey Trails Map #116.
Directions: Take I-287 to Exit 57 and continue on Skyline Drive to its western end at Greenwood Lake Turnpike (County Route 511) in Ringwood. Turn right and proceed for 8.2 miles to an intersection with Lakeside Road. Turn right and follow Lakeside Road (still designated County Route 511) for 2.4 miles to the Greenwood Lake Marina, just south of the New Jersey-New York boundary. Turn left and park on the left side of the dirt access road, west of Lakeside Road. Do not, under any circumstances, park on the private property of the Greenwood Lake Marina, on the east side of Lakeside Road.

This is one of the most spectacular hikes in the New Jersey-New York metropolitan area. Although it begins with a fairly strenuous 600-foot climb, the rest of the hike does not involve any major elevation changes. There are, however, many short, steep ups and downs, some of which require you to use your hands as well as your feet. The estimated time of four hours will allow you plenty of time to pause and enjoy the wonderful scenery that you'll encounter along the route.

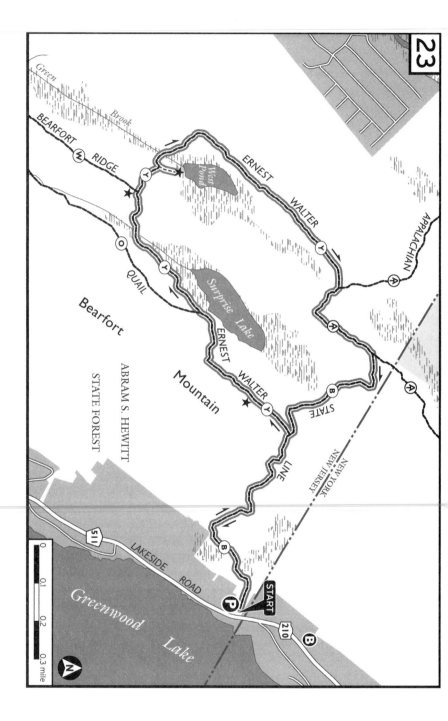

At the parking area, a triple blue-on-white blaze marks the start of the State Line Trail. Bear left onto this trail, which follows a wide, rocky path up Bearfort Mountain. The ascent is moderate at first, and the trail soon levels off. With a private home visible directly ahead, the trail turns right and begins to climb more steeply. Take care to follow the blue-and-white blazes, as there are many side trails that branch from the main route.

In about three-quarters of a mile, you'll reach an intersection with the yellow-blazed Ernest Walter Trail. Bear left and follow the yellow-blazed trail uphill. Soon, you begin to traverse a long, glacially smoothed outcrop of Schunemunk conglomerate "puddingstone" rock. This unusual reddish-matrix conglomerate rock – studded with pebbles of pink sandstone and white quartz – is characteristic of the Bearfort Ridge. As you climb along the rock outcrop, views open up over Greenwood Lake to the east.

Continue to the top of the outcrop, which offers a panoramic view over the six-mile-long lake, 600 vertical feet below. The hills of Sterling Forest are in the background and, on a clear day, you can see the Sterling Forest Fire Tower in the distance. You'll want to spend some time here, taking in the magnificent view and resting from the steep climb.

View of Greenwood Lake from the Ernest Walter Trail

When you're ready to resume the hike, continue along the Ernest Walter Trail, which briefly dips into the woods, but soon comes out again on another long conglomerate outcrop. After passing through an area studded with pitch pines, with more views over Greenwood Lake, the trail bears right and descends to cross the outlet of a wetland to the right of

Hikers at Surprise Lake

the trail. A short distance beyond, it reaches the eastern shore of pristine, spring-fed Surprise Lake. Again, you'll want to stop here to experience the beauty of this wilderness lake. Swimming is not permitted, however.

The yellow trail heads south from the lake, immediately reaching the start of the orange-blazed Quail Trail. When the trails diverge just ahead, take the right fork to continue along the Ernest Walter Trail. In a short distance, you'll begin to pass through a dense rhododendron grove. In several places, the thick rhododendrons actually form a canopy over the trail!

After descending a little, the trail crosses Cooley Brook, the outlet of Surprise Lake, on rocks and logs. This crossing may be difficult if the water is high. The trail now climbs to reach an east-facing viewpoint from a rock outcrop studded with pitch pines at the northern terminus of the white-blazed Bearfort Ridge Trail. The hills of Sterling Forest and the Wyanokie Plateau are directly ahead, with an arm of the Monksville Reservoir beyond. On a clear day, you can see the skyscrapers of Manhattan in the distance. If there are no leaves on the trees, you might be able to see Surprise Lake through the trees to the left.

Continue along the yellow-blazed Ernest Walter Trail, which heads west, crossing many sharp ridges of the mountain. This section of trail is particularly rugged, with many short but steep ups and downs. At the

Greenwood Lake

Greenwood Lake was originally known by the Native Americans as Quampium (which means "long water"). When it was acquired by European settlers in 1707, it was renamed Long Pond. In 1765, Peter Hasenclever directed the construction of a dam across the southern end of the pond to provide power for his ironworks downstream in the Hewitt area. A more substantial dam was constructed in 1837. This dam – which was built to provide water to the Morris Canal – resulted in an expansion of the size of the lake to 1,920 acres and an increase of 12 feet in its elevation.

After it was enlarged by the 1837 dam, Greenwood Lake became an attractive vacation locale, particularly for residents of New York City. Beginning in 1851, many hotels and seasonal cottages were built near the lake. In 1876, the New York and Greenwood Lake Railroad was completed from Jersey City to the lake. Steamboats met the trains and took passengers to the various resorts around the lake. These steamboats included the Greenwood Lake Transportation Company's *Arlington* and *Milford*, and their side-wheeler, *Montclair*, which had two decks and carried over 200 passengers. The high point of vacation traffic to the lake was in 1883, when over half of the railroad's revenue came from passenger traffic.

As automobiles became more popular in the early 20th century, rail passenger service to the lake decreased in importance, and the rail line to Greenwood Lake was abandoned in 1935. The popularity of this area as a seasonal recreational destination continued until the 1940s, when much of the previously seasonal housing stock (particularly along the New York side of the lake) was converted into year-round residences. Today, Greenwood Lake is used for boating, swimming and water skiing, primarily by residents of nearby communities.

---

bottom of the second steep descent, you'll come to a T-intersection. A yellow arrow on a tree points right to a "view." Turn right and follow a side trail for about 150 feet to a rock outcrop overlooking pristine West Pond. You'll want to spend a little time at this special spot, enjoying the view!

When you're ready to continue, retrace your steps to the trail junction and continue ahead, heading west along the Ernest Walter Trail. You'll soon come to a third, very steep descent, at the base of which the trail crosses Green Brook, the outlet stream of West Pond. The trail now proceeds through an attractive forest of hemlocks, pines and deciduous trees. After a while, there are seasonal views of West Pond through the trees to the right.

About half a mile from Green Brook, the trail crosses a small stream, the outlet of a wetland to the left. Just beyond, a rock outcrop to the left of the trail affords a view over the wetland. An unusual huge split boulder adds interest to this spot, which is another good place to take a break.

Soon, the trail traverses a long, narrow, smooth rock. A short distance beyond, it turns right and descends to end at a junction with the white-blazed Appalachian Trail (A.T.). Turn right onto the Appalachian Trail, which almost immediately climbs a steep ledge. You're now heading east, again crossing several sharp ridges. At a limited viewpoint to the east, the trail turns left and heads north.

After about a third of a mile on the A.T., you'll reach another limited viewpoint, with both east- and west-facing views from an open rock ledge. The A.T. now descends a long, sloped rock and reaches a junction with the blue-and-white-blazed State Line Trail (the junction is marked by paint blazes on a rock). Turn right and follow the State Line Trail, which crosses several ridges and then begins a steady descent. In about half a mile, you'll reach the junction with the yellow-blazed Ernest Walter Trail that you encountered earlier in the hike. Continue along the State Line Trail, which descends steadily to the parking area on Lakeside Road where the hike began.

West Pond

24 Storm King State Park

This loop climbs to the summits of Butter Hill and Storm King Mountain, with many spectacular viewpoints over the Hudson River and the Highlands.

Difficulty: Moderate to strenuous
Length and Time: About 2.5 miles; about two and one-half hours.
Map: New York-New Jersey Trail Conference West Hudson Trails Map #113.
Directions: From the Bear Mountain Circle (at the north end of the Palisades Interstate Parkway and the west end of the Bear Mountain Bridge), proceed north on U.S. Route 9W for 8.5 miles to a parking area on the right, at a sharp bend in the road. (This is the second parking area along Route 9W in Storm King State Park, but the only one which is designated by a blue "Parking Area" sign; it has a yellow-on-blue historical marker entitled "Freedom Road" and an adjacent marker commemorating the completion of the Storm King By-Pass Highway.)

From the parking area, walk north along the grassy shoulder of the road. Soon, you will see a triple-orange blaze, which marks the start of the Butter Hill Trail. Follow the orange blazes as they bear right, away from the road, and begin to ascend steeply. Soon, views over the Hudson River begin to appear to the right. The mountain across the river is Bull Hill (Mt. Taurus), and the point of land jutting into the river is Little Stony Point.

In 0.2 mile, you'll reach three stone pillars, with a stone foundation behind the pillars. These are the remains of Spy Rock House, the summer cottage of Dr. Edward L. Partridge, who served on the Palisades Interstate Park Commission from 1913 to 1930. The trail now descends slightly, then continues to climb Butter Hill, first gradually, then more steeply. At

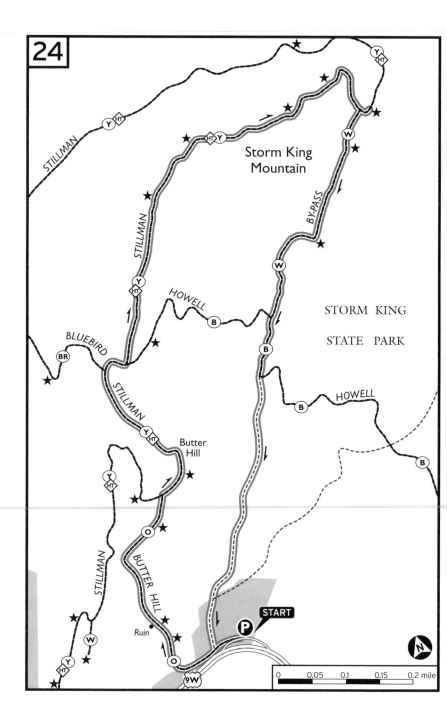

the top of the steep climb, you'll reach open rock ledges that afford a wide panorama to the east, south and west. Route 9W is visible straight ahead to the south, with the fire-scarred North Ridge of Crows Nest Mountain to its left. The Hudson River is to the east. You'll want to pause here for a little while to enjoy this expansive view, but the best is yet to come.

These three stone pillars mark the site of Spy Rock House

After a short level stretch, the Butter Hill Trail ends at a junction with the yellow-blazed Stillman Trail, also the route of the teal diamond-blazed Highlands Trail (some of the blazes at the junction are blue diamonds). Turn right and follow the Stillman Trail up to the summit of Butter Hill, where a rock outcrop just to the left of the trail provides a 360° view. The East Hudson Highlands are visible across the river, with towers marking the summits of Beacon Mountain to the north. Bull Hill is directly to the east. On the west side of the river, the North Ridge of Crows Nest Mountain is directly to the south, with Black Rock Forest visible to the southeast. Schunemunk Mountain may be seen to the west, with the Moodna Viaduct (on the Metro-North rail line to Port Jervis) towering over the valley just north of the mountain. In the distance to the northwest are the Shawangunks and, behind them, the Catskills. To the north, the Newburgh-Beacon Bridge spans the Hudson River.

After enjoying this spectacular view, continue ahead on the yellow-blazed Stillman Trail, which descends slightly. Soon, you'll reach a junc-

The north-facing view over the Hudson River, Pollopel Island and the Newburgh-Beacon Bridge from the Stillman Trail

tion with the blue-and-red-blazed Bluebird Trail, marked by a large cairn. Turn right, uphill, and continue on the Stillman Trail. A short distance ahead, after passing through a burned-out area, you'll reach the northern end of the blue-blazed Howell Trail, which leaves to the right. Bear left here, continuing along the yellow-blazed trail, which follows a relatively level route for the next 0.7 mile. After a short, steep climb, you'll reach a limited view to the north. About five minutes ahead, though, you'll come to a much better viewpoint looking north over the Hudson River. Pollopel Island is directly below, with the ruins of Bannerman's Castle on its high point. The rail line running along the east shore of the Hudson is Metro-North's Hudson Line (also the route of Amtrak trains to Albany).

Continue ahead, past the summit of Storm King Mountain, with some more views from rock ledges to the left. After a short descent, you'll reach a panoramic north-facing viewpoint, with superb views. To the east, Breakneck Ridge (marked by the rail tunnel) is visible across the river. The stone building at the foot of Breakneck Ridge (partially obscured by the vegetation) caps a shaft of the Catskill Aqueduct, which tunnels 1,100 feet below the river. North Beacon Mountain (with communications towers) and South Beacon Mountain (with a fire tower) are to the northeast. To the northwest, the village of Cornwall can be seen along the west bank of the river.

Storm King and the Birth of the Environmental Movement

In 1962, the Consolidated Edison Company (Con Edison) proposed to construct a large pumped storage hydroelectric plant on lands owned by the Palisades Interstate Park Commission (PIPC) at the base of Storm King Mountain, with power lines extending across the river to Putnam County. Initially, the plan was met with opposition from PIPC, the Hudson River Conservation Society and the West Point Military Academy. However, when Con Edison agreed to move the plant to private land on the north face of Storm King and to put the transmission lines under the Hudson River, these groups dropped their objections to the plan.

Others did not, however. A leader in the fight again the plant was Leo Rothschild, Conservation Chairman of the New York-New Jersey Trail Conference, who decried "the desecration of the northern gate of the Hudson Highlands." In 1963, the Scenic Hudson Preservation Conference (Scenic Hudson) was formed to fight this proposed desecration of the natural beauty of the Highlands.

Despite opposition from environmentalists, in 1965 the Federal Power Commission (FPC) granted Con Edison a license to construct the plant. But Scenic Hudson challenged the FPC's decision by bringing suit in the United States Court of Appeals for the Second Circuit. Later that year, the Second Circuit reversed the decision, ruling that Scenic Hudson had standing to sue as an "aggrieved party" and that the FPC "must include as a basic concern the preservation of natural beauty." After holding additional hearings, the FPC issued a decision in 1970, again granting Con Edison a license to construct the plant.

More legal challenges were raised, however, and eventually Con Edison's new chairman, Charles Luce, decided to consider a mediated settlement. Finally, in 1980, a settlement was announced that provided for the project to be abandoned, with the land acquired by Con Edison for the project to be donated to PIPC and the Town of Cornwall. The settlement was characterized by the *New York Times* as "a peace treaty for the Hudson."

The Second Circuit's landmark decision established the right of citizen groups to sue a government agency to protect natural resources and scenic beauty. It set a national precedent for environmental issues and has been credited with launching the modern environmental movement.

The Stillman Trail now continues to descend, soon reaching a junction with the white-blazed By-Pass Trail. Turn left at this junction and walk about 25 feet to a rock ledge that affords a broad south-facing view down the Hudson River. The village of Cold Spring is visible across the river to the southeast, and Constitution Island juts into the river just beyond.

Now return to the junction and continue along the white-blazed By-Pass Trail, which descends along the side of the mountain, first gradually and then more steeply. There are several views of the river from rock ledges to the left, but they are not as broad as the views from the junction with the Stillman Trail. After crossing a seasonal stream, the By-Pass Trail climbs briefly to end at a junction with the blue-blazed Howell Trail, which comes in from the right.

Bear left and continue ahead on the Howell Trail, which soon begins to follow an old road. In about 500 feet, the blue-blazed trail turns sharply left, leaving the old road, but you should continue ahead on the road. Although it is now unmarked, the road is distinct and easy to follow. It climbs briefly, then descends steadily. As it approaches Route 9W, the old road climbs rather steeply to end just beyond the parking area where the hike began.

The south-facing view over Cold Spring and Constitution Island from the Stillman Trail

25 Worthington State Forest

This loop hike steeply climbs Mt. Tammany, with panoramic views, and follows scenic Dunnfield Creek.

Difficulty: Strenuous
Length and Time: About 3.5 miles; about three hours.
Map: New York-New Jersey Trail Conference Kittatinny Trails Map #120.
Directions: Take I-80 west towards the Delaware Water Gap. Immediately beyond milepost 1, take the exit for "Dunnfield Creek/ Appalachian Trail" and bear left at the fork. Continue past the underpass on the left and turn right into a parking area at signs with "P" and "hiker" symbols. (If you miss the exit from I-80, continue ahead and take Exit 1, the last exit in New Jersey. Turn left at the end of the ramp, and continue on the service road parallel to I-80 past the visitor center. Turn left at the underpass, go under I-80, turn left again, and turn right into the parking area at the signs with "P" and "hiker" symbols.)

Near the entrance to the parking area, you will see a sign for the Tammany Trail (also known as the Red Dot Trail). You will be taking this red-on-white-blazed trail all the way up Mt. Tammany. Follow the trail up wooden steps and bear left when you reach junctions with several side trails that lead to another parking area. The trail briefly levels off on a wide path, but it soon reaches stone steps that mark the start of a rather steep climb. Passing through a dense forest of hemlocks and deciduous trees, the trail ascends steadily on a rocky footpath.

After climbing over rock outcrops, you'll reach the first panoramic viewpoint, from open rocks just to the right of the trail. You can see up and down the Delaware River, with Arrow Island in the river to the left, and Mt. Minsi directly across the river in Pennsylvania. You've climbed

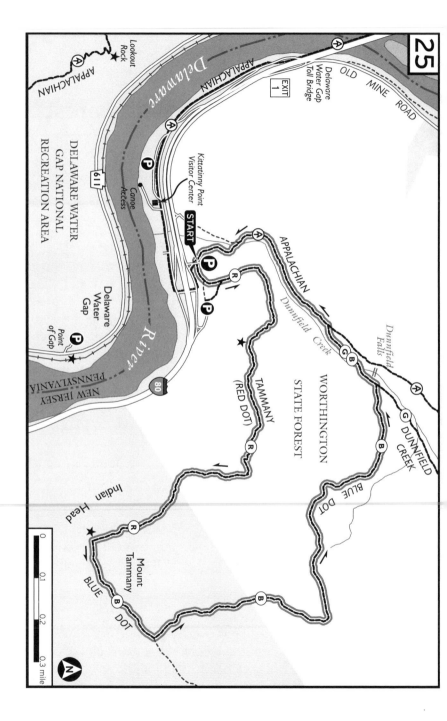

about 400 vertical feet to reach this point, and you'll want to rest from the steep climb and take in the view.

When you're ready to continue, follow the trail upwards on a more gradual grade through an open forest, with an understory of blueberries. In about 10 minutes, the trail bears right to cross a streambed (often dry), and the climb steepens. You'll go up a set of rock steps and continue through a talus field. Just beyond, there is a short level stretch, but the steady climb soon resumes.

As you approach the top of the mountain, the grade moderates, and there are views through the trees to the right. Finally, you'll reach the end of the Red Dot Trail, marked by a triple blaze. Turn right and follow a rock outcrop downhill for about 100 feet to another panoramic viewpoint over the Delaware River and Mt. Minsi, with the rolling hills of Pennsylvania in the background. You've now climbed nearly 1,200 vertical feet, and you'll want to take another break here.

View north along the Delaware River from viewpoint at top of Mt. Tammany

After you've rested from the climb, retrace your steps to the trail. Just ahead, you'll see a triple-blue blaze that marks the start of the Blue Dot Trail. Follow this trail, which heads northeast along the ridge of Mt. Tammany on a rocky but relatively level path. In a quarter mile, it turns sharp-

The Delaware Water Gap, looking north, about 1912. The Kittatinny Hotel is in the foreground on the Pennsylvania side, with the Water Gap House above it. The building along the river to the right of the Kittatinny Hotel is the Delaware Water Gap station of the Delaware, Lackawanna and Western Railroad.

ly left at a wooden sign for the "Blue Trail" and soon begins a rather steep descent on a rocky, eroded woods road. After a while, the descent moderates somewhat, but the road remains quite rocky for most of the descent. Towards the base of the descent, sections of the trail have been relocated off the eroded road and onto a parallel footpath.

A little over a mile from the summit, you'll arrive at a junction with the green-blazed Dunnfield Creek Trail. Turn left and follow the joint blue and green blazes, which follow a wide path parallel to Dunnfield Creek. Just ahead, you'll notice an open area with a bench that overlooks an attractive waterfall on the right. Continue ahead a short distance until you reach a wooden footbridge that spans the creek. Here, a short unmarked trail on the right leads to the base of the waterfall (if it's hot out, you might want to dip your feet in the water!). This is another good spot to take a break.

When you're ready to continue, cross the footbridge and proceed north along the trail, which parallels the creek on a wide path. This is the most scenic portion of the hike, as you pass through the narrow gorge of

The Delaware Water Gap

As you look down over the Delaware River from the rock ledge atop Mt. Tammany, you have a glorious view of a dramatic geological spectacle almost completely framed in maturing mountainside forest and pristine watershed. Only the long gray scar of I-80, a disused railroad bridge, and the smaller gash of Pa. Route 611 mar the natural scenery. It is a memorable vista.

But equally remarkable is what you don't see, can't see, because time and technology have so completely erased it.

For the half century between the Civil War and World War I, the Delaware Water Gap was a most desirable summer destination for the well-to-do of the Northeast, second only to Saratoga Springs, N.Y. The Pennsylvania side contained many hotels, and the town of Delaware Water Gap, Pa. was a thriving resort. The bottomlands and knolls along the river were covered with farms supporting the tourist trade.

In the peak year of 1912, three railroads and two interurban trolley lines carried half a million vacationers to their summer retreats from heat, humidity and pollution-borne diseases. From the Mt. Tammany viewpoint, you could have seen five railroad bridges, one of which had been converted into a toll roadway. Your view would have been dominated by two elaborate wooden structures on the Pennsylvania side – the 500-room Kittatinny Hotel set on a rise behind the tracks and, farther upstream, the 275-room Water Gap House.

The original Delaware, Lackawanna and Western (DL&W) Railroad main line crossed south of Mt. Tammany into the town of Portland, Pa. The Lehigh and New England Railroad built a bridge into Portland from Columbia, N.J., and a covered roadway crossed nearby. Between Portland and the Gap was the famed Lackawanna Cut-Off Viaduct, completed in 1911, which reduced the travel time from New York to the Gap by half an hour. The New York, Susquehanna and Western Railroad had a bridge further north.

After World War I, the Gap became a less-fashionable resort. In 1915, the Water Gap House burned down, and the Kittatinny Hotel burned in 1931. As the tourist trade disappeared, farms were abandoned. The successional forest took over, and now the view from Mt. Tammany invokes awe at the vast forces of nature and the landforms of geology. The gods of commerce have fled, and their shrines are buried in the forest undergrowth.
-George Petty

Waterfall along Dunnfield Creek

Dunnfield Creek, studded with rhododendrons, with the waters of the cascading creek below to your left.

In another quarter mile, the Blue Dot and Dunnfield Creek Trails end, and you continue ahead along the creek, now following the white-blazed Appalachian Trail. Soon, the trail bears left, leaving the wide path, and crosses Dunnfield Creek on a steel bridge with a wooden deck. Just ahead, you'll reach the parking area where the hike began.

26 Schunemunk Mountain

This loop hike climbs to a ridge composed of unusual conglomerate rock, with many viewpoints from open rock ledges dotted with pitch pines.

Difficulty: Strenuous
Length and Time: About 8.0 miles; about five and one-half hours.
Map: New York-New Jersey Trail Conference West Hudson Trails Map #114.
Directions: Take the New York State Thruway to Exit 16 (Harriman). Proceed north on N.Y. Route 32 for about seven miles to the Village of Mountainville, and turn left onto Pleasant Hill Road (County Route 79). At the bottom of the hill, turn left again onto Taylor Road, then bear right and cross the bridge over the Thruway. The trailhead parking area is on the right side of the road, just beyond the junction with Creekside Lane.

From the parking area, cross the road and proceed south on the joint Jessup (yellow), Sweet Clover (white) and Highlands (teal diamond) Trails, which climb gently to the crest of a field and then descend to a woods road. To the right, you can see Schunemunk Mountain, which you'll soon climb.

Turn right on the woods road, going past a chain that blocks off the road. When the white-blazed Sweet Clover Trail leaves to the left, continue ahead, now following the yellow blazes of the Jessup Trail. (You're also following the Highlands Trail, but the teal-diamond Highlands Trail blazes appear mainly at intersections.) The Jessup Trail crosses a field diagonally to the right, crosses a footbridge over a stream re-enters the woods, and soon climbs to a woods road, where it turns right.

Follow the yellow blazes along the woods road for about half a mile. Watch for a sharp left turn, where the trail leaves the road and climbs to

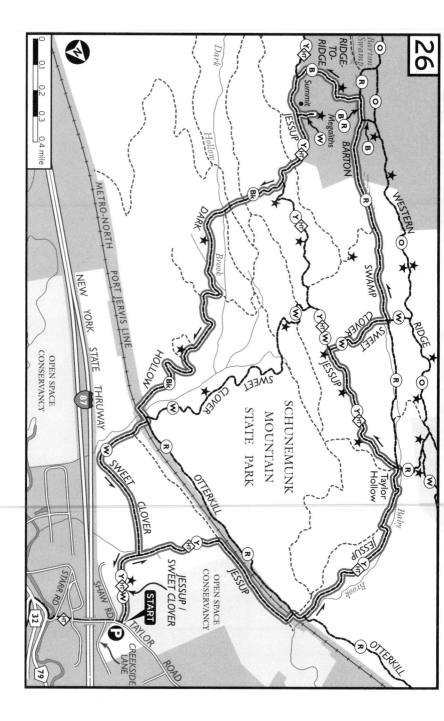

cross the railroad tracks. This is an active rail line, so be sure to stop, look and listen for approaching trains before crossing.

On the other side of the tracks, the Jessup Trail turns right, briefly joining the red-blazed Otterkill Trail. It soon reaches the cascading Baby Brook and turns left to parallel the brook. The Otterkill Trail turns right and crosses the brook on a footbridge, but you should continue ahead along the yellow-blazed Jessup Trail, which climbs steadily along the brook. In the next three-quarters of a mile, you'll climb about 700 feet.

Cascade in Baby Brook

After joining a woods road, the trail detours to the right to pass by a beautiful cascade. This is a good place to take a break. Continue ahead along the Jessup Trail, which soon reaches a junction with the red-on-white-blazed Barton Swamp Trail. The Barton Swamp Trail proceeds ahead and to the right, but you should turn left to continue on the yellow-blazed Jessup Trail.

The Jessup Trail now climbs – steeply in places – along a ridge formed of the unusual conglomerate bedrock, studded with pebbles of white quartz and pink sandstone, that is characteristic of Schunemunk Mountain. The trail winds through pitch pines and soon reaches the first in a series of panoramic viewpoints. The Hudson River may be seen to the northeast, with the Newburgh-Beacon Bridge visible in the distance, and the East Hudson Highlands beyond. To the west, you can see the western ridge of Schunemunk Mountain.

Continue heading south along the ridge. After climbing another conglomerate outcrop, you'll reach a second viewpoint. You're high enough now that you can see over the western ridge of the mountain. The Shawangunks are visible in the distance to the northwest, and on a clear day you can see the Catskills beyond.

View of Hudson River from Schunemunk Mountain

After descending slightly and passing through an area with deciduous trees, the Jessup Trail climbs again and reaches a third viewpoint at a junction with the white-blazed Sweet Clover Trail. This is the highest and broadest of the three viewpoints on this section of the Jessup Trail, and you'll want to pause and take in the panoramic 270° view.

When you're ready to continue, turn right onto the white-blazed Sweet Clover Trail, which soon begins to descend. After climbing over a few minor ridges, the trail passes through dense mountain laurel thickets, and the descent steepens. At the base of the descent, you'll cross Baby Brook

The Geology of Schunemunk Mountain

As you approach the ridge of Schunemunk Mountain, you will probably be struck by the unusual rock formations along the ridge. While most bedrock in the region, including the mountain's lower slopes, is the older grayish basalt and granite, Schunemunk is crowned by reddish-purple rocks with many smaller, lighter embedded stones. Geologists call this kind of rock conglomerate, and the variety found here — on the highest ground in Orange County — is called Schunemunk conglomerate or, more popularly, puddingstone.

Its presence here and nowhere else on the nearby mountains testifies to Schunemunk's geological distinctiveness. The mountain formed by itself, part of neither the nearby Hudson Highlands nor the Shawangunk Ridge to the northwest. Its closest relatives among the region's mountains, in fact, are the much higher Catskills.

Like the shales and sandstones of the Catskills, with which they sometimes share their color, the Schunemunk conglomerates were once sands and pebbles washed down from the mighty Taconic Mountains. About 400 million years ago, the summits of the Taconics — many over 20,000 feet — were the highest on the planet.

The Silurian period that formed these mountains gave way to the Devonian, and the Taconics gradually eroded into the inland sea to their west. Most of these sediments compacted into river deltas that became the Catskill bedrock, atop the older rocks that today underlie the valleys west of Schunemunk. Some accumulated on the beaches, creating the similar yet distinct Shawangunk conglomerate.

When the sea dried up, it is likely that the Catskill and Schunemunk sediments formed a continuous layer. So they remained until 260 million years ago, when the uplift that created the Allegheny Mountains of Pennsylvania and raised the Catskills (then a plateau, but later dissected by erosion) broke the connection. Similar ridgetop conglomerates are also found in a line extending 40 miles to the southwest into New Jersey, including the Bearfort Ridge along Greenwood Lake and extending past Green Pond to Lake Hopatcong.

The ridgetop isn't Schunemunk's only geological anomaly. The adjacent Woodcock Hill and other nearby hills are made of billion-year-old Precambrian bedrock, much older than any other bedrock found nearby. This bedrock was formed either from upthrusts of deeper rock or from detached blocks carried here from elsewhere.

-*Dan Case*

(the crossing can be a little tricky when the water is high) and reach a junction with the red-on-white-blazed Barton Swamp Trail.

Turn left and follow the Barton Swamp Trail as it proceeds south along a nearly level route between the two ridges of Schunemunk Mountain. After about 1.3 miles, the blue-on-white-blazed Ridge-to-Ridge Trail joins from the right. When the two trails diverge a short distance beyond, turn left, now following the blue-on-white blazes of the Ridge-to-Ridge Trail.

The Ridge-to-Ridge Trail steeply climbs the eastern ridge of the mountain. After a very steep pitch, the trail turns right along a ledge and reaches a panoramic west-facing viewpoint. You'll want to take a short break here to catch your breath and enjoy the view! The trail continues to climb more gradually. Where it proceeds over bare rock surfaces, the trail is marked with blue paint blazes on the rocks and with cairns (small piles of rocks). After traversing an open area of exposed conglomerate bedrock, the Ridge-to-Ridge Trail ends, on the crest of the eastern ridge, at a junction with the yellow-blazed Jessup Trail and the teal-diamond-blazed Highlands Trail.

A hiker on the ridge of Schunemunk Mountain

Turn left and follow the joint Jessup/Highlands Trail, which soon reaches the 1,664-foot-high summit of Schunemunk Mountain (marked on the rock with white paint), which affords a 360° view. The Jessup Trail bears left and descends, almost immediately reaching a junction with a

The conglomerate rock at the summit of Schunemunk Mountain

white-blazed side trail (also marked by cairns) that leads to the Megaliths – a group of huge blocks that have split off from the bedrock. This is another good place for a break, as the interesting geologic features are complemented by a fine viewpoint to the west.

The Megaliths

When you feel rested, return to the Jessup/Highlands Trail and turn left. In another third of a mile, the black-on-white-blazed Dark Hollow Trail leaves to the right. Turn right onto the Dark Hollow Trail, which crosses several small streams and soon begins a steady descent. The first part of the descent is quite steep, after which the trail crosses Dark Hollow Brook, bears left and reaches a short level stretch. Just before the descent resumes, there is another great view to the east and northeast over the Hudson River and East Hudson Highlands.

After another steep stretch, you'll cross a brook and bear left again. Soon, the trail joins a woods road, which it follows for most of the remainder of the descent. At one point, the trail proceeds straight ahead, cutting off a loop of the road. The final viewpoint of the hike is reached as the trail begins a steep descent to rejoin the woods road.

The Dark Hollow Trail ends at the base of the descent, just before the railroad tracks. Turn left onto the red-blazed Otterkill Trail, which descends to cross Dark Hollow Brook below an attractive waterfall, then climbs to reach a junction with the white-blazed Sweet Clover Trail. Turn right onto the Sweet Clover Trail and cross the railroad tracks (use extreme caution, as the crossing is on a curve in the tracks, and it is difficult to see or hear approaching trains). Continue to follow the Sweet Clover Trail as it descends through the woods, turns right onto a woods road, then bears left and follows a grassy road through fields. When you reach the junction with the yellow-blazed Jessup Trail, turn right, then left, following the joint Sweet Clover/Jessup Trails back to the parking area where the hike began.

Fall

Tenafly Nature Center | Campgaw Mountain County Reservation | Garret Mountain Reservation | Sourland Mountain Preserve | Norvin Green State Forest | Point Mountain Reservation | Ramapo Mountain State Forest and Camp Glen Gray | Mohonk Preserve | Harriman State Park (Claudius Smith's Rock/Parker Cabin Mountain Loop) | Harriman State Park (Raccoon Brook Hill/Pine Meadow Lake) | Norvin Green State Forest | Palisades Interstate Park, New Jersey Section | Catskill Forest Preserve

27 Tenafly Nature Center

This loop hike circles the nature preserve, passing a glacial erratic and an interesting pond.

Difficulty: Easy

Length and Time: About 4.0 miles; about two and one-half hours.

Dogs: Not permitted on Tenafly Nature Center property.

Map: Tenafly Nature Center map (available from nature center or online at www.tenaflynaturecenter.org).

Directions: Take U.S. Route 9W to the traffic light at East Clinton Avenue in Tenafly. Proceed west on East Clinton Avenue for 1.7 miles and turn right onto Engle Street. Continue on Engle Street until it ends at a T-intersection with Hudson Avenue. Turn right and follow Hudson Avenue to its end at the nature center, where parking is available. GPS address: 313 Hudson Avenue, Tenafly, NJ 07670.

After obtaining a trail map from the visitor center, proceed ahead on the Main Trail, a wide dirt road which is the continuation of Hudson Avenue. In about 300 feet, turn right onto the Red Trail (blazed with red triangles), which proceeds south. After several turns, the trail begins to follow along a stream.

Be alert for a trail junction by several huge fallen trees, where the Purple Trail begins. Turn right and follow the Purple Trail, which immediately crosses the stream on a footbridge. When you reach a T-intersection (with a sign pointing to "Highwood Ave."), turn left, continuing along the Purple Trail (the trail to the right is the Blue Trail, which leads to an adjacent residential street). After crossing a stream on a footbridge, the Purple Trail ends at a T-intersection with the yellow-blazed Allison Trail. Turn right onto the Allison Trail and follow it to a junction with the orange-

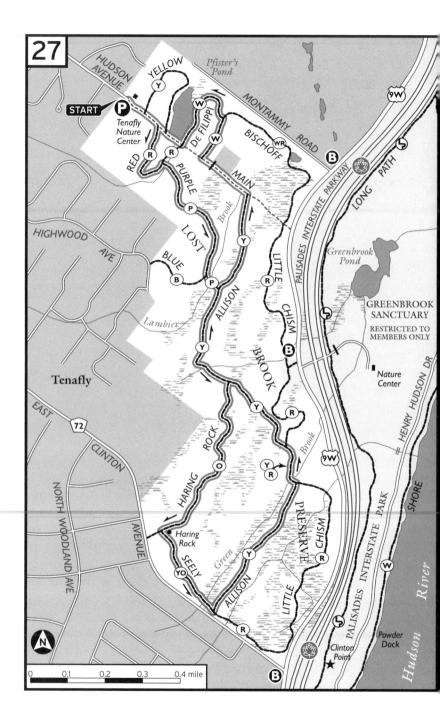

Haring Rock

blazed Haring Rock Trail (marked by a sign on the right). Turn right and continue south on the Haring Rock Trail.

As you reach the southern boundary of the nature center, you'll notice a large boulder to the left of the trail. This is the Haring Rock, a glacial erratic, after which the trail is named. Here, a triple yellow/orange blaze marks the start of the Seely Trail. Turn left and follow this trail, which heads southeast, parallel to East Clinton Avenue (visible through the trees on the right). After crossing a footbridge over the Green Brook, the Seely Trail ends at a junction with the yellow-blazed Allison Trail, which comes in from East Clinton Avenue.

Turn left and follow the Allison Trail northward, parallel to the Green Brook. In about half a mile, the Allison Trail turns sharply left and is joined by the red-blazed Little Chism Trail. Both trails recross the Green Brook on a footbridge, then turn right and parallel the brook. Soon after the trails turn left, away from the brook, you'll reach a junction where the two trails diverge. The Little Chism Trail leaves to the right, but you should continue ahead on the yellow-blazed Allison Trail.

Saving the East Hill Tract

The Tenafly Nature Center Association was formed in 1961 to develop a "Living Workshop" on 65 acres at the top of Hudson Avenue. For its first 15 years, the Nature Center administered only this 65-acre tract, but it soon became the steward of a much larger parcel.

In 1959, Norman Blankman, a real estate developer, purchased from John D. Rockefeller, Jr. a 274-acre wooded tract that adjoined the Nature Center property. He proposed building cluster housing and office complexes on this tract. Local residents fought the plan, and Mr. Blankman's applications for variances (the land was zoned for single-family homes on one-acre lots) were twice rejected.

Then, in 1973, Blankman sold the property to Centex Homes, Inc. of Texas for $8.5 million. Centex proposed building a 1,780-unit housing development on the land – said at the time to be the largest privately owned tract within ten miles of New York City. Again, local residents were outraged by the plan, and this time, a community-wide effort began to raise sufficient funds to acquire what became known as the East Hill Tract and thereby permanently block any plan for development. After much effort – and litigation that went all the way to the New Jersey Supreme Court – the purchase price of $9.35 million was raised, and on November 1, 1976, the 274-acre tract was acquired by the Borough of Tenafly.

The acquisition was made possible by a Green Acres grant of $2.95 million from the State of New Jersey – the largest such grant ever awarded up to that time – and by other public and private funds, including substantial contributions by local residents. Portions of the tract were conveyed to the local Jewish Community Center and to the Palisades Interstate Park Commission (both of which had contributed funds towards the purchase price), and remaining acreage was leased to the Tenafly Nature Center to manage as a nature preserve.

The Nature Center also manages 31 acres formed by a 200-foot-deep strip of land along the westerly side of Route 9W, most of which was donated by John D. Rockefeller, Jr., as well as several other smaller parcels.

Today, extending over 380 acres, the Tenafly Nature Center is the largest nature preserve in Bergen County. It includes over seven miles of maintained trails which are open to the public for hiking and other types of passive recreation.

When you reach the junction with the orange-blazed Haring Rock Trail (marked in this direction by a sign to "E. Clinton Ave."), continue ahead on the yellow trail, now covering an 0.3-mile section of trail that you previously hiked in the reverse direction. When you reach the junction with the Purple Trail, remain on the yellow trail (following the sign to "Hudson Ave."), now once again proceeding along a stretch of trail that you have not covered previously on this hike. About a third of a mile beyond, the yellow-blazed Allison Trail ends at the Main Trail, a wide dirt road.

Boardwalk along the shore of Pfister's Pond

Turn left onto the Main Trail, passing the historic Laimbeer House, a private residence which dates back to the 1870s. Beyond the house, the road is blocked to vehicular traffic, but you should continue ahead, following the wide path. Just beyond a sign "Nature Center Regulations," the De Filippi Trail (marked by white triangles) begins on the right. Turn right, leaving the Main Trail, and follow the De Filippi Trail northward. When you reach a junction with the white/red-blazed Bischoff Trail, turn left to continue along the white-triangle-blazed De Filippi Trail, which soon begins to run along the shore of Pfister's Pond. Sections of the trail that traverse wet areas are built on boardwalk.

Just beyond a wooden shelter used for programs (camping is not permitted), the De Filippi Trail ends at the Main Trail (the junction is marked by a stone monument to Dr. Joseph A. De Filippi). Turn right onto the Main Trail and follow it back to the parking area where the hike began.

Pfister's Pond

28 Campgaw Mountain County Reservation

This loop hike climbs gradually to the summit of Campgaw Mountain, with a sweeping view of Bergen County and the New York City skyline.

Difficulty: Easy to moderate
Length and Time: About 3.3 miles; about two hours.
Map: New York-New Jersey Trail Conference North Jersey Trails Map #115.
Directions: Take N.J. Route 208 North to the Summit Avenue exit in Franklin Lakes. Turn left at the end of the ramp, following the sign for Franklin Lakes. At the next traffic light, turn left onto Franklin Avenue. Continue to the following traffic light, and turn right onto Pulis Avenue. Follow Pulis Avenue for 1.4 miles and turn left onto Campgaw Road. In about a mile and a half, you'll pass the Law and Public Safety Institute and the entrance road to the Darlington Golf Course on the right. Just beyond, turn left onto the entrance road leading into Campgaw Mountain County Reservation, which crosses over I-287. When you reach a fork in the road after 0.4 mile, bear left and continue for another 0.2 mile, then turn left and park at the southern end of the main parking area, near a large portable restroom.

From the southern entrance to the parking area, proceed west, crossing the park entrance road. You'll notice three yellow blazes and three blue blazes on a pole to the right of a chained-off gravel road. These blazes mark the start of the Indian Trail (yellow) and the Rocky Ridge Trail (blue).

The Rocky Ridge Trail immediately goes off to the left, but you should continue ahead along the gravel road, following the yellow blazes of the Indian Trail. You'll soon cross under high-voltage power lines and go around a yellow steel gate.

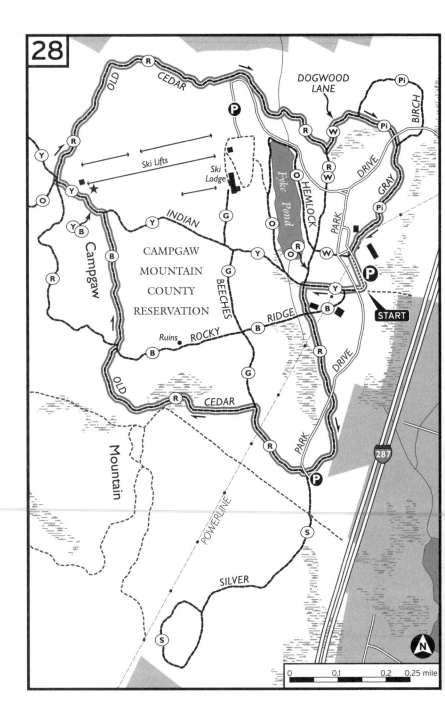

About 500 feet from the start, you'll notice three red-on-white blazes on either side of the trail, which mark the start and end of the Old Cedar Trail. Turn left, leaving the gravel road, and follow the red-on-white blazes. The Old Cedar Trail now proceeds through an oak-beech forest, passing a park building to the left. It soon crosses the wide route of the blue-blazed Rocky Ridge Trail, continues through a low area with abundant surface roots, and recrosses under the power lines.

After crossing the park entrance road diagonally to the right, the Old Cedar Trail follows a path between the park entrance road on the right and I-287 on the left. It crosses several wet areas on wooden bridges, goes over an old stone wall, then turns right and passes several picnic tables. Half a mile from the start, just before a cul-de-sac parking area on the left (where the Silver Trail begins), the red-on-white blazed trail recrosses the paved road diagonally to the right and goes over an intermittent stream on a wooden footbridge. After a short climb, it bears right, then turns left and again passes under the power lines.

A short distance beyond, the green-blazed Beeches Trail proceeds straight ahead, but you should turn left, continuing to follow the red-on-white blazes of the Old Cedar Trail. You've now left the developed portion of the park, and the trail begins a steady, gradual ascent. It bears right to cross a stream on rocks and then turns left to parallel it. Soon, the trail bears right, away from the stream, and continues its winding, gentle ascent.

As you reach the crest of the ridge, the blue-blazed Rocky Ridge Trail comes in from the right. Just beyond, the Old Cedar Trail turns left, but you should proceed straight ahead, now following the blue blazes of the Rocky Ridge Trail, which continues along the ridgeline on a rocky footpath, soon beginning a steady, gentle descent. The trail goes by several tees and yellow-rimmed metal baskets for disc golf, one of the activities offered in the park.

After passing through an area with many cedar trees, the yellow-blazed Indian Trail joins from the right. Just beyond, an unmarked path on the right leads to an open area, but you should proceed ahead, continuing to follow the blue and yellow blazes along the edge of the woods.

In another 250 feet, you'll reach a tree with three blue and two yellow blazes (which signify the terminus of the Rocky Ridge Trail and a sharp left turn on the Indian Trail). Turn right, leaving the marked trails, and cross the open area to reach an expansive east-facing viewpoint at the

The broad east-facing view from the top of the ski slope

top of the ski slope. To the left are the hills of Harriman Park, and in the center is northern Bergen County, with Mahwah in the foreground. The Palisades can be seen on the horizon, and the New York City skyline is visible to the right on a clear day. This is a good place to take a break.

After you've rested a little and enjoyed the view, return to the trail on the west side of the clearing (a triple-blue blaze is visible from the viewpoint). Turn right and continue along the yellow-blazed Indian Trail, which heads northwest.

In another 300 feet, after crossing a woods road, follow the Indian Trail as it turns right and joins the red-on-white-blazed Old Cedar Trail. A short distance beyond, the Indian Trail leaves to the left, but you should continue ahead on the Old Cedar Trail, which curves to the east and descends gradually. In about half a mile, it reaches the northwest corner of the large parking lot for the ski area. The trail turns left and follows the stone curbing along the edge of the parking lot and the entrance road.

Just before the merge of the exit road from the parking lot, the trail bears left, reenters the woods, and descends along the hillside. It turns left

Campgaw Mountain County Reservation

Campgaw Mountain County Reservation was acquired by Bergen County in 1954. In a March 1954 newspaper article, Clifford Mische, Executive Director of the Bergen County Park Commission, was quoted as saying that the County had "established a firm policy that [this] vast tract of rugged mountainous land... will remain essentially in its natural state and be preserved as a wildlife sanctuary." Another article in November 1955 emphasized that there would be "no hot dog stands nor swimming pools nor amusements nor zoos. The rugged land is to be bisected by nature trails, and the birds and animals there now are to be encouraged to stay."

The intent to retain the parkland in its natural state was not entirely adhered to, however. Development of the park, which included the establishment of campsites and picnic areas at the base of the mountain, began in 1960. Some conservationists opposed the addition of these facilities, complaining that the park "was being overdeveloped with the creation of numerous campsites that drove away wildlife." However, for the most part, the mountain itself was spared from development. The ski area was built in 1968, and the disc golf course was established in 2005.

The name "Campgaw" is a variant of names found in deeds and other property descriptions dating back to the 1700s. It was chosen by the Park Commission because it is "an historical name peculiar to the area."

In 1954, a portion of the park (as well as other adjacent land) was condemned by the Federal government to establish a Nike anti-aircraft missile base. The Control Area was located at the southern end of the park (in Franklin Lakes), and the Launch Area was nearly two miles away, at the northern end of the park in Mahwah. The missiles were to be fired against Soviet aircraft that might be sent to drop nuclear bombs on the United States. The missile base was closed in 1971 (the Control Area is now the park's Saddle Ridge Riding Center, while the site of Launch Area has been developed for private homes).

---

and crosses Fyke Brook on a wooden bridge. The Old Cedar Trail then curves left, bears right, and gradually ascends to reach a junction with the white-blazed Dogwood Lane Trail.

Turn left at this junction and follow the white-blazed Dogwood Lane Trail for about 500 feet to its terminus at a cairn. Continue ahead on the pink-blazed Gray Birch Trail, which comes in from the left. The trail crosses the park entrance road, briefly parallels another stone wall, and follows a level path through the woods. In a quarter of a mile, it turns right, begins to parallel power lines on the left, and soon reaches the northern end of the main parking area. Turn left and proceed to the southern end of the parking area, where the hike began.

Bridge over Fyke Brook

29 Garret Mountain Reservation

This loop hike visits less-used areas of this popular park, passing several outstanding views over northern New Jersey and the New York City skyline.

Difficulty: Easy to moderate
Length and Time: About 3.3 miles; about two hours.
Map: Available online at www.nynjtc.org/map/garret-mountain-reservation-trail-map.
Directions: Take I-80 to Exit 57A. Proceed south on N.J. Route 19, and take the first exit (Valley Road). Turn right at the top of the ramp, then make the first right turn, which leads into the parking area for Lambert Castle. Continue past the castle, then turn sharply left and proceed to the southern end of the parking area. (If you have additional time, you may also wish to visit the historic castle, which is open Wednesday-Sunday from 1:00 to 4:00 p.m. An admission fee is charged to enter the castle, but there is no charge for parking.)

From the southern end of the parking area, follow the yellow-blazed Garret Mountain Trail, which proceeds rather steeply uphill on a macadam path and stone steps. The trail turns right onto a wide, paved path, which switchbacks up to the top of the mountain.

At the top of the climb, you'll pass through an opening in a stone wall. Turn sharply right here, briefly following the stone wall, then turn right again. You're now heading north. The trail soon begins to descend on a rocky path and stone steps. After paralleling the paved park road (which runs to the left) for a short distance, you'll notice a well-worn side trail to the right. Follow this trail, which leads to an expansive east-facing viewpoint from the edge of a cliff. (A police firing range is located directly below, so don't be startled to hear some gunshots!) Paterson may be seen directly below, with much of southern Bergen County beyond, and the

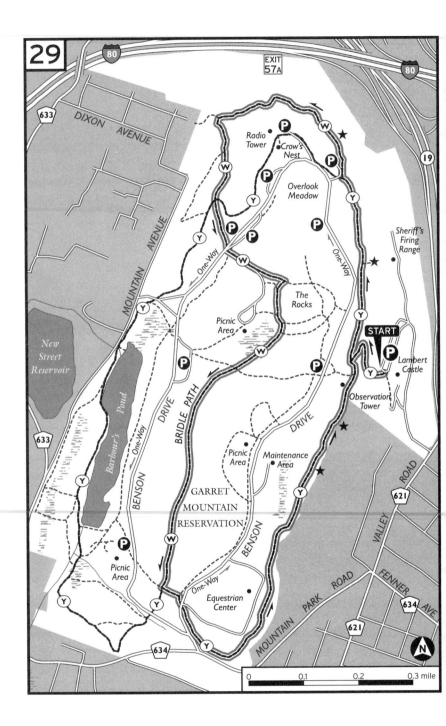

The east-facing view over Bergen County and the New York City skyline from Garret Mountain

New York City skyline visible in the distance on a clear day. The Verrazano-Narrows Bridge is at the extreme right of this broad panorama.

After spending some time here, enjoying the view, return to the yellow trail and turn right. The trail soon passes a small gravel parking area to the left and, about 300 feet beyond, follows along the right side of a grassy field. At the end of the field, the trail descends on a footpath to reach an intersection with the White Trail at the entrance to an overlook. Turn right onto the White Trail, which follows a paved path along the right side of the overlook. It turns right and descends stone steps, then turns left and follows the stone wall along the edge of the overlook. The view to the south and east is more limited here, but downtown Paterson is visible directly below, and High Mountain may be seen to the north.

At the end of the wall, the trail descends into the woods, then climbs slightly to skirt an open area, with a radio tower visible through the trees to the left. The trail continues to descend, soon bearing left. At the base of the descent, the trail briefly parallels an intermittent stream to the right, then turns left and ascends, soon joining a vague woods road. At a huge boulder, the trail turns left, leaving the woods road, and climbs on a footpath.

After leveling off, the White Trail reaches a junction with the yellow-blazed Garret Mountain Trail at a rock ledge that overlooks a ravine to the right. Follow the White Trail as it bears left, soon reaching a gravel parking area along a paved park drive. Here, the trail bears right, turns left

View of High Mountain from overlook on Garret Mountain

to cross the park drive, and continues ahead on a gravel road. In 200 feet, the white blazes bear left at a fork and follow a bridle path for 250 feet. The White Trail then turns right onto another bridle path, passing a line of unusual flat-sided boulders to the left.

In 250 feet, the White Trail bears right at a fork and continues along the bridle path. Then, in another 800 feet, the white blazes bear left onto a footpath, but soon rejoin the bridle path. The White Trail continues along the bridle path for another third of a mile until it ends at a junction with the yellow-blazed Garret Mountain Trail.

Turn left here, now once again following the yellow-blazed trail, which runs along another bridle path. As the trail approaches the paved park road, the bridle path bears left, but you should continue ahead, climb the embankment and cross the paved road. Follow the yellow blazes which indicate that the trail turns right and runs along the grassy shoulder of the road, bearing left past two road intersections. (Do not follow the paved road leading ahead to the park stables.) In about 800 feet, near the park boundary, the yellow-blazed trail turns left, leaving the road, and ascends into the woods on a footpath.

Just before reaching the access road to the stables, the trail bears right and passes between several concrete tank supports. It curves to the left and begins to run along the ridge of Garret Mountain, with the stables

Catholina Lambert and His Castle

Lambert Castle was built by Catholina Lambert — a wealthy businessman who made his fortune in the silk industry. Born in 1834 in Yorkshire, England, he was the son of working-class parents who labored in mills. Catholina began working at a mill at the age of 10. When he finished a seven-year apprenticeship in 1851, he traveled to America and found a job in a silk mill in Boston for $4 a week. Four years later, he was offered a partnership in the firm, and after another three years, he bought out the partner and became head of Dexter, Lambert and Company. In 1866, Lambert consolidated the firm's operations in Paterson, which had become the silk capital of America.

Catholina Lambert married Isabelle Shattuck in 1857. Tragically, five of their eight children died in infancy or childhood. Three children survived into adulthood, but only one son, Walter, outlived his parents.

In 1892, Lambert decided to build a castle, which he named *Belle Vista*, to serve as his home. It was made of granite as well as sandstone quarried from the surrounding hills, and the construction cost has been estimated at $500,000 (at a time when the average wage was $1 a day). The 70-foot-high observation tower was added in 1896.

Lambert's finances took a turn for the worse in 1913, when the Paterson silk strikes began. He lost a large part of his wealth and had to mortgage his estate and sell his large art collection, as well as some of his mills, but he managed to pay all of his debts.

Catholina Lambert lived in his castle for over 30 years, until he died in 1923 at the age of 89. In 1925, his son Walter sold the Castle and the surrounding estate to the City of Paterson for $125,000, and it was used for two years as a summer camp for children suffering from tuberculosis. The Passaic County Parks Commission acquired the Castle in 1928. It became part of the 575-acre Garret Mountain Reservation and was used as the Commission's headquarters until the 1960s.

Between 1995 and 2000, the Castle was restored. Today, it serves as the headquarters of the Passaic County Historical Society and houses a museum that is open to the public. The observation tower was restored in 2010.

to the left. At the end of the stables, the trail bears left, makes a short but steep descent, and then turns right, continuing along the ridge.

About 0.2 mile beyond the stables, the trail reaches an unobstructed viewpoint to the east from the edge of the ridge. The view is similar to that afforded by the first viewpoint that you reached earlier in the hike, but you're a little further away from the urban bustle of the City of Paterson. This is a good place to take a break.

Follow the trail as it continues north along the ridge, passing several more viewpoints. Soon, you'll reach a stone observation tower, built in the 1890s by a wealthy silk manufacturer as part of Lambert Castle, at the base of the mountain. The trail skirts to the right of the tower, which has recently been restored, following a stone wall. Near the end of the wall, the trail turns left. Just ahead, at a break in the wall, turn right and descend the paved path and steps that lead back to the parking area where the hike began.

Observation tower of Lambert Castle

30 Sourland Mountain Preserve

This hike loops around the preserve, passing through several interesting boulder fields.

Difficulty: Easy to moderate

Length and Time: About 5.6 miles; about three and one-half hours.

Map: Sourland Mountain Preserve map (available from kiosk at trailhead or online at www.somersetcountyparks.org).

Directions: Take I-80 West to Exit 43 and proceed south on I-287. Take Exit 17 and continue south on U.S. Route 206 for about 7.6 miles. Turn right onto Amwell Road (County Route 514) (do not turn right at New Amwell Road) and proceed for 2.8 miles to East Mountain Road. Turn left onto East Mountain Road and follow it for 1.9 miles to the entrance to Sourland Mountain Preserve, on the right. GPS address: 425 East Mountain Road, Hillsborough, NJ 08844.

Sourland Mountain is a ridge which straddles the borders of Somerset, Hunterdon and Mercer Counties. Due to the harshness of the land and its unsuitability for farming, large portions of the ridge have remained undeveloped. The largest protected portion of the ridge is in Somerset County, where about 4,000 acres have been set aside as a preserve, administered by the Somerset County Park Commission.

The preserve offers three loop trails, marked with white blazes with the logo of the Somerset County Park Commission. The white-triangle-blazed Maple Flats Trail and the white-circle-blazed Pondside Trail are short, easy loop hikes. The five-mile-long, white-square-blazed Ridge Trail is more challenging, and it permits one to spend several hours exploring this beautiful preserve. In addition, the red-circle-blazed Roaring Brook Trail meanders through the southwest section of the preserve, connecting at both ends with the Ridge Trail. Finally, there are several

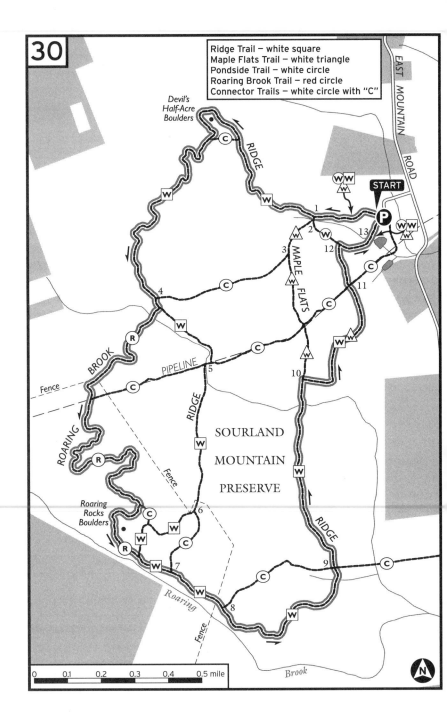

Ridge Trail – white square
Maple Flats Trail – white triangle
Pondside Trail – white circle
Roaring Brook Trail – red circle
Connector Trails – white circle with "C"

30

Devil's Half-Acre Boulders

EAST MOUNTAIN ROAD

START

P

RIDGE

MAPLE FLATS

BROOK

PIPELINE

RIDGE

ROARING

Fence

Roaring Rocks Boulders

Fence

SOURLAND

MOUNTAIN

PRESERVE

Roaring

Fence

Brook

0   0.1   0.2   0.3   0.4   0.5 mile

N

short connecting trails, marked with "C" blazes on a white background. This hike follows the Ridge Trail and the Roaring Brook Trail (none of the connecting trails are included in the route of this hike).

From the kiosk at the edge of the parking area (trail maps of the preserve are usually available here), head west across a grassy field. At the edge of the woods, you will notice a wooden post with three blazes – white triangle, white circle and white square. This marks the start of the three loop trails, which head uphill into the woods, paralleling a brook to the left.

Follow the joint trails for about five minutes until you reach post #1 (all intersections are marked with white-on-green reflective numbers on wooden posts). Here the white-triangle and white-circle trails turn left, crossing the stream on a footbridge, but you should continue ahead on the white-square-blazed Ridge Trail.

The white-square-blazed trail proceeds steadily uphill (you'll climb a total of about 400 vertical feet during the first part of the hike), skirting a small boulder field. It goes through a heavily wooded area, far removed from the homes and farms that you passed on your way to the park. After about 10 minutes of steady climbing, the trail briefly levels off, and a connecting trail (marked with "C" blazes on a white background) begins on the left. You should continue ahead on the white-square-blazed trail, which soon resumes its steady climb.

The trail goes through a narrow passage between these boulders

After another level stretch, followed by a short climb, you'll come to an area of huge boulders (designated on the park map as the "Devil's Half-Acre Boulders"). The first gigantic boulder is just to the left of the trail, but you'll encounter many other large boulders in the next half hour or so. This is the most interesting part of the hike, so take your time to enjoy the unusual boulders. At one point, the trail goes through a narrow passage between two huge boulders. Here, you'll encounter the other end of the connecting trail that you passed on the way up, but continue ahead on the white-square-blazed trail. Towards the end of the boulder field, be alert for another unique feature of this trail – a large tree that has grown out of a horizontal crack in a boulder!

This tree has grown out of a horizontal crack in a boulder

The trail continues through a forest that features many tulip trees – tall, straight trees, with no branches below the treetops. You'll notice a number of multiple tulip tree trunks growing out of the same roots.

Finally, after about an hour of hiking, you'll reach post #4. To the left, a connecting trail leads back towards the parking area, but you should bear right to continue along the white-square-blazed trail. In another 200 feet, you'll come to another junction. Here, the white-square-blazed trail bears left, but you should turn right onto the red-circle-blazed Roaring Brook Trail, which crosses a stream and proceeds through another boulder field, climbing gently.

The Sourland Mountains

The Sourland Mountains were formed by the magma intrusion that lifted up the first Watchung mountain range. Erosion later reduced the height of the softer red sandstone on top of the intrusion, and in most areas of Somerset County, the first Watchung ridge disappears below the surface. However, in the Sourlands, a layer of clay in the overlying sandstone formed a hard rock known as argillite. This hard rock sheltered the Sourlands and kept them higher than the surrounding terrain.

Near the top of the ridgeline, erosion has exposed impressive outcrops of dense diabase bedrock, from which freeze-thaw weathering has split off great boulders. A few large boulders of sedimentary rocks, baked hard by the heat of the igneous intrusion, lie nearby.

These isolated hills stand out today amid gently rolling farmland, much of which has been converted to housing development. Early settlers ignored its steep and rocky slopes as unfit for farming. Eventually the ridgetops and hillsides were logged, and marginal farms and orchards appeared in the clearings, but by the end of the nineteenth century these were abandoned. The successional forest returned, and the mountain became an undisturbed wilderness.

After only a few hundred steps uphill from the Sourland Mountain Preserve trailhead, the visitor begins to recognize that this is a very special place. Compared to other Jersey forests, the mature trees are taller and thicker, and the understory is dense with shrubs, saplings and young trees of various ages. In all green seasons, there is evidence of a wide variety of native wildflowers; through the trees the staccato cry of the pileated woodpecker echoes; and overhead the red-tailed hawk cries "keeeer." Audubon Society hikers have reported sighting colorful songbirds, both migratory and breeding species. The understory has a large population of spicebush, which botanists say is characteristic of the aboriginal forest. While the preserve is not pristine old growth forest, it is a natural museum of our native trees, flowers and birds – open every day, free of charge.   -*George Petty*

In about 15 minutes, you'll pass through a gap in a chain-link fence and enter an area that was formerly owned by the 3M Company but now has been added to the park. In a short distance, the trail crosses the Texas Eastern gas pipeline.

Soon, the trail winds through another boulder field, passing a number of interesting huge boulders. For much of the way, the trail route is relatively level, but it eventually descends a little.

After following the Roaring Brook Trail for about 45 minutes, you'll reach a junction where a connecting trail (marked by "C" blazes) begins on the left. You should bear right to continue on the Roaring Brook Trail, which soon begins a steady descent towards Roaring Brook. Just before reaching the brook, the Roaring Brook Trail ends at a junction with the white-square-blazed Ridge Trail. Turn right and follow the Ridge Trail, which continues to descend, with Roaring Brook directly to your right.

In a short distance, you'll reach a junction marked by post #7 and a huge cairn. Here, another connecting trail (marked by "C" blazes) begins on the left. Continue ahead, following the white-square blazes of the Ridge Trail.

In about five minutes, you'll go through a gap in another chain-link fence. Just beyond the fence, you'll notice post #8. Yet another connecting trail (marked by "C" blazes) goes off to the left, but you should bear right to continue on the white-square-blazed Ridge Trail. Soon, the trail bears left and heads away from Roaring Brook.

In another 15 minutes, you'll cross a boardwalk over a stream and pass an old stone-and-concrete wall (possibly built as a dam) to the left of the trail. Just beyond, you'll come to a four-way intersection marked by post #9, where you should continue straight ahead.

The next stretch of trail is nearly level, and it features a long boardwalk and many short stretches of boardwalk. In another 20 minutes or so, you'll reach post #10. Here, you'll encounter the white-triangle-blazed Maple Flats Trail once more. Turn right and follow both white-square and white-triangle blazes, soon crossing another long section of boardwalk.

A short distance beyond, you'll again cross the gas pipeline (marked by post #11). Continue straight ahead, soon reaching post #12, where the white-circle-blazed Pondside Trail joins from the left. Here, you should turn right, now following all three trails – white triangle, white circle and white square. Soon, you'll emerge onto a grassy area and descend towards a small pond. Bear left around the pond, pass post #13, and you'll reach the parking area where the hike began.

31 Norvin Green State Forest
Torne Mountain Loop

This loop hike climbs to the summit of Torne Mountain, with excellent views.

Difficulty: Moderate
Length and Time: About 1.7 miles; about one and one-half hours.
Map: New York-New Jersey Trail Conference North Jersey Trails Map #115.
Directions: Take I-287 to Exit 53 (Bloomingdale) and turn left onto Hamburg Turnpike. Upon entering Bloomingdale, the name of the road changes to Main Street. In 1.3 miles (from I-287), you will reach a fork in the road. Bear right, and in another 0.1 mile turn right (uphill) onto Glenwild Avenue (following the sign to "West Milford"). Continue ahead for 3.2 miles to a parking area on the right side of the road.

At the eastern end of the parking area, at the sign "Welcome to Bloomingdale," cross Glenwild Avenue. On the south side of the road, you will notice a blue-blazed post, marked "HB." Follow the blue-blazed Hewitt-Butler Trail, which climbs the hill and then turns right, heading west and parallel to the road, for about a quarter of a mile. Here, with the road visible to the right, you will come to an intersection with the red-blazed Torne Trail. Turn left on this red trail, proceeding south. The trail climbs briefly, levels off, and then descends through a valley, which soon becomes a very rocky and boulder-filled gully.

In about half a mile, the red-blazed Torne Trail ends at a second junction with the blue-blazed Hewitt-Butler Trail, which crosses the gully amidst large boulders. Turn right and head west and uphill, following the blue markers.

After climbing steeply for a short distance, you'll reach a junction with a black-dot-on-blue side trail. Turn right to continue on the blue-blazed

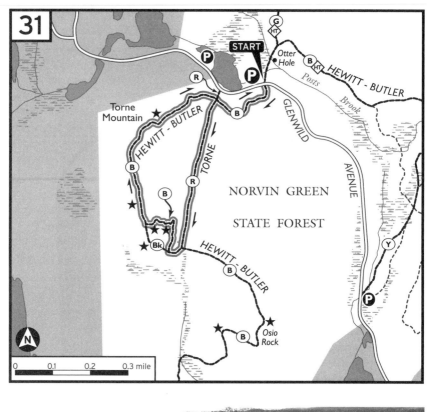

Two balanced glacial erratics at a viewpoint along the Hewitt-Butler Trail.

Ice Age Artifacts

The huge boulders sit along the trail like giant question marks. How these rocks, known as glacial erratics, got there has been the source of speculation for millennia. Some early cultures thought that witches moved them, but by the nineteenth century, the prevailing theory was that they had been washed there by the Biblical Great Flood. Geologists called them "erratics" because they were found far from the bedrock in which they originated. Some could be traced hundreds of miles from their source, bringing into question the Great Flood theory.

In the mid 1800s, Louis Agassiz, a Swiss naturalist who studied erratics and glaciers, postulated a theory of massive sheets of ice covering huge parts of the globe during a period of extreme cold. His theory was first greeted with skepticism, but subsequent research supported most of his findings. Agassiz referred to glaciers as "God's great plough."

As these glaciers began to retreat over 10,000 years ago, they left a newly sculpted landscape, with features such as the Great Lakes and Niagara Falls (as well as the contours of this state forest). The glaciers carried with them and deposited along the way both small pieces scoured from bedrock and larger rock fragments – the erratics. These huge rocks that were stranded far from their original locations serve as geological road maps to the movement of the glaciers that dropped them, and they play a central role in the understanding of glaciers and of the Ice Age itself.

One of the first to embrace Agassiz's theory was Charles Darwin, but Agassiz, who had become a professor at Harvard, did not reciprocate. He became a leading critic of Darwin's theory on evolution, contending that the glacial sheets had been so extensive that they destroyed all life. Thus, he argued, there could not be a link between life forms of the pre-glacial age and those of the present.

Research in the last century has led scientists to conclude that the Ice Age postulated by Agassiz, which peaked 20,000 years ago to cover about 30 percent of the globe, was only the most recent of several Ice Ages, with at least four glacial periods occurring during the last million years.

When Agassiz died in 1873, a monument was brought from Switzerland for his grave in Boston – a piece of an erratic from the glacier where he had done his primary research.   -*Jim Simpson*

Hewitt-Butler Trail, which briefly follows a level path, then continues to climb. Soon, it comes out on open rocks, with views to the southeast over Osio Rock. After climbing on a switchback, the trail reaches a broader viewpoint to the south and southeast. Then, after climbing some more, you'll come to a southeast-facing viewpoint, with the New York City skyline visible in the distance.

The south-facing view from the Hewitt-Butler Trail

A short distance beyond, you'll reach another junction with the black-dot-on-blue side trail. Turn right, continuing to follow the blue-blazed Hewitt-Butler Trail, which soon comes out on open rocks, with views to the west and south. You'll notice a single cedar tree, a stone bench and two balanced glacial erratics at this interesting spot. The trail continues through a wooded section and reaches a final viewpoint, this one looking to the north and west. Buck Mountain is visible to the north (when there are no leaves on the trees), with the Pequannock Watershed to the west. The trail now bears right and descends rather steeply. In about a quarter mile, it reaches the first junction with the red trail. Continue ahead on the blue trail, now retracing your steps, until the trail crosses Glenwild Avenue to reach the parking area where the hike began.

32 Point Mountain Reservation

This loop hike follows mowed paths along cultivated fields, parallels the scenic Musconetcong River, and climbs to the summit of Point Mountain, with views of small towns, fertile farmland, and the Musconetcong River valley.

Difficulty: Moderate

Length and Time: About 4.1 miles; about three hours.

Map: Hunterdon County Parks Department map (available online at www.co.hunterdon.nj.us or from kiosk at trailhead).

Directions: Take I-80 to Exit 26 (Budd Lake/Hackettstown) and proceed west on U.S. Route 46 for 7.4 miles to Hackettstown. Turn left onto N.J. Route 182 and follow it for 1.0 mile, then turn right onto N.J. Route 57. Follow Route 57 for 6.2 miles and turn left onto Penwell Road (at a sign for "Penwell"). Proceed for 0.4 mile to a bridge over the Musconetcong River. About 0.1 mile beyond the bridge, turn right onto a gravel driveway just before a stone house (the small park sign at this location is difficult to see) and continue uphill for about 0.2 mile to the parking area. GPS address: 402 Penwell Road, Port Murray, NJ 07865.

From the parking area, proceed south on the orange-blazed Ridge Trail, which follows a wide mowed path to the left of cultivated fields, with views of Point Mountain ahead in the distance. In about a third of a mile, where the orange-blazed trail turns left, continue ahead on the blue-blazed Riverwalk Trail. The blue-blazed trail turns right at the end of the field, follows along its southern end, then turns left and descends on a footpath to the Musconetcong River. After crossing a tributary stream, the trail widens to a woods road. When you reach a fork, bear right to continue along the blue-blazed trail.

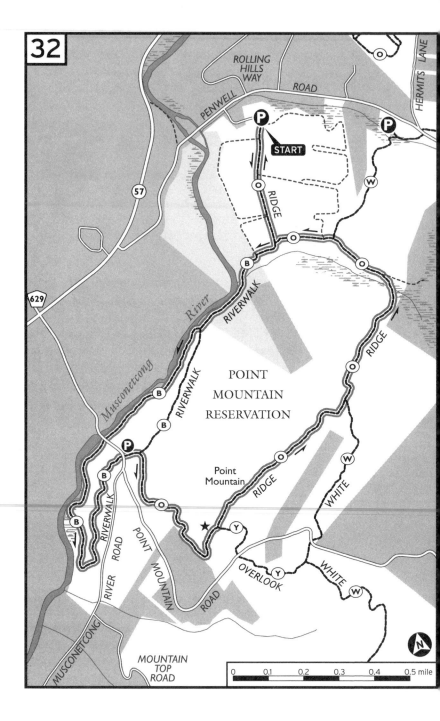

The trail follows a mowed path to the left of cultivated fields, with Point Mountain ahead in the distance

In a third of a mile, the Riverwalk Trail reaches another fork. The trail ahead is also marked blue, but you should turn right, leaving the woods road, follow a footpath for 50 feet to the river, then turn left and proceed along the river, still following blue blazes. For the next half mile, the trail follows a footpath that closely parallels the scenic river, which features attractive cascades.

Musconetcong River

Point Mountain

As one heads west along the Jersey Highlands, the hills decline in height, eventually disappearing under sedimentary rocks near Reading, Pennsylvania. Point Mountain is the most westerly peak in the Highlands over 900 feet in elevation.

At the highest point of the hike, after a steep climb, a typical Highlands gneiss rock outcrop offers panoramic views from southwest to due north across the Musconetcong River and its valley. The countryside is rural – farmed fields dot the landscape close to the river, sharing the hillsides with streets and houses, and with new growth forest at higher elevations.

But 150 years ago, this landscape was surprisingly different. An 1874 map shows a sawmill where Point Mountain Road crosses the Musconetcong River, and there were grain mills and sawmills on the southeast slopes of the mountain. In the days before electricity and oil, running streams provided the power for industry. The climate was colder, with heavier snow cover, and undisturbed soil retained ground water, so the mill streams flowed reliably through the summer. There was an iron mine just to the south of the mountain, and wagon roads carried logs to the mill, charcoal to the furnace, and farm produce to market. Portions of today's hiking trails follow these former roads. An old stone farm fence parallels the trail along the top of the ridge, bordering what was once a flat meadow suitable for pasture.

Today, no tree in the forest is thicker than 14 or 15 inches. This is an indication that 80 to 90 years ago the entire mountain, both slopes and ridgetop, was either farmed or logged clean. As you look over the valley and surrounding hills – now half open fields and half growing forest – it is startling to think that, a century and a half ago, every square foot of surface that could be reached with a plow, mower or saw was bare of trees.

The Musconetcong River turns west just below the north end of the mountain. The 1874 map calls the small peninsula that juts into the river here "Squires Point," and a 1914 map calls it "The Point." It is probable that the name Point Mountain is derived from its location near that bend.

-George Petty

After passing a huge sycamore tree, the trail crosses Point Mountain Road and soon heads slightly inland, following a footpath through wild rose thickets. This trail section is often somewhat overgrown, although it is well blazed and relatively easy to follow. After approaching the river once more, the trail bears left, away from the river, and begins to run through a deciduous forest. Soon, the trail bears sharply left and begins to head northeast, paralleling Musconetcong River Road, visible through the trees to the right.

About two miles from the start, the Riverwalk Trail recrosses Point Mountain Road and enters a parking area on the east side of the road. Here, the trail turns right and begins to climb on a rocky footpath, reaching a trail junction in 250 feet. Continue ahead, uphill, now following the orange-blazed Ridge Trail. After the trail makes a sharp right turn, the grade steepens, and the trail continues to ascend on a rocky, rugged treadway, with rock and wood steps provided for part of the way.

After the trail bears sharply left in sight of a private home ahead, the grade moderates, and the trail soon reaches a panoramic viewpoint over the Musconetcong River valley from a rock outcrop to the left of the trail. The tranquil view includes farms and small towns. This is a good place to take a break and rest from the climb – the one steep ascent on the hike.

View of the Musconetcong River valley from Point Mountain

The Ridge Trail now briefly descends to a junction with the yellow-blazed Overlook Trail. Here, it bears left and climbs to regain the ridge. Follow the orange-blazed trail as it continues along the ridge, with occasional views through the trees to the left. After about half a mile of ridgetop walking, the trail bears right and descends slightly. It parallels an old stone wall for about 600 feet, passing a junction with the White Trail, which leaves to the right. Continue ahead on the orange-blazed Ridge Trail, which soon turns left and climbs back to the ridge.

Soon, the trail begins a steady descent from the ridge. After crossing a stream, it turns left and follows a woods road downhill. Near the base of the descent, the White Trail goes off to the right. Continue ahead on the orange-blazed trail, which emerges onto a field and follows a mowed path along its left side. At the end of the field, it bears left and reaches a junction with the blue-blazed Riverwalk Trail, which begins on the left. Turn right and follow the orange-blazed trail along the right side of fields, retracing your steps to the Penwell Road parking area, where the hike began.

33 Ramapo Mountain State Forest and Camp Glen Gray

This loop hike passes interesting and historic millstones and climbs to a panoramic viewpoint over Bergen County and the New York City skyline.

Difficulty: Moderate
Length and Time: About 6.0 miles; about four hours.
Map: New York-New Jersey Trail Conference North Jersey Trails Map #115.
Directions: Take I-287 to Exit 57 (Skyline Drive). Proceed north on Skyline Drive for about one mile to the upper parking area for Ramapo Mountain State Forest on the left side of the road, just beyond at milepost 1.4 (opposite the entrance to Camp Tamarack).

From the northwest end of the parking area, cross Skyline Drive. You will see a triple orange blaze on a tree, marking the start of the Schuber Trail, as well as a triple white blaze, which marks the start of the Todd Trail. The Schuber Trail will be your return route, but for now, follow the white-blazed Todd Trail, which heads southeast along Skyline Drive for 200 feet. It turns left into the woods, winds downhill on a rocky footpath, and ascends from a shallow ravine. In half a mile, the trail turns right onto a woods road and soon bears left at a fork onto another woods road. A short distance beyond, you will notice three yellow blazes that mark the start of the Yellow Trail.

Turn left and follow the Yellow Trail (marked with yellow diamonds), which heads north, soon reaching Todd Lake. Here, the trail bears left and follows along the west shore of the lake, passing a rock ledge with a stone wall at lake level, with a view over the water. After climbing steeply to a rock outcrop near the north end of the lake (from which a municipal water tower is visible to the right), the Yellow Trail begins a steady, rather

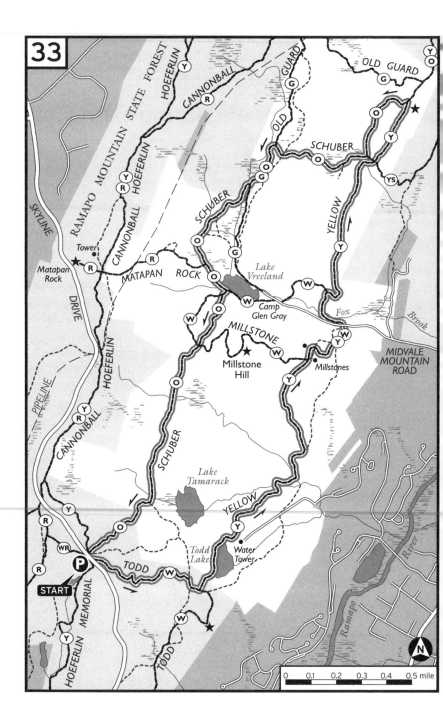

steep descent to a valley, where it crosses two streams (with attractive cascades when the water is high).

The trail now begins a steady, gradual climb. After paralleling a stone wall on the right, the trail bears right and heads north, continuing to climb steadily. Eventually, the trail levels off on a shoulder of the ridge, with views through the trees of Campgaw Mountain to the east.

About two miles from the start of the hike, continue on the Yellow Trail as it joins the white-blazed Millstone Trail. Just beyond the junction, several abandoned millstones in various stages of completion may be seen to the right of the trail. This area was once the site of a millstone quarry, and the stones that you see were either damaged during quarrying or abandoned when the quarry operation shut down. After crossing an old woods road at a sign "HT 12," the two trails pass a millstone in nearly perfect condition 25 feet to the right.

A millstone in nearly perfect condition

Continuing to descend, the trails pass an old stone wall, which marks the boundary of Camp Glen Gray, and cross paved Midvale Mountain Road diagonally to left at Kiosk #4. (These kiosks were installed by Camp Glen Gray, in cooperation with the Trail Conference and Bergen County; this is the first of five kiosks that you will pass along the route of the hike.) The trails head into the woods and bear left to parallel Fox Brook,

A hiker at the footbridge over Fox Brook

then turn right and cross two branches of the brook on footbridges. The trails now begin to climb, reaching a junction in a level area. Here, the Millstone Trail leaves to the left, but you should turn right, staying on the Yellow Trail. The trail briefly follows an old woods road, then turns left at a huge, flat-sided boulder and heads north, climbing steadily through a wooded valley.

After reaching the crest of the rise, the trail descends briefly and continues along a level woods road. It crosses a stream on a wooden footbridge and, just beyond, passes the ruins of some old Scout buildings. Just ahead, it turns right onto a wide woods road (briefly joining the route of the Yellow-Silver Trail). In 100 feet, it turns left and begins to ascend, soon passing a stone foundation on a rock ledge.

At the high point of the ridge (996 feet), reached a little over three miles from the start, you'll come to a junction, marked by a cairn and a wooden post with a sign "HT 2." Turn right to reach an expansive viewpoint over northern Bergen County from a rock outcrop. On a clear day you can see the New York City skyline on the horizon to the right. You've now gone a little more than halfway, and this is a good place to stop and take a break.

The expansive view over northern Bergen County from the Yellow Trail

After enjoying the panoramic view, return to the wooden post at the junction, and continue straight ahead (west), now following the orange blazes of the Schuber Trail, which head downhill, soon joining a grassy woods road. (Do *not* follow the joint Yellow/Schuber Trail, which heads north from the viewpoint.) About half a mile from the viewpoint, at Kiosk #7, the Yellow-Silver Trail begins on the left, but you should bear right to continue along the Schuber Trail, which crosses a wooden bridge over the outlet of Sanders Pond, to the right of the trail. Just beyond, a sign "HT 1" on the left marks the site of the historic Sanders Farm, settled in 1810. The stone foundations of a farm building are still visible.

After climbing over a knoll, the Schuber Trail descends to cross the historic Cannonball Road at Kiosk #10. It continues straight ahead on a footpath, descending to North Brook, where it turns left and joins the Old Guard Trail, blazed with a green tulip leaf on a white background.

The trails climb to a rock outcrop overlooking the brook and continue to parallel the brook. Soon, they skirt the Tindall Cabin of Camp Glen Gray and reach Kiosk #6. Here, the Old Guard Trail proceeds ahead, but you should turn right to continue on the Schuber Trail, which crosses a footbridge over the brook and bears left, passing more stone foundations of the historic Sanders Farm.

Camp Glen Gray

Camp Glen Gray was established in 1917 by the Montclair Council, Boy Scouts of America. It was named for "Uncle" Frank Gray, a schoolteacher, who spent his summers at the camp, living in a cabin that became known as the Library. In 1931, the Montclair Council merged with Scout councils in neighboring communities to form the Eagle Rock Council, and that council merged in 1976 with several other councils to form the Essex Council. In 1999, Essex Council, in turn, merged with three other councils to form the Northern New Jersey Council.

The new, expanded council viewed the camp as surplus property and decided to sell it. Concerned Scouters feared that the camp, which had served Scouts for over 80 years, would be no more. They formed a committee to do whatever they could to keep the camp open. Among those who joined the effort was John C. Whitehead, Chairman of the Lower Manhattan Redevelopment Corporation, who grew up in Montclair and served on the staff of Camp Glen Gray as a boy.

As a result of these Scouters' efforts to keep the camp open, the Trust for Public Land (TPL) acquired the camp from the Boy Scouts in 2002 for $5.1 million and sold it to Bergen County. In coordination with Bergen County, TPL entered into an agreement with Friends of Glen Gray ("FOGG") which authorized FOGG to continue the operation of the camp. Although Camp Glen Gray is no longer a Boy Scout camp, and the campsites and cabins may be rented by the general public, most overnight use of the camp is still by Boy Scout units.

Hikers were always informally allowed to walk through the camp property, but with the takeover of the property by Bergen County, the public acquired the right to use the hiking trails that traversed the camp. The Trail Conference was invited to improve the trails, and meetings were held between John Moran, North Jersey Trails Chair for the Trail Conference, and representatives of the camp. Several historic Scout trails, such as the Millstone Trail and the Old Guard Trail, were rehabilitated and integrated into the pre-existing system of public trails. The result is an expanded and enhanced trail network that criss-crosses the camp and can be enjoyed by all.

After skirting the Augie Schroeder Memorial Campsite (the former camp archery range) to the left, the Schuber Trail joins Mary Post Road. It passes McMullen Field on the right, crosses a wooden bridge, and gradually curves to the left, going past more cabins and campsites of Camp Glen Gray (for more information about the camp, consult www.glengray.org).

Soon, the Schuber Trail reaches the shore of Lake Vreeland. After crossing a culvert over South Brook, with the lake to the left and a wet area to the right, the trail passes the Mothers' Pavilion on the left. Just beyond, the Schuber Trail turns right onto a woods road, leaving the lake shore. Here, the white-blazed Millstone Trail joins briefly. In 100 feet, you'll reach a fork, where you should bear left to continue on the orange-blazed Schuber Trail. After passing the Explorer Cabin on the left, the trail bears left again and continues to climb on a footpath.

The Explorer Cabin at Camp Glen Gray

In another quarter of a mile, just beyond the crest of the rise, you'll cross the white-blazed Millstone Trail. The Schuber Trail now descends to cross a stream on rocks. It climbs over a rise and descends to cross another stream on cinder blocks and rocks. Just beyond, the trail passes the ruins of the former rifle range of Camp Tamarack. Here, the trail turns right and then immediately bears left. It climbs to the southwest on a winding footpath and ends at Skyline Drive, opposite the large upper parking area where the hike began.

34 Mohonk Preserve
Millbrook Mountain

This loop hike climbs to the summit of Millbrook Mountain along spectacular cliffs of Shawangunk conglomerate that offer expansive views over the surrounding countryside.

Difficulty: Moderate

Length and Time: About 6.5 miles; about four and one-half hours.

Map: New York-New Jersey Trail Conference Shawangunk Trails Map #105.

Directions: Take the New York State Thruway to Exit 18 (New Paltz). Beyond the toll booths, turn left onto N.Y. Route 299 and continue west through the Village of New Paltz. When you cross the bridge over the Wallkill River at the west end of the village, continue ahead on Route 299 (do not turn right towards the Mohonk Mountain House). In another 5.5 miles (from the Wallkill River bridge), Route 299 ends at a T-intersection with Route 44/55. Turn right here and follow Route 44/55 for half a mile to the Mohonk Preserve Visitor Center, on the right side of the road. Stop at the visitor center to purchase a pass, obtain a free map and view the interesting exhibits. Then continue ahead on Route 44/55. The road makes a very sharp hairpin turn and climbs to the Trapps Bridge (a steel overpass). Continue for 0.3 mile past Trapps Bridge and turn right into the West Trapps Trailhead Parking Area.

From the eastern end of the parking area, follow the yellow-blazed West Trapps Connector Trail, a gravel road which leads east, parallel to Route 44/55. In about a quarter of a mile, you'll reach the Trapps Bridge. Ascend the rock stairway that leads up to the bridge, turn right, and cross the bridge. About 150 feet beyond the bridge, three light-blue blazes mark the start of the Millbrook Ridge Trail. Turn left and follow this trail – marked with paint blazes on the rocks – which steeply climbs over rock

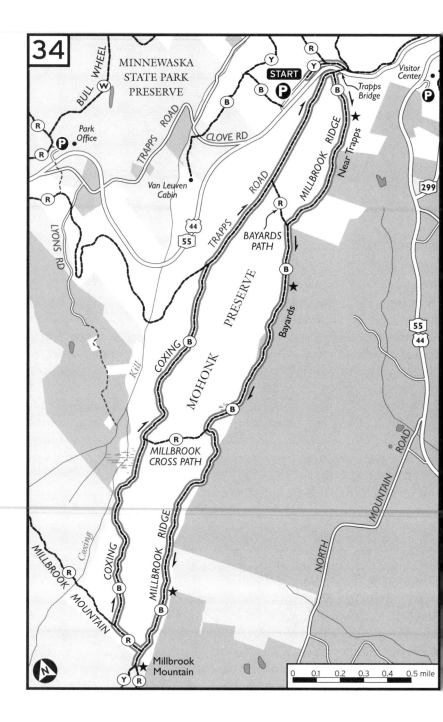

34

MINNEWASKA
STATE PARK
PRESERVE

BULL WHEEL

TRAPPS ROAD

CLOVE RD

Park
Office

Van Leuven
Cabin

LYONS RD

Kill

START
P

Visitor
Center
P

Trapps
Bridge

Near-Trapps

MILLBROOK RIDGE

299

TRAPPS ROAD

44
55

BAYARDS
PATH

Bayards

55
44

PRESERVE

MOHONK

COXING

MILLBROOK
CROSS PATH

COXING

MILLBROOK RIDGE

Coxing

MILLBROOK MOUNTAIN

NORTH MOUNTAIN ROAD

N

Millbrook
Mountain

0   0.1   0.2   0.3   0.4   0.5 mile

slabs dotted with pitch pines. Soon, you'll reach a north-facing viewpoint (the first of many along the ridge).

A short distance beyond, after some more climbing, you'll reach the crest of the ridge (known as the Near Trapps). Here, there is an even broader view from a point called the Hawk Watch. To the left, you can see Dickie Barre, with the Catskill Mountains in the distance beyond. To the right, there is a sweeping view over the Wallkill Valley, with New Paltz visible in the distance. This is a good spot to rest and take a break from the climb.

A hiker taking in the view from the Hawk Watch

The trail now levels off and continues through a wooded area along the ridge, with scrub oak and pitch pine and an understory of blueberry bushes. Soon, you'll reach another viewpoint on the left, with the Sky Top tower of the Mohonk Mountain House visible to the north, and the intersection of Routes 299 and 44/55 directly below.

About a mile from the start, you'll descend slightly and reach a junction with the red-blazed Bayards Path, which leaves to the right. Continue ahead on the light-blue-blazed Millbrook Ridge Trail, which bears left and climbs to the top of the next ridge, known as the Bayards. The trail follows along the ridge, passing several viewpoints over the Wallkill Valley. A long, relatively level section follows, with the trail cutting through groves of

Mohonk Preserve and the Legacy of the Smiley Family

The Millbrook Ridge, from the Trapps Bridge to Millbrook Mountain, was originally part of the Mohonk Mountain House property, acquired in 1869 by Albert K. Smiley and his twin brother Alfred H. Smiley. The brothers, who were Quakers and teachers by profession, built and operated both the Mohonk Mountain House and the Minnewaska Mountain Houses. Over the years, the Smileys acquired over 17,500 acres along the Shawangunk Ridge, protecting and conserving this geologically unusual and scenically beautiful feature. The Mohonk Mountain House is still owned and operated by the Smiley family (today, it is headed by Albert K. "Bert" Smiley, great-grandnephew of the original Albert K.), but the Minnewaska hotels closed about 1980, and the property on which they were located (including the summit of Millbrook Mountain) is now part of Minnewaska State Park Preserve.

By the early 1960s, the taxes on the Mohonk Mountain House property had increased significantly. The Smileys decided to sell 5,300 acres of land that surrounded the hotel – including The Trapps (considered one of the premier rock-climbing destinations in North America) and the Millbrook Ridge – to the Mohonk Trust, a non-profit, tax-exempt organization now known as the Mohonk Preserve. Originally closely associated with the Mountain House and the Smiley family, the Mohonk Preserve today is an independent organization that manages over 7,500 acres of land on the Shawangunk Ridge, forming New York State's largest privately owned, member-and-visitor-supported nature preserve.

In 2011, 874 acres of Smiley-owned lands on the New Paltz side of the mountain were sold to the Open Space Institute (OSI). The hotel retains about 1,350 acres. The property sold to OSI includes the four-story Testimonial Gateway, a stone archway near the intersection of Gate House Road and Route 299 that once served as the hotel's main entrance. It was created by local stonecutters in 1908 as a fiftieth wedding anniversary gift to the original Albert K. Smiley and his wife Eliza, and was funded by contributions of 1,200 friends of the Smileys, including many long-time guests at the hotel. This 874-acre parcel is currently managed by the Mohonk Preserve, which has agreed to acquire 534 acres from OSI by 2015.

-Daniel Chazin and Charlotte Fahn

mountain laurel and blueberry bushes. Suddenly, the trail emerges onto a rounded outcrop with a view ahead (through the trees) of the dramatic cliff of Millbrook Mountain – the destination of the hike.

After bearing right and descending through mountain laurel and hemlock, the Millbrook Ridge Trail arrives at a junction with the red-blazed Millbrook Cross Path. You've now gone about two miles from the start. Continue ahead on the light-blue trail, which bends left and climbs to regain the crest of the ridge. Soon, it crosses a rock outcrop with several small glacial erratics. It continues on a relatively level footpath through laurel and hemlocks and emerges onto an open area.

After traversing a rocky path through hemlocks, the trail arrives at the base of a cliff. It climbs over rocks to the right of the cliff and continues on a footpath below the crest of the ridge. Soon, the trail bears left, climbs through a boulder field, and proceeds through an open area, with blueberries and pitch pines, to reach the crest of the ridge. This is the start of the most interesting and dramatic part of the hike.

The trail turns right and continues to climb along exposed rock outcrops, with views to the south and east over the Wallkill Valley as far as the Hudson Highlands. Sky Top may be seen to the northeast, and the Catskills in the distance to the north. Just beyond, the trail follows a narrow path to the right of a sloping rock slab. Next, the trail climbs to the very edge of the cliff, with a sheer 300-foot drop. Using extreme caution, you can peer over the sharp cliff edge and see the vast boulder field below – probably the moraine of a small glacier that remained after the main ice sheet had melted away. This is another good place for a break.

The trail continues to run along the cliff edge, then heads slightly inland. Finally – a little over three miles from the start – you'll arrive at a junction with the red-blazed Millbrook Mountain Trail (marked by a sign for "Lake Minnewaska"). This is your return route, but first, continue ahead on the trail (now blazed red) for a few hundred feet to a sign "Entering Minnewaska State Park Preserve," turn left and climb the rock slab to the edge of the cliff – the summit of Millbrook Mountain, which offers an even broader view than those you've seen until now. After taking in the view, return to the trail junction and turn left onto the red-blazed trail.

In 0.2 mile, turn right onto the light-blue-blazed Coxing Trail, which descends steadily over rock slabs dotted with pitch pines, then bears left and continues to descend through blueberry bushes, mountain laurel and

View of the Wallkill Valley from the Millbrook Ridge

hemlock. After leveling off and crossing a wet area on puncheons, the trail widens to a woods road.

About two miles from its start, the Coxing Trail ends at a junction with the dirt Trapps Road, a carriage road built by the proprietors of the Mohonk and Minnewaska Mountain Houses. Turn right and follow this level road for about a mile to the Trapps Bridge. Cross the bridge, turn left and descend the stairway, and follow the connector trail back to the parking area where you began the hike.

35

Harriman State Park
Claudius Smith's Rock/
Parker Cabin Mountain Loop

This loop hike climbs to several panoramic viewpoints, including the historic Claudius Smith's Rock, and goes along the shores of Lakes Sebago and Skenonto.

Difficulty: Moderate to strenuous.
Length and Time: About 8.5 miles; about six hours.
Map: New York-New Jersey Trail Conference Harriman-Bear Mountain Trails Map #118.
Directions: Take N.J. Route 17 North to the New York State Thruway and take the first exit, Exit 15A (Sloatsburg). Turn left at the bottom of the ramp onto N.Y. Route 17 North, and continue for 4.9 miles, passing through the villages of Sloatsburg and Tuxedo. Just past the Tuxedo railroad station, turn right onto East Village Road, cross the railroad tracks, and turn left into a commuter parking lot. Parking is free on weekends; on weekdays, a parking fee is charged.

The hike may be reached by public transportation – Metro-North Port Jervis Line trains from Hoboken to Tuxedo (you can take NJ Transit trains from Penn Station in New York City and transfer at Secaucus Junction). You can also take the Short Line bus to Tuxedo from the Port Authority Bus Terminal in New York City. From the station, head north along the station platform to East Village Road, turn right, and follow the description below.

From the parking area, turn left and proceed east along paved East Village Road, immediately crossing the Ramapo River. Continue to follow the road as it bears right, paralleling the New York State Thruway, then turns left and crosses under the Thruway. At the next T-intersection, turn left and head north on Grove Drive for about 800 feet. As the road curves

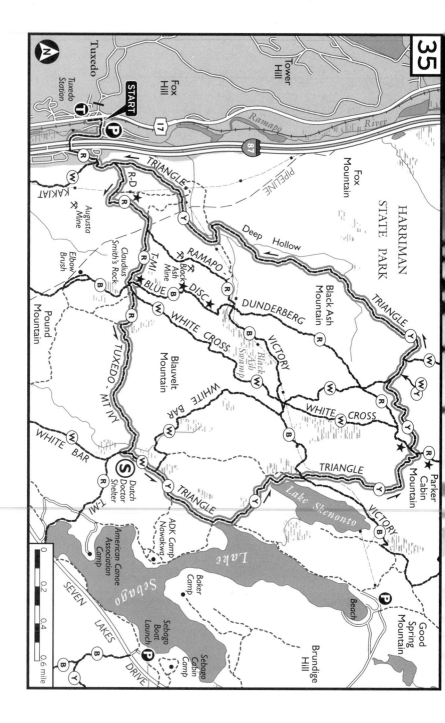

to the left, follow the red-dot-on-white blazes of the Ramapo-Dunder-berg (R-D) Trail, which turn right and enter the woods.

The trail climbs on a switchback and turns left, soon reaching a junction with the yellow-triangle-blazed Triangle Trail, which continues ahead. This trail will be your return route, but you should now turn right and continue on the red-and-white-blazed R-D Trail.

After crossing a grassy woods road, the trail begins a steep climb. At the top of the climb, the trail bears left and soon reaches a panoramic west-facing viewpoint from a rock outcrop to the left of the trail. The village below is Tuxedo, where you began the hike.

The west-facing view over Tuxedo from the rock outcrop along the R-D Trail

The trail now descends briefly, then turns right onto a woods road. A short distance beyond, you'll reach a junction. The R-D Trail continues ahead, but you should turn right onto the red-dash-on-white-blazed Tuxedo-Mt. Ivy (T-MI) Trail (be careful here, as both trails have red-on-white blazes!). The T-MI Trail climbs on a woods road, crosses a swampy area, and soon arrives at the base of the massive Claudius Smith's Rock. Claudius Smith, after whom this rock formation is named, was a thief who was reputed to have used the "caves" at its base as a hideout during the Revolutionary War. He was captured by an officer of the Continental Army and hanged at the jail in Goshen in 1779.

"Cowboy" of the Ramapos

Claudius Smith's Rock offers a commanding view of the surrounding countryside. It is believed that, during the early years of the American Revolution, the site's namesake used it frequently. But his interests were more strategic than scenic: he was the leader of a gang of marauders that preyed on suspected Patriot sympathizers.

Life during the war was difficult, and it was especially trying for those living in the areas between New York City – a stronghold of the British – and the Hudson Highlands – the main defensive line of the Continental forces. Lower Westchester County and southern Orange County (which included present-day Rockland County) were referred to as "neutral ground," but it was more a no-man's land, with roving attacks by marauders. The Patriot raiders were called "skinners," and the Loyalists were referred to as "cowboys." Perhaps the most notorious of the Loyalist cowboys in Orange County was Claudius Smith.

Smith was born on Long Island (Smithtown in Suffolk County is named for his forebears), but his family later moved to Smith Clove (now Monroe). With the onset of the conflict, he and his gang began raiding in the Ramapo Valley, selling stolen livestock to the British. Among their reputed hideouts was this rock formation. The top of the rock was used as an observation point, and the two dens at its base – formed from the overhanging rock – were used for shelter. The lower den was for livestock.

Smith was caught while trying to steal Continental Army livestock in 1777 and was detained in Kingston, but he escaped in a daring foray by his comrades. He continued his raiding until, after a particularly brutal attack attributed to his gang, a price was put on his head. He fled to the British lines and traveled to Long Island, considered a safer haven for Tories. A militia party in Connecticut learned of his location and, with an eye to the reward, snatched him in a raid across Long Island Sound. Smith was brought to Goshen, tried and executed in January 1779.

Legend has it that Smith, wild in his youth, stepped out of his shoes before being hanged to belie a mother's harangue that he would "die like a trooper's horse, with your shoes on." Three of his four sons joined his gang, and two would die during the war. A fourth son (the eldest) served with the Patriots.

-Jim Simpson

Claudius Smith's Rock

When you're finished exploring the overhanging rock "caves," continue along the T-MI Trail for a short distance until you reach a junction with the blue-on-white Blue Disc Trail. Turn left and follow the Blue Disc Trail up to the top of this massive rock formation, with its expansive west-facing view. You'll want to take a break here to enjoy the view!

After taking in the view, retrace your steps to the junction with the T-MI Trail, and turn left, following the red-dash-on-white blazes. The trail descends gradually, making a horseshoe turn at the base of the descent to skirt a swamp to the left of the trail. It then climbs over a low ridge and descends through a rocky area to cross Spring Brook and reach a junction with the White Bar Trail, about 1.2 miles from Claudius Smith's Rock.

Turn left at this junction and follow the White Bar Trail, which runs along a woods road. Soon, you'll pass the Dutch Doctor Shelter, on a small rise to the right of the trail. Overnight camping is permitted at this and several other similar shelters in Harriman State Park.

A short distance beyond the shelter, you'll reach another junction. Here, the White Bar Trail curves to the left, but you should continue straight ahead, now following the yellow triangle blazes of the Triangle Trail. The Triangle Trail – which you will be following for the next five miles – proceeds through an area with a dense understory of mountain laurel and blueberry bushes.

In about half a mile, you'll cross a stream leading into Lake Sebago and briefly follow the shore of this scenic lake. The trail then bears left, away from the lake, climbs over two low hills, and descends to Lake Skenonto. It soon reaches a rock outcrop that overlooks the tranquil south arm of the lake. This is a good place to take a break.

A hiker at Lake Skenonto

The Triangle Trail continues parallel to the lake shore, crossing the main inlet stream of the lake and joining a woods road. After a short distance, it crosses another woods road – the route of the Victory Trail (blue V on white) – and heads back into the woods.

The Triangle Trail now begins a steady climb of Parker Cabin Mountain. On the way, it crosses under a power line and passes an interesting overhanging rock to the right, while ascending through a shallow ravine. After a short, steep climb, you'll reach the summit ridge of Parker Cabin Mountain, where a rock outcrop affords an expansive southeast-facing view over Lake Sebago.

View of Lake Sebago from Parker Cabin Mountain

On the summit ridge, the Triangle Trail reaches a junction with the red-dot-on-white-blazed R-D Trail. Turn left at the junction, and briefly follow both yellow triangle and red-dot-on-white blazes. When the two trails split, bear right, continuing to follow the Triangle Trail, which now begins a steady descent through mountain laurel. After a relatively flat section, the White Bar Trail joins from the left, then leaves to the right in about 500 feet.

Follow the Triangle Trail as it descends to cross a stream, then levels off. For the next two and one-half miles, the Triangle Trail passes through a little-used area of the park. At first, the trail is relatively level but, after crossing a wide stream, it widens to a woods road and descends gradually.

It passes through a hemlock grove, crosses Deep Hollow Brook, then – in another quarter of a mile – turns very sharply left onto another woods road and recrosses the brook. The second crossing of the brook may be a little difficult if the water is high.

The trail now bears right, crosses under power lines, and goes through a hemlock grove, soon crossing several small streams and a gas pipeline. Upon reaching the power lines once more, it bears right, crosses under the power lines and parallels them for a short distance, then finally turns left and recrosses under the power lines for the final time.

After a short climb, the Triangle Trail ends at a junction with the Ramapo-Dunderberg Trail. Continue ahead, following the red-dot-on-white blazes and retracing your steps to the trailhead on Grove Drive. Turn left onto Grove Drive, make a right under the Thruway, and follow East Village Road back to the parking lot where the hike began.

36 Harriman State Park
Raccoon Brook Hill/Pine Meadow Lake

This loop hike at the southern end of the park climbs Raccoon Brook Hill and Diamond Mountain, with several panoramic viewpoints, and runs along cascading Stony Brook and scenic Pine Meadow Lake.

Difficulty: Moderate to strenuous
Length and Time: About 7.2 miles; about four and one-half hours.
Map: New York-New Jersey Trail Conference Harriman-Bear Mountain Trails Map #118.
Directions: Take N.J. Route 17 North to the New York State Thruway and take the first exit, Exit 15A (Sloatsburg). Turn left at the bottom of the ramp onto N.Y. Route 17 North, and continue through the Village of Sloatsburg. Just past the village, turn right at the traffic light, following the sign for Harriman State Park. Cross an overpass over railroad tracks and continue along the Seven Lakes Drive, passing under the Thruway overpass, and soon entering Harriman State Park. Proceed for another three-quarters of a mile to the Reeves Meadow Visitor Center, on the right side of the road. Park in the Visitor Center's parking lot (if the lot is full, parking is permitted on the shoulder on the south side of Seven Lakes Drive).

From the parking lot, head east (left when facing the woods), passing the Visitor Center to the left. You are following the red-on-white-blazed Pine Meadow Trail, which parallels Stony Brook, on the left. For most of the way, the trail follows a woods road parallel to the brook, but a portion of the trail has been rerouted onto a narrower footpath to avoid flooded or eroded sections of the road.

In 0.4 mile, you will reach a fork. The yellow-blazed Stony Brook Trail, which proceeds straight ahead, will be your return route, but you should

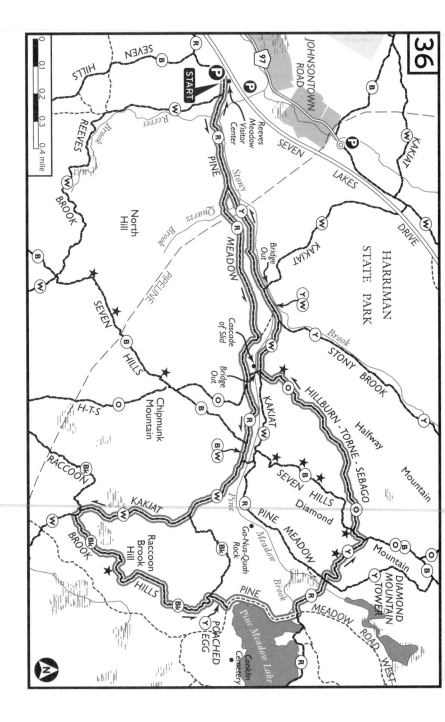

bear right and continue along the red-on-white-blazed Pine Meadow Trail, which begins a steady climb. Soon, the trail dips slightly to cross Quartz Brook. A footbridge over the stream has been constructed to the right, but when the water is low, the stream can easily be crossed on rocks. After crossing a gas pipeline right-of-way, the trail continues to follow a wide path along the hillside, high above Stony Brook (which can be heard below to the left). In another half a mile, an unmarked trail on the left leads down to the Stony Brook Trail, but you should bear right to continue ahead on the red-blazed Pine Meadow Trail.

About 1.2 miles from the start, the orange-blazed Hillburn-Torne-Sebago Trail joins briefly. Continue ahead on the red-on-white-blazed Pine Meadow Trail. Soon, the blue-on-white-blazed Seven Hills Trail joins from the right. In another 500 feet, you'll reach a junction. Here, the Pine Meadow and Seven Hills Trails bear left to cross Pine Meadow Brook on a footbridge, but you should turn right onto the white-blazed Kakiat Trail (don't cross the footbridge).

The Kakiat Trail climbs gradually for about a third of a mile until it reaches the start of the black-on-white-blazed Raccoon Brook Hills Trail on the left. You'll be following this trail in a short while, but for now, continue ahead on the white-blazed Kakiat Trail. The trail levels off and passes some huge boulders on the right. It then turns left to cross an intermittent stream and continues through a dense mountain laurel thicket, with an understory of blueberry bushes.

After climbing a narrow passage through rocks and passing jumbled boulders on the right, the Kakiat Trail is joined by the black-on-white-blazed Raccoon Brook Hills Trail. The two trails run together for about 100 feet, and when they diverge, turn left and follow the Raccoon Brook Hills Trail. The trail descends gradually for a short distance, crosses an intermittent stream, then climbs steeply to an open rock ledge, with pitch pines and scrub oak. There is a view to the southwest from here, and it might seem like the summit – but it's not. Just ahead, you'll encounter another steep, rocky climb, with a wooden ladder placed at a particularly steep spot near the top.

At the top of the climb (elevation 1,150 feet), the trail comes out on a rock ledge with a panoramic southwest-facing view. This spot – the western summit of the mountain – is the halfway point of the hike, and it's a good place to take a break. The trail continues along the crest of the ridge, soon once again coming out on open rocks, with more views. It

The ladder on the Raccoon Brook Hills Trail

then descends through thick mountain laurel, comes out on an open area, and climbs slightly to reach the eastern summit. Pine Meadow Lake is on the right, but the lake cannot be seen from the summit when there are leaves on the trees.

The Raccoon Brook Hills Trail now begins a steep descent. At the base of the descent, a junction is reached with the yellow-on-white-blazed Poached Egg Trail. Here, the Raccoon Brook Hills Trail turns left, but you

Pine Meadow Lake and the Conklin Family

Pine Meadow Lake was born in hard times. It was the depth of the Great Depression, and millions were without work. But a new administration was in office in Washington with a New Deal – a series of programs to provide relief. One of these programs, the Civilian Conservation Corps (CCC), would bring a small army of the jobless to this secluded meadow – a mountain family's homestead since the early 1700s – and transform it into a picturesque lake.

The CCC was designed to employ young men of families on relief while providing labor for projects involving conservation and parkland development. Workers were assigned to camps and received $30 a month, with the majority of the funds sent directly to their dependent families.

Work to build Pine Meadow Lake began in May 1933, just a month after the CCC was formed, with about 200 workers clearing trees and brush and constructing a 650-foot-long dam. By September 1934, they had built not only the dam, but roads, buildings and the infrastructure for a series of camps to be constructed by another New Deal program, the Works Progress Administration. (The camps themselves were never built.)

As the lake began to fill, the last remaining residents, descendants of the Conklin family that had first settled the meadow in the eighteenth century, realized it was time to leave. Major William A. Welch, General Manager and Chief Engineer of the Palisades Interstate Park, who had first envisioned a lake there over a decade earlier, promised the Conklins that they could stay as long as they liked. But with their fields gone, their subsistence living was threatened. The Park attempted to preserve their log cabin, built in 1779, but it was gone by 1942.

Ramsey Conklin, the family patriarch, moved to an old schoolhouse in Ladentown, but soon came back to the mountains, now making his home on Limekiln Mountain. He disappeared one day in 1952, and his body was found by hunters five months later. He was interred in the family cemetery on the south side of the lake – the last to be buried there.

-Jim Simpson

should continue ahead on the Poached Egg Trail. This short trail proceeds through a rocky area to reach Pine Meadow Road West – an unmarked dirt road, built in the 1930s by the Civilian Conservation Corps (CCC).

Turn left onto Pine Meadow Road West, which runs near the shore of Pine Meadow Lake. In about a third of a mile, the road comes out on the lake shore. You'll want to stop here and enjoy the beauty of this scenic lake. Built by the CCC in 1934, it was designed to serve children's camps that would be developed around the lake, but these camps were never established.

Pine Meadow Lake

Continue ahead and cross the dam of the lake (which was designed to accommodate a two-lane road). About 200 feet beyond the dam, turn left onto the red-on-white-blazed Pine Meadow Trail, which descends on a rocky woods road. At the base of the descent, the Pine Meadow Trail crosses a stream on a culvert and climbs along a footpath to reach a junction with the yellow-blazed Diamond Mountain-Tower Trail, which goes off both to the right and to the left.

Turn onto the left branch of the yellow trail and climb Diamond Mountain, first on switchbacks and then more steeply. As you reach the top, there is an excellent view back over Pine Meadow Lake. At the crest of the ridge, the Diamond Mountain-Tower Trail ends at a junction with the blue-on-white-blazed Seven Hills Trail and the orange-blazed Hillburn-

Pine Meadow Lake from Diamond Mountain

Torne-Sebago Trail. Turn left and follow the blue and orange trails, which soon reach a panoramic viewpoint to the west and north.

A short distance beyond, where the trails separate, bear right and follow the orange-blazed Hillburn-Torne-Sebago Trail, which begins to descend. The trail heads downhill for the next quarter mile, steeply in places (including a very steep descent through a cleft in a rock). It then levels off and follows the ridge of Halfway Mountain for about half a mile. At a west-facing viewpoint, the trail begins a gradual descent to Pine Meadow Brook.

At the brook, the Hillburn-Torne-Sebago Trail bears left and crosses a footbridge, but you should turn right (don't cross the footbridge) and follow the white-blazed Kakiat Trail, which proceeds over and around huge boulders. In another quarter of a mile, you'll reach a junction with the yellow-blazed Stony Brook Trail. Turn left, now following both white and yellow blazes, and cross a footbridge over Pine Meadow Brook. A short distance beyond, the Kakiat Trail leaves to the right, crossing a footbridge over Stony Brook, but you should continue ahead on the yellow-blazed

Stony Brook Trail. This section of the trail, which closely parallels the cascading brook, is particularly scenic.

After crossing a gas pipeline right-of-way and then a footbridge over Quartz Brook, the Stony Brook Trail ends at a junction with the red-on-white-blazed Pine Meadow Trail. Continue ahead on the Pine Meadow Trail, which parallels Stony Brook and leads back to the parking lot where the hike began.

Stony Brook

37 Norvin Green State Forest
Carris Hill/Wyanokie High Point Loop

This loop hike climbs to panoramic viewpoints on Carris Hill and Wyanokie High Point and returns via pleasant footpaths and woods roads.

Difficulty: Moderate to strenuous
Length and Time: About 5.8 miles; about four and one-half hours.
Map: New York-New Jersey Trail Conference North Jersey Trails Map #115.
Directions: Take I-287 to Exit 53 (Bloomingdale) and turn left onto Hamburg Turnpike. Upon entering Bloomingdale, the name of the road changes to Main Street. In 1.3 miles (from I-287) you will reach a fork in the road. Bear right, and in another 0.1 mile turn right (uphill) onto Glenwild Avenue (following the sign to "West Milford"). Continue ahead for 3.2 miles to a parking area on the right side of the road.

From the eastern end of the parking area, at the sign "Welcome to Bloomingdale," follow the blue-blazed Hewitt-Butler Trail, which heads north and descends to Posts Brook at Otter Hole, an attractive cascade and waterfall. Here the trail crosses the brook on large boulders.

Just beyond the brook, the light-green-blazed Otter Hole Trail leaves to the left, and the Hewitt-Butler Trail is joined by the Highlands Trail, with teal diamond blazes. Continue ahead, following the blue and teal diamond blazes along a rocky woods road. When you reach the next Y-intersection, take the right fork. The trail continues to ascend for a short distance, and then begins a steady descent.

In about half a mile, the trail turns left, leaving the woods road, and continues to descend. At one point, the yellow-blazed Wyanokie Crest Trail joins briefly, but continue ahead on the blue-blazed trail (also blazed with teal diamonds).

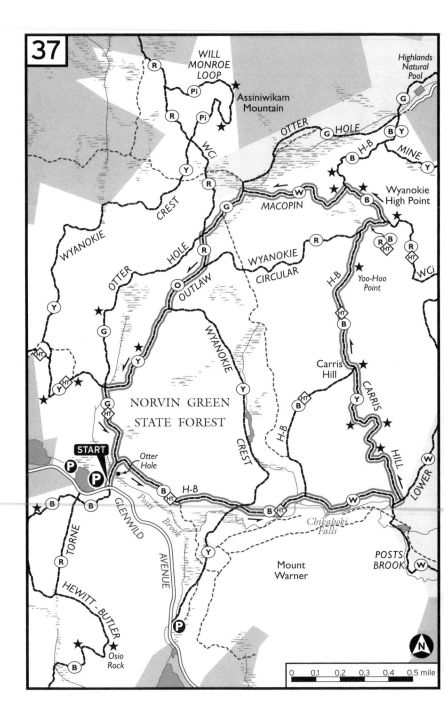

37

WILL
MONROE
LOOP

Highlands
Natural
Pool

Assiniwikam
Mountain

OTTER HOLE

MINE

WYANOKIE

CREST

OTTER HOLE

MACOPIN

WYANOKIE
CIRCULAR

Wyanokie
High Point

Yoo-Hoo
Point

OUTLAW

WYANOKIE

NORVIN GREEN
STATE FOREST

Carris
Hill

CREST

CARRIS

HILL

LOWER

START

Otter
Hole

H-B

Chikahoki
Falls

POSTS
BROOK

GLENWILD

Posts Brook

AVENUE

Mount
Warner

TORNE

HEWITT - BUTLER

Osio
Rock

N

0   0.1   0.2   0.3   0.4   0.5 mile

After leveling off and passing through a wet area, the trail approaches Posts Brook, crosses a tributary stream on rocks (with a log bridge provided if the water is high), and reaches a junction with the white-blazed Posts Brook Trail. The Hewitt-Butler and Highlands Trails leave to the left, but you should continue ahead on the white trail, which closely parallels the brook.

Soon, the trail reaches the top of Chikahoki Falls and descends to the brook, with a good view of the falls. The trail closely parallels the brook for a short distance, then bears left and heads uphill, away from the brook. After a while, it again descends to the brook and passes through an area with a thick understory of ferns.

Chikahoki Falls

A short distance beyond, you'll come to a junction with the Lower Trail, blazed with a black "L" on white. Turn left and follow the Lower Trail a short distance to a junction with the yellow-blazed Carris Hill Trail. Turn left again, now following the yellow blazes.

After traversing a level, rocky area, the Carris Hill Trail crosses a stream and begins a rather steep climb. The grade soon moderates, but after a third of a mile, it again climbs steeply over rocks, reaching a viewpoint to the southeast from a rock outcrop just to the right of the trail. The trail continues to climb to another rock outcrop, with a broader view. Here, it bears right and ascends to the left of a 40-foot-high massive rock face.

At the top of the ascent, a short detour to the right leads to a magnificent viewpoint to the east. The Wanaque Reservoir, contained by the Raymond, Wolf Den and Green Swamp dams, is in the foreground, with the Ramapo Mountains beyond, and a long viaduct of I-287 visible to the right. On a clear day, the New York City skyline may be seen on the horizon. This is a good place to pause and enjoy the spectacular view.

View of the Wanaque Reservoir from the third viewpoint on the Carris Hill Trail

The yellow trail now climbs more gradually, soon reaching another viewpoint (partially blocked by trees), with a ten-foot-high balanced glacial erratic silhouetted against the sky. The trail curves to the right and proceeds through laurel and blueberry bushes to reach a fifth viewpoint, this one to the south, with pitch pines and a large glacial erratic. It continues through laurel and blueberry bushes to end, on a rock outcrop with

Once a Valley, Now a Reservoir

A hike along the trails of Norvin Green State Forest should satisfy any hiker's appetite for the outdoors, but the landscape here, highlighted by the fluid blues of Wanaque Reservoir, shapes another need: the thirst for clean water by the cities of northern New Jersey.

The reservoir is not a natural feature. Rather, it is the result of damming the Wanaque River. As early as the late 1870s, the City of Newark began to look at this river, as well as the Ramapo and Pequannock Rivers, as possible sources of water for the growing city. The reservoir, though, was not completed for another half a century.

The area, which the native Lenape tribe called Wanaque or Wyanokie (two iterations of the Algonquin word for "valley of sassafras"), had first been settled by Dutch farmers in the late 1690s. In the early 1800s, iron mines were opened and furnaces built to process the ore, but the industry fell into decline by 1890. It was replaced by paper mills and factories that manufactured gunpowder.

Around this time, Newark, Paterson and other burgeoning industrial centers were looking for new sources of water, and the Wanaque River became the prime candidate. The Passaic River had been their main water source, but that river had become polluted, and a new source of clean water was needed. In 1916, the state legislature created the North Jersey District Water Supply Commission to acquire the necessary land and construct the dams that would create the reservoir.

Clearing of the ground began in 1920. To build the reservoir, over 70 buildings had to be demolished, four cemeteries had to be relocated, and many miles of roads and rail lines had to be rerouted. Raymond Dam, the main dam of the reservoir, was the first to be constructed. It rises over 67 feet above the bedrock. A series of secondary dams filled in terrain that dipped below the projected level of the reservoir.

After eight years of construction and a year to fill the reservoir, water from the reservoir was delivered to customers for the first time on March 30, 1930. The reservoir and its watershed now comprise the largest water supply system in the state, providing up to 200 million gallons of water a day to over three million people in northern New Jersey.

-*Jim Simpson*

Balanced glacial erratic at the fourth viewpoint on the Carris Hill Trail

views to the north and west, at a junction with the blue-blazed Hewitt-Butler Trail and the teal-diamond-blazed Highlands Trail.

Continue ahead (do not turn left), now following blue and teal diamond blazes, and descend steeply toward a sign for "Weis." The trail continues to descend through mountain laurel thickets, climbs a little, then descends gradually, heading north along the ridge. In about half a mile, you'll reach a rock outcrop with a view ahead of Wyanokie High Point – a rocky dome with pitch pines. This location is known as "Yoo-Hoo Point."

The joint Hewitt-Butler/Highlands Trail now descends to a junction, where the red-on-white-blazed Wyanokie Circular Trail joins. Continue ahead, now following the route of three trails, and soon begin a rather steep climb.

At the next junction, turn right, following the sign to "Hi-Point," and climb steeply, following the red-on-white blazes of the Wyanokie Circular

View of Wanaque Reservoir from Wyanokie High Point

Trail and the teal diamond blazes of the Highlands Trail. In a short distance, you'll reach the summit of Wyanokie High Point, which features a panoramic 360° view amid pitch pines. To the north and west, you can see Saddle, Assiniwikam and Buck Mountains, and the New York City skyline is visible to the east on a clear day.

After spending some time savoring the view, retrace your steps, following the red-and-white and teal diamond blazes as they descend very steeply over bare rock. Extreme care is required here if the rocks are wet. When you reach the junction with the Hewitt-Butler Trail, turn right and follow the blue blazes. After a short, gradual climb, the trail reaches a balanced boulder on a rock ledge. It then descends briefly through laurel thickets to a junction with the white-blazed Macopin Trail.

Turn left and follow the Macopin Trail, which descends through laurel and blueberry bushes. In half a mile, it crosses a stream and ends at a junction with the light-green-blazed Otter Hole Trail. Turn left onto the Otter Hole Trail, which climbs on a woods road.

Near the top of the climb, the red-on-white-blazed Wyanokie Circular Trail crosses. Turn left onto the Wyanokie Circular Trail, which ascends on a footpath through dense mountain laurel thickets. At the crest of the rise, a large boulder marks a trail junction. Here, the red-on-white blazes turn left, but you should bear right, now following the orange blazes of the Outlaw Trail, which begins here.

The Outlaw Trail heads across the level ridge and ends in a quarter of a mile at a junction with the yellow-blazed Wyanokie Crest Trail. Turn right and follow this trail, which descends through a second-growth forest of deciduous trees.

In a third of a mile, after a short climb, the trail emerges at a viewpoint that overlooks Buck Mountain to the west. The trail now descends through dense laurel thickets, crosses a stream on rocks and reaches a junction with the light-green-blazed Otter Hole Trail.

Turn left onto the Otter Hole Trail (also the route of the teal-diamond-blazed Highlands Trail), which follows a pleasant woods road. After a steady descent, you'll reach a T-intersection with the blue-blazed Hewitt-Butler Trail. Turn right here, now retracing your steps, and follow the Hewitt-Butler Trail across Posts Brook at the Otter Hole and back to the parking area where the hike began.

38 Palisades Interstate Park, New Jersey Section
Giant Stairs/Long Path Loop from State Line Lookout

This loop hike descends the Palisades cliffs, follows a challenging, rocky path along the Hudson River, passes a scenic waterfall, and climbs to reach a panoramic viewpoint over the river.

Difficulty: Strenuous
Length and Time: About 4.5 miles; about four hours.
Map: New York-New Jersey Trail Conference Hudson Palisades Trails Map #109.
Directions: Take the Palisades Interstate Park north from the George Washington Bridge. Continue for 1.7 miles beyond Exit 2, and turn right at a sign for the State Line Lookout. Follow the access road for about half a mile until it ends at a large parking lot near the lookout. (If you are coming from the north on the Parkway, bear left just beyond Exit 3 and follow the signs for the lookout.)

This hike explores the northern end of the New Jersey Section of the Palisades Interstate Park. It is, perhaps, the most rewarding loop hike in the park, as it incorporates a number of scenic features and, for nearly the entire distance, you are far away from the noise of the Parkway. But it is also the most difficult hike in the park, as it involves not only steep climbs and descents on uneven rock steps, but also nearly a mile of walking near the shore of the river on jumbled rocks. Make sure you allow enough time to complete the hike before dark, and wear sturdy footwear with rubber soles. Don't attempt the hike if it is wet or icy outside.

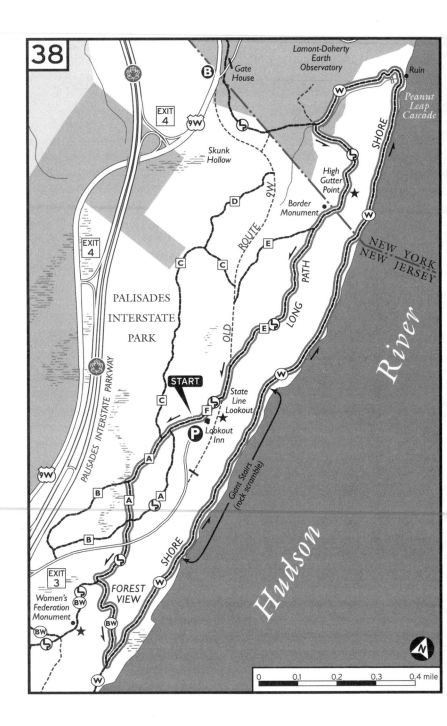

The hike begins at the rear of the parking area at the State Line Lookout, at a sign for the "Ski Trails." Follow the wide path, marked with the aqua blazes of the Long Path, into the woods. You'll soon reach a junction where the Long Path turns left and Trail A comes in from the left and proceeds ahead. Continue ahead on the wide path. Just beyond, you'll come to another junction. Here, Trail C begins to the right, but you should continue ahead on Trail A. About five minutes into the hike, you'll reach another junction, marked by an old rock monument to the left (the faded words "Shore Path" may be visible). Trail B proceeds ahead, but you should turn left to continue on Trail A.

After proceeding straight ahead at the next intersection, you'll come to the lookout access road. Cross the road and continue ahead on the aqua-blazed Long Path, which heads south, parallel to the cliffs. There is a good viewpoint over the river just to the left of the trail (use caution here, as there is a steep dropoff). Just beyond, the trail starts a steep descent on rock steps, built by the park in the early years of the twentieth century. Use extreme caution when descending these steps, as they are somewhat uneven. The steps can be particularly hazardous when wet or covered with leaves.

Looking south over the Hudson River from viewpoint on the Long Path

After crossing a small stream on a wooden bridge, you'll reach a trail junction. The Long Path turns right, but you should bear left, now following the blue/white-blazed Forest View Trail. A sign indicates that it is 0.3 mile from this point to the Shore Trail, but the distance will probably seem much longer. The steep descent continues, first on more rock steps, then on switchbacks, some of which are well graded, but others are rocky and uneven.

You'll finally reach the bottom of the descent, marked by a large boulder. Here you should turn left and head north on the white-blazed Shore Trail. Soon, you'll emerge onto an open area covered with vines. Take a moment to contemplate this magnificent "sea of green."

A short distance beyond, you'll reach a field of jumbled boulders. This is the beginning of the Giant Stairs, the most challenging section of the hike. After taking in the panoramic view to the north along the river and over the striking Palisades cliffs, bear left and follow the white blazes as they begin to climb over the rocks. Pay careful attention to the white paint blazes, some of which are in the shape of a half-moon.

The Giant Stairs

For the next half mile, the trail follows a rocky path about 100 vertical feet above the river. You'll have to use care in deciding where to take each step. In about half an hour, the trail emerges onto a huge talus field, made up of large boulders that have fallen down from the cliffs above. This is the site of the massive rockslide that took place at 7:28 p.m. on Saturday, May 12, 2012, in which a large section of the cliff face broke off and

The Sculptress of Peanut Leap Cascade

Hikers will notice the ruins of a pergola at the base of Peanut Leap Cascade, just north of the New Jersey-New York state line. This structure, along with a formal "Italian Garden," was designed by sculptress Mary Lawrence Tonetti (who created a monumental statue of Christopher Columbus for the 1893 Columbian Exposition in Chicago) to entertain friends from the New York art world. Her father, H.E. Lawrence, owned an estate at nearby Snedens Landing (along the Hudson River, a short distance to the north). Her guests would take a train to Dobbs Ferry, on the east side of the river, and continue by ferry across the Hudson to Snedens Landing.

In 1884, Lydia Lawrence, Mary Lawrence Tonetti's mother, bought the land surrounding the cascade to forestall the building of a pier and picnic pavilion at this location. Soon afterwards, Mary received $5,000 from her father to embellish the property. With the assistance of renowned sculptor Augustus Saint-Gaudens and well-known architects Stanford White and Charles McKim, she designed and built a pergola and gardens around the cascade, in order to enhance its natural beauty. Subsequently, she and her husband, sculptor Francois Tonetti, added pools and steps at various levels.

In 1909, Lydia Lawrence donated three acres just north of the cascade to the Palisades Interstate Park Commission (PIPC), thus allowing public access to the property. The family retained the 3.6-acre parcel to the south, which included the cascade, until donating it to PIPC in 1979. At the time, the family also established the "Tonetti Waterfall Fund," which provided about $50,000 to be used towards the upkeep of the area. The following year, PIPC's Summer Youth Work Program built a trail from the Long Path near the top of the cliffs down to the cascade.

The Shore Trail originally ascended the cliffs south of the state line and did not connect with the trail to the Peanut Leap Cascade. In 1999, Hurricane Floyd washed out this section of the Shore Trail, and it was not considered feasible to rebuild it. The Shore Trail was then relocated to continue along the shore to the cascade, from where it climbed the cliffs, using the trail built in 1980, and ended at the Long Path.

-Ruth Rosenthal

Peanut Leap Cascade

tumbled down to the river. There are panoramic views across the river, and the lighter-faced rock column on the cliff indicates where the rock fell from.

At the end of the talus field, the trail reenters the woods. In about ten minutes, it comes out on another talus slope and then, after briefly passing through a wooded section, it emerges onto a third talus slope, marked by a huge tree stump. Again, you're afforded a panoramic view over the river, and you'll want to stop to rest from this difficult section of the hike and enjoy the view.

The trail now descends and eventually comes out close to the river level. You'll encounter one more rocky section, but this one is much easier to negotiate. After about a mile of walking on a relatively smooth footpath along the river, you'll go through a gate in a rusted chain-link fence. A short distance beyond, you'll reach the Peanut Leap Cascade. Adjacent to this waterfall, which is truly spectacular after heavy rains, are the ruins of the Italian Garden, built around 1900 by sculptress Mary Lawrence Tonetti, whose family owned an estate at nearby Snedens Landing.

After spending some time at this interesting and beautiful spot, follow the white-blazed Shore Trail as it turns left, away from the river, and climbs on wooden steps and switchbacks. It parallels the stream leading to the waterfall for a short distance and soon ends at a junction with the aqua-blazed Long Path. Turn left onto the Long Path, which you will follow all the way back to the State Line Lookout.

The Tappan Zee Bridge and Hook Mountain from High Gutter Point

The Long Path crosses the stream on two wooden bridges. A short distance ahead, it turns sharply right and begins a steep climb on stone steps. At the top of the climb is High Gutter Point, a panoramic viewpoint up and down the river. To the north, you can see the Tappan Zee Bridge and Hook Mountain, the northernmost point on the Palisades along the Hudson. You'll want to take a break here to rest from the steep climb and enjoy the view, but use caution, as the drop-off is very steep.

The trail continues ahead, passing several more viewpoints, then climbs more stone steps, goes through a gate in a chain-link fence that marks the boundary between New York and New Jersey, and briefly parallels the fence. When the trail bears left, away from the fence, continue ahead for about 50 feet to see a stone monument, placed in 1882 to mark the state line.

State Line Monument

Return to the aqua-blazed Long Path, which turns left just beyond the monument, then takes the left fork at the next intersection (along with Ski Trail E). It follows an old woods road for about half a mile to reach the Old Route 9W (a wide concrete road), then turns left along the road and follows it for a short distance back to the State Line Lookout, where the hike began.

39 Catskill Forest Preserve
Plateau Mountain

This loop hike climbs to the summit of Plateau Mountain via the Warner Creek Trail, with many panoramic views.

Difficulty: Strenuous
Length and Time: About 8.0 miles; about six hours.
Map: New York-New Jersey Trail Conference Catskill Trails Map #141.
Directions: Take the New York State Thruway to Exit 19 (Kingston). After the tollbooths, turn right and continue on N.Y. Route 28 West. Follow Route 28 for about 22.5 miles to N.Y. Route 214 in Phoenicia. Turn right onto Route 214, then, in another 0.2 mile, turn left to continue on Route 214. Proceed north on Route 214 for another 7.7 miles to Notch Inn Road, which is just before the highest point on the road. Turn right onto Notch Inn Road, a dirt road, and follow it uphill, passing between old stone abutments. In about 0.4 mile, the road levels off. Park in one of the pull-offs on the left side of the road, beyond the first house (the road is blocked off to vehicles a short distance beyond).

The first part of this hike follows the Warner Creek Trail, built by volunteers of the Catskill Mountain Club, a member of the New York-New Jersey Trail Conference. It is one of the most outstanding trails in the Catskills, featuring a well-designed route with (for the most part) moderate grades, as well as a series of scenic viewpoints.

To start the hike, proceed ahead (uphill) on the continuation of Notch Inn Road, marked with yellow blazes, for about three-quarters of a mile, until you reach the height of land (the trail bypasses an eroded section of the road). Here, you should turn left onto the blue-blazed Warner Creek Trail (also the route of the Long Path), which begins to climb towards Daley Ridge and Plateau Mountain.

The climb is gentle at first, but the grade soon steepens as the trail switches back, first to the right, then to the left. Along the way, you'll pass many interesting boulders and other rock formations.

After about 20 minutes, you'll reach a short side trail to the right, blazed with yellow markers, which leads to the first of the five viewpoints along the trail. The view is to the southwest, and the prominent peak directly ahead is Edgewood Mountain. You'll want to take a break here to rest from the climb.

The Warner Creek Trail passes this massive rock wall on its way up Plateau Mountain

As you continue up the ridge, you'll pass a massive rock wall just to the left. After climbing some more, you'll come to a yellow-blazed side trail that leads to the next viewpoint – to the southeast, over Olderbark Mountain. A third viewpoint is a short distance beyond, but this one is partially obscured by vegetation.

You're now approaching the crest of Daley Ridge, having climbed about 1,300 vertical feet from the trailhead. The grade moderates, and spruce and fir trees become the predominant vegetation. The trail continues along this relatively level ridge for about half a mile and then descends a little.

After resuming your climb, now heading up Plateau Mountain, you'll reach a fourth viewpoint, also marked by a short yellow-blazed side trail

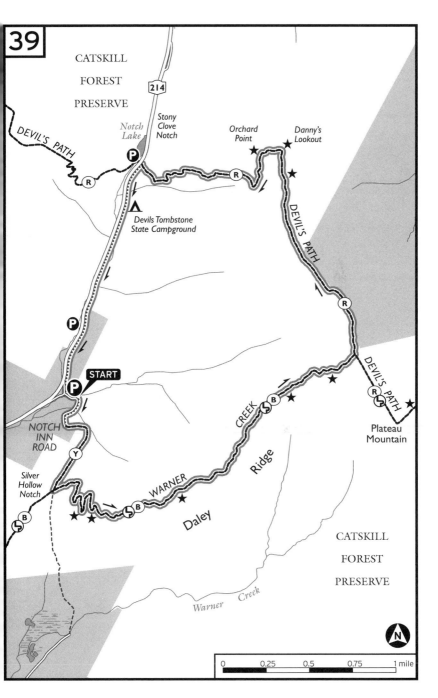

39

CATSKILL
FOREST
PRESERVE

DEVIL'S PATH

214

Notch Lake

Stony Clove Notch

Orchard Point

Danny's Lookout

DEVIL'S PATH

Devils Tombstone State Campground

START

NOTCH INN ROAD

Silver Hollow Notch

WARNER CREEK

Ridge

Daley

Plateau Mountain

DEVIL'S PATH

CATSKILL
FOREST
PRESERVE

Warner Creek

N

0   0.25   0.5   0.75   1 mile

A hiker at the fourth viewpoint overlooking Daley Ridge and Olderbark Mountain

to the right. The south-facing view from here is even broader. To the right, you can see Daley Ridge, which you just climbed, and Olderbark Mountain is the long ridge to the left.

Soon, you'll come to a sign marking the 3,500-feet contour, with camping and fires prohibited above this elevation (except in winter). Here, a yellow-blazed trail to the right leads about 500 feet to a spring. If you need more water, you might want to take this short detour (but be sure to purify the water).

The trail now climbs very steeply to the last of the five viewpoints, also marked by a short yellow trail to the right. From here – the highest overlook on the Warner Creek Trail – you can look down over Daley Ridge onto Stony Clove Notch, traversed by Route 214, where you began your hike.

Before reaching the summit ridge of Plateau Mountain, the trail narrows as it traverses a dense spruce-and-fir forest, typical of the higher elevations in the Catskills. This trail section has been named the "Dark Woods."

The Warner Creek Trail ends, three miles from its trailhead, at a junction with the red-blazed Devil's Path. Turn left and follow the Devil's Path for a mile and a half along the long, flat summit ridge of Plateau Mountain (elevation 3,840 feet). This is the longest nearly level ridge in the

Constructing the Warner Creek Trail on Plateau Mountain

Originally, the Long Path wasn't supposed to be a trail – just a series of points of interest for hikers to find their own routes between. When the dormant concept was revived in the early 1960s as a marked trail, much of it followed roads, even in the Catskills. Enough "forever wild" Forest Preserve land existed, however, for trail planners to see the possibilities for relocating nearly all the Long Path through the Catskills onto footpaths. By the 1990s, most of the Long Path in the Catskills, except for the section between Woodland Valley and Stony Clove Notch (which would connect the Catskill Park's two largest wilderness areas), had been moved off the roads.

In 2000, the Long Path route from Mount Tremper to Silver Hollow Notch was opened. It would take several more years for the state to approve the rest of the route into the Indian Head Wilderness that this hike traverses. Construction got underway in April 2006.

The trail was built by Trail Conference volunteers, organized by Pete Senterman, Catskills Trail Chair, and assisted by staff of the New York State Department of Environmental Conservation (DEC). During the scouting of the route, Pete Senterman named the ridge followed by the trail up the mountain "Daley Ridge," for a veteran Catskill trail maintainer who had recently lost his battle with cancer. Volunteer Doug Egeland found a spring along the way, shortening a long, dry stretch of the Long Path. A professional Adirondack Mountain Club crew added longer switchbacks on the steep climb out of Silver Hollow Notch.

Due to the multiple route-scouting trips required, coordination with the DEC, and a major storm that necessitated recutting most of the trail, the trail didn't open until the fall of 2007. "That's why it turned out so well," says Cal Johnson, a Catskill Trail Supervisor for the Trail Conference, who played a major role in scouting and building the trail.

In the long term, he'd like to make it possible for loop hikers to avoid the roadwalk on Route 214. He's already scouted a route that begins at the Devil's Tombstone parking area, follows the old Catskill Mountain Railroad bed through the notch and climbs to Silver Hollow Notch. The Trail Conference is currently working with the DEC to secure their approval for the route.

-Dan Case

Catskills traversed by a marked hiking trail, and it offers a unique hiking experience as you traverse the thick evergreen forest on the trail.

As you approach the western end of the ridge, you'll come to three panoramic viewpoints. The first two viewpoints (one of which is known as Danny's Lookout) offer a view over Kaaterskill High Peak to the north, while the view from the third viewpoint (Orchard Point) is to the west and south, with Hunter Mountain visible straight ahead.

The west-facing view from Orchard Point on Plateau Mountain

The Devil's Path now descends to Stony Clove Notch and Route 214. After a precipitous drop over a rock ledge, the grade moderates for a short distance but, for most of the way, the descent is rather steep. You descend a vertical distance of about 1,600 feet in only a mile and a half, with the grade averaging about 20%! The footing is rocky and uneven, so use caution and take your time, especially if the ground is wet.

At the base of the descent, you'll reach Route 214. Turn left and follow the road for 1.2 miles to Notch Inn Road, then turn left and climb Notch Inn Road to your car.

Winter

Old Croton Aqueduct | Van Cortlandt Park | Flat Rock Brook Nature Center | Rockefeller State Park Preserve | Morristown National Historical Park | Westchester Wilderness Walk | Sterling Forest State Park | Mahlon Dickerson Reservation | Minnewaska State Park Preserve | Ward Pound Ridge Reservation | Harriman State Park (Iron Mines) | Abram S. Hewitt State Forest | Harriman State Park (Dunderberg Spiral Railway and Bald Mountain)

4O Old Croton Aqueduct

This level hike follows the route of the historic Old Croton Aqueduct from Tarrytown to Yonkers, with return via Metro-North train.

Difficulty: Easy

Length and Time: About 8.5 miles; about four and one-half hours (includes return trip by train).

Map: Old Croton Aqueduct State Historic Park Map and Guide, published by Friends of the Old Croton Aqueduct, www.aqueduct.org.

Directions: Take the New York State Thruway to Exit 9 (Tarrytown) and head north on South Broadway (U.S. Route 9). (If coming from the west, Exit 9 is the first Thruway exit after crossing the Tappan Zee Bridge.) Continue on South Broadway for about 0.4 mile, then turn right onto Prospect Avenue. You will note the Aqueduct route heading south from Prospect Avenue, parallel to and just west of Martling Avenue (the first intersection east of South Broadway). There is a parking area atop the Aqueduct just south of Prospect Avenue; park here.

The hike may be reached by public transportation – Metro-North Hudson Line trains from Grand Central Terminal in New York City to Tarrytown. For directions from the Tarrytown station to the start of the hike, see the last paragraph of the description.

This hike follows the historic route of the Old Croton Aqueduct, built between 1837 and 1842 to supply water to New York City. Supplanted by several newer aqueducts, the Old Croton Aqueduct was taken out of service in 1965. The level footpath atop the Aqueduct "tube" has for many years been a favorite of walkers, and the Westchester County section of the Aqueduct became a state park in 1968. Except for occasional posts at

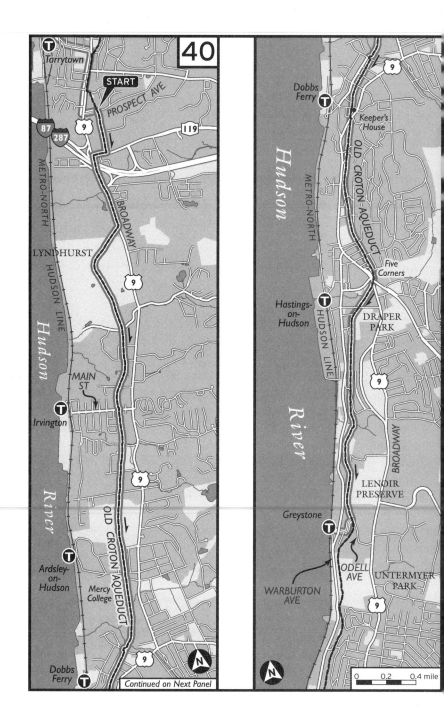

START

40

Tarrytown

PROSPECT AVE

87
287
9

119

METRO-NORTH

Dobbs
Ferry

Keeper's
House

OLD CROTON AQUEDUCT

Hudson

METRO-NORTH

BROADWAY

LYNDHURST

9

HUDSON LINE

Hudson

River

Five
Corners

Hastings-
on-
Hudson

DRAPER
PARK

HUDSON LINE

9

River

MAIN
ST

Irvington

9

9

BROADWAY

OLD CROTON AQUEDUCT

River

Greystone

LENOIR
PRESERVE

Ardsley-
on-
Hudson

Mercy
College

ODELL
AVE

UNTERMYER
PARK

WARBURTON
AVE

9

Dobbs
Ferry

9

N

Continued on Next Panel

N

0   0.2   0.4 mile

A stone ventilator along the Aqueduct

road intersections with the letters "OCA," there are few markings along the route, so you should be careful to follow the directions below.

Begin the hike by proceeding south from Prospect Avenue along the route of the Aqueduct. Just before the next intersection, you will notice a chimney-like stone tower with the number "14." These towers, known as ventilators, were constructed along the Aqueduct about every mile. They

Old Croton Aqueduct

The embankments and ventilators of the Old Croton Aqueduct, noted in the hike description, are clues to the presence of an American engineering masterwork beneath the hiker's feet. The Aqueduct was designed on the same principles as the aqueducts of ancient Rome: the water flowed through a covered masonry channel by the force of gravity. It was engineered to drop at a steady gradient of 13½ inches per mile. This nearly imperceptible descent was maintained over the Aqueduct's length of 41 miles.

The Aqueduct was constructed by several thousand Irish immigrants, who toiled under grueling conditions for low wages. Chief Engineer John B. Jervis was determined to build for the ages. The general method of construction was cut-and-cover trenching, with the roof of the water tunnel about four to six feet below the surface. Whenever necessary to maintain the Aqueduct's steady gradient, however, the horseshoe-shaped, brick-lined water "tube" and the stone foundation on which it sat were built into hillsides and blasted through rock outcrops. Embankments of packed earth faced with finely laid stone carried the Aqueduct over lowlands and stream valleys, and stone culverts were provided at their base to allow the passage of small streams. Stone-arch bridges were used for major stream crossings and to permit local roads to pass beneath the Aqueduct.

For some 50 years, the original Croton Aqueduct was the sole source of pure water for New York City. In 1890, the New Croton Aqueduct – with triple the capacity of the "old" Croton Aqueduct – was opened. The original Croton Dam is now submerged in the waters of the present-day Croton Reservoir, created by the 1906 New Croton Dam.

To supply its ever-expanding need for water, New York City tapped sources west of the Hudson River, completing the Catskill Aqueduct in 1917 and the Delaware Aqueduct in 1945. These two watersheds now supply about 90% of the city's water, in addition to serving several counties to the north and west. By 1965, the Old Croton Aqueduct had been taken out of service, but in 1987, a three-mile section was reopened to supply water to Ossining. The Old Croton Aqueduct was designated a National Historic Landmark in 1992, its 150th anniversary.

-Charlotte Fahn

were equipped with an open grate on top and allowed fresh air to circulate over the water passing through the Aqueduct.

When you reach the next intersection, White Plains Road (Route 119), you will have to detour from the Aqueduct route, which is interrupted by the New York State Thruway just ahead. This will involve about half a mile of walking along busy streets, but it is the only detour you'll encounter on the entire hike. Turn right and follow White Plains Road for one block to South Broadway (Route 9), then turn left and cross the bridge over the Thruway. Continue south along South Broadway past the Double-Tree Hotel and the entrance to the Kraft Foods Technical Center. About 500 feet beyond this entrance, at the top of a rise, there is a break in the stone wall on the right side of the road. Turn right here onto a wide dirt path blocked off by wooden posts and enter the grounds of Lyndhurst, an American Gothic Revival "castle" built about 1840 and once owned by railroad magnate Jay Gould.

Along the Aqueduct in Irvington

Continue ahead, following the dirt path through Lyndhurst. Soon after you leave the Lyndhurst property, you'll pass ventilator #15. The Aqueduct soon begins to follow a high stone wall to the left, then continues across an embankment.

In another half mile or so, you'll cross several paved roads and enter a quiet residential area of the village of Irvington. The Aqueduct follows a wide right of way past large, attractive homes. Then, about two miles from the start, you'll pass through a parking area adjacent to a school and cross Main Street in Irvington. Continue ahead through a municipal parking area and immediately pass ventilator #16.

A short distance beyond, you'll cross a high embankment over Barney Brook (formerly known as Jewells Brook). After crossing two streets, you'll notice the domed Octagon House, built in the 1860s, to the right. Next, the Aqueduct passes through the Nevis estate, now the property of Columbia University. The brick mansion with white columns on the right side of the trail was built by Colonel James Hamilton III, son of Alexander Hamilton, in 1835.

After passing ventilator #17, you'll traverse the campus of Mercy College and then cross two more embankments. At the end of the second embankment, climb steps to Cedar Street in the village of Dobbs Ferry, cross the street and continue through a parking area. The Aqueduct now

The stone-arch bridge over the quarry railway in Hastings. From "Illustrations of the Croton Aqueduct" by Fayette B. Tower (New York: Wiley and Putnam, 1843). Courtesy of Friends of the Old Croton Aqueduct.

parallels Main Street in Dobbs Ferry, with views over the Hudson River to the right.

In a few blocks, you'll reach an interpretive sign which explains the history and engineering of the Aqueduct. The adjacent green trailer is the park office, and the barn and garage are used as maintenance facilities. Across Walnut Street is the Keeper's House, a brick building – now being restored as a visitor center – that formerly served as a residence and office for Aqueduct caretakers. Just beyond, the Aqueduct crosses to the east side of Broadway and follows an embankment through a residential area, with more views over the Hudson River.

View of the Hudson River and the Palisades from the Aqueduct

In another mile, the Aqueduct – now in the village of Hastings-on-Hudson – crosses back to the west side of Broadway at the Five Corners. Using the crosswalks provided, cross Chauncey Lane, Farragut Avenue and Broadway, turn left and cross the driveway of Grace Episcopal Church, then immediately turn right onto the route of the Aqueduct at a green "OCA" post (which may be obscured by vegetation). After crossing another high embankment, you'll go through a parking area and begin to parallel Aqueduct Lane to the right, with Draper Park to the left.

A sign on the left for the "Quarry Lane Trail" marks the start of a short path that goes down and passes under the Aqueduct. Here, the Aqueduct is supported by a stone-arch bridge, built in 1840 over a railway that served a former marble quarry to the east of the Aqueduct. It is worth taking this short side trail to get a view of this beautifully preserved stone arch bridge.

Near the end of a long, uninterrupted stretch of the Aqueduct route, you'll pass ventilator #18. About half a mile later, as the Aqueduct curves to the left, you'll come to a particularly fine unobstructed view over the Hudson River and the Palisades. Just beyond, you'll enter the City of Yonkers. After passing a side trail that leads into the Lenoir Preserve and then an abandoned stone building on the left, you'll reach Odell Avenue, which crosses the Aqueduct in the middle of a broad curve in the road.

Turn right and follow Odell Avenue downhill to Warburton Avenue, then descend through the park on steps to reach the Greystone Metro-North station. Northbound trains to Tarrytown leave every hour – 56 minutes past the hour on weekends and off-peak hours on weekdays (for schedules, call 800-METRO-INFO or go to www.mta.info). Be sure to sit on the left side of the train to enjoy beautiful views of the Hudson River. The train ride takes only 14 minutes. When you arrive in Tarrytown, proceed to the southern end of the station and follow Franklin Street up the hill. When you reach South Broadway, turn right and proceed for two blocks to Leroy Avenue. Turn left onto Leroy Avenue, then turn right into the parking lot for an office building. Just ahead, you will see the Aqueduct embankment on the right side of the parking lot. Follow the Aqueduct for one block to the parking area where the hike began.

41 Van Cortlandt Park

This loop hike passes the historic Van Cortlandt House Museum, follows the abandoned Putnam rail line and the Old Croton Aqueduct, and goes by the scenic Van Cortlandt Lake.

Difficulty: Easy (except for one steep descent)
Length and Time: About 3.0 miles; about two hours (allow additional time for tour of Van Cortlandt House Museum).
Map: Van Cortlandt Park map (available at Nature Center).
Directions: Take the Henry Hudson Parkway to Exit 23A (N.Y. Route 9 South, Broadway) and proceed south on Broadway to 242nd Street, where the elevated rail line ends. Parking is available along Broadway north of 242nd Street (alternate-side-of-the-street restrictions).

To reach the trailhead by public transportation, take the New York City Subway #1 train to its final stop, 242nd Street.

At the northernmost entrance to the 242nd Street station on the east side of Broadway, descend a short stairway into the park and turn left onto a wide path. After passing a restroom building to the left and green buildings that surround the park's pool on the right, you'll come to the Van Cortlandt House Museum (open Tuesday to Friday from 10 a.m. to 3 p.m., and on weekends from 11 a.m. to 4 p.m.). This historic stone building, built in 1748, is the oldest building in the Bronx. George Washington actually slept here! There is an admission charge for a self-guided tour of this fascinating building, which has been beautifully restored.

After touring the building and its grounds, head east along a service road, passing playing fields to the left and the park's Nature Center to the right. At the end of the fields, as the service road curves to the left, turn right and follow a dirt path that descends through the woods to the

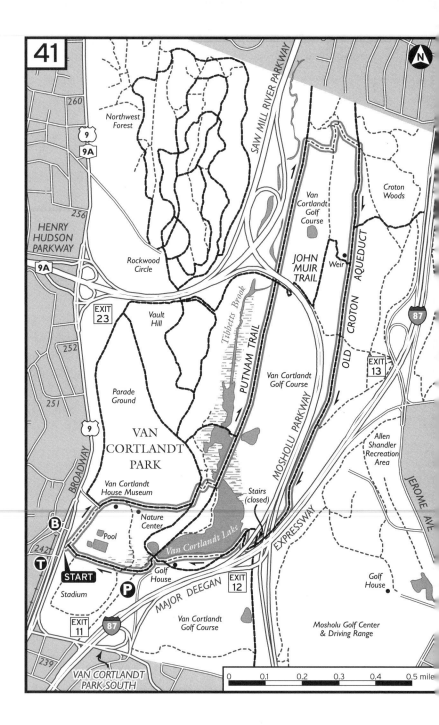

Putnam Trail. To the right, you'll notice 13 stone pillars, known as the Grand Central Stones. These were placed there by the New York Central Railroad prior to the construction of Grand Central Terminal to determine which type of stone weathered best.

Grand Central Stones

Turn left onto the Putnam Trail, which follows the right-of-way of the abandoned Putnam Division of the New York Central Railroad. Built in 1880 as part of a projected through route to Boston, the line offered commuter service for many years. Although passenger service was abandoned in 1958, occasional freight service was operated until 1981. Remnants of the former rail use remain, including railroad ties and several lineside telegraph poles.

After crossing a wide bridge over Tibbetts Brook, continue heading north along the Putnam Trail, which follows a wooded route between the Van Cortlandt Golf Course (on the right) and the brook (on the left). Although you're in the center of the Bronx, the sights (and even the sounds) of civilization are largely absent along this stretch of the hike! In about half a mile, though, after passing beneath an overpass of the Mosholu Parkway, you'll begin to parallel the Henry Hudson Parkway to the left.

When you reach the end of the fence that separates the Putnam Trail from the golf course, turn right, leaving the railbed, and follow the fence

Van Cortlandt House

along the northern end of the golf course for a short distance. Continue along the wide path which bears left and heads north, then – at the next intersection – bear right and follow an eroded path uphill. Ahead, you'll notice a massive stone retaining wall in the distance. This is the outer wall of an embankment that protects the Old Croton Aqueduct, which you will soon be following. Opened in 1842, it provided the first source of pure drinking water to New York City and remained in service as a source of water for New York City until 1955.

After climbing on the path, you'll reach another intersection. Turn right and proceed south, soon beginning to follow the route of the Aqueduct, with a low stone wall in the woods to the left. In about ten minutes, you'll reach a large stone structure. Known as a weir, this structure allowed the water in the aqueduct to be diverted into the adjacent stream, thus permitting the section to the south to be maintained. Just beyond, the pink-blazed John Muir Trail leaves to the right, but you should continue ahead on the wide Aqueduct route.

Soon, the aqueduct begins to parallel the Mosholu Parkway, which is below to your right. When you reach a T-intersection, turn right and con-

The "Old Put"

For over a mile, the hike follows the route of the former Putnam Division of the New York Central Railroad, originally conceived as a link in a through route from New York City to Boston via Hartford. To this end, the New York & Boston Railroad was chartered in 1869 to construct a 58-mile line from High Bridge in the Bronx to Brewster in Putnam County, but it quickly ran into financial difficulties. The franchise was taken over in 1878 by the New York City & Northern Railroad, and the line to Brewster was completed in 1881. The line was extended to 155th Street in Manhattan, and in 1882, through service was established to Hartford, Connecticut.

The route was acquired by the New York Central Railroad in 1894, and through service to Hartford and Boston was discontinued in 1907. The extension to Manhattan was soon taken over by the Ninth Avenue El, after which Putnam Division trains terminated at Sedgwick Avenue, a short distance south of High Bridge. Passengers could transfer at High Bridge to trains that took them to Grand Central Terminal.

The "Old Put," as it was fondly known, was sandwiched between the Hudson and the Harlem Divisions of the New York Central, both of which operated directly into Grand Central Terminal and had faster and more frequent service. By 1958, fewer than 500 daily passengers rode the commuter trains on the Putnam Division, and the New York State Public Service Commission authorized the abandonment of passenger service. The last passenger train ran on May 29, 1958. However, local freight service on the portion of the line that traverses Van Cortlandt Park was provided until 1981, when the line was completely abandoned. Most of the right-of-way has since been converted to a multi-use trail (in Westchester County, it is known as the South County Trailway and the North County Trailway, and in Putnam County, it is the Putnam County Trailway).

---

tinue south on a macadam path along the Mosholu Parkway (you now leave the Aqueduct route). The path soon bears left and climbs to the Major Deegan Expressway, where it follows the sidewalk across a bridge that spans the Mosholu Parkway. The bridge offers broad west-facing views over Van Cortlandt Lake, directly below, and Riverdale in the distance.

At the end of the bridge, a stone staircase descends to the right. This staircase is currently closed for repairs, but you can bypass it by following a steep dirt path down the side of the hill. Use extreme caution, as the path can be very slippery when muddy and wet.

At the bottom, bear right, then follow a marked bike path as it curves left and passes beneath a highway ramp overpass. Continue along the southern edge of scenic Van Cortlandt Lake. When you reach a Y-intersection, bear right, continuing to follow a wide paved path along the lakeshore. Soon, you'll pass in front of the golf clubhouse. Just beyond, at a

Van Cortlandt Lake

gap in a wooden fence, turn right and descend to the Putnam Trail (note the steel bridge to the right, which spans an arm of the lake).

Turn left onto the Putnam Trail for a very short distance. Almost immediately, you'll reach the rusting steel supports of the canopy for the former Van Cortlandt railroad station. Turn left here, then immediately bear right onto a paved path and continue through the underpass beneath the railbed (note the date "1904" inscribed in the abutment). On the opposite side, continue ahead on a path lined with Belgian blocks (do not follow a boardwalk on the right), then bear right at a fork and follow a wide path that heads west to the 242nd Street station, where the hike began.

42 Flat Rock Brook Nature Center

This loop hike runs along a scenic brook and passes a broad overlook.

Difficulty: Easy

Length and Time: About 2.0 miles; about one hour.

Dogs: Not permitted on Flat Rock Brook Nature Center property.

Map: Flat Rock Brook Nature Center trail map (available at Nature Center or online at www.flatrockbrook.org); New York-New Jersey Trail Conference Hudson Palisades Trails Map #108.

Directions: Take N.J. Route 4 to the Jones Road exit in Englewood. Turn right at the top of the ramp, and continue to the first stop sign, which is Van Nostrand Avenue. Turn right onto Van Nostrand Avenue and continue past the "dead end" sign to the Nature Center at the top of the hill. GPS address: 443 Van Nostrand Avenue, Englewood, NJ 07631.

The Flat Rock Brook Nature Center manages a 150-acre tract in Englewood that has been protected from development. It includes the 75-acre Allison Woods Park, established in 1924 under the will of William O. Allison, and an additional 75 acres acquired by the City of Englewood over a ten-year period beginning in 1968. The preserve has 3.6 miles of trails, and the hike described below forms a loop around the property.

From the parking area, proceed to the Nature Center building, where you can view nature exhibits and pick up a free trail map. Find the trailhead of the White Loop Trail, marked by a triple white blaze, directly opposite the entrance to the Nature Center building. Head north on this trail, which follows a wide path. The Red Loop Trail soon crosses, but you should continue ahead on the White Loop Trail, which gradually ascends the hill on switchbacks. At the top of the hill, you'll come to the Outdoor

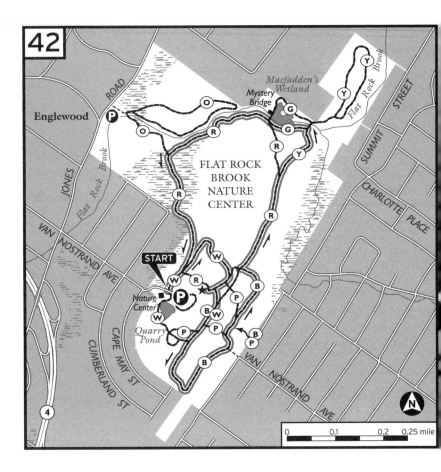

Classroom. Here, the Red Loop Trail joins from the left. You should turn right, now following the joint White and Red Loop Trails.

Soon, the Purple Trail leaves to the left. Continue along the joint White and Red Loop Trails, but when the White Loop Trail turns sharply left, proceed straight ahead on the Red Loop Trail for 50 feet to a southwest-facing overlook, marked by a rock parapet. You can hear the sounds of the traffic on I-95 below, and on a clear day, you can see the First Wat-chung Mountain in the distance.

Retrace your steps to the junction and turn right to continue on the White Loop Trail. Just ahead, at a T-intersection, the White Trail turns right and joins the Blue Loop Trail. A short distance beyond, the Purple

Macfadden's Wetland

What is today known as "Macfadden's Wetland" dates back at least as far as 1876, when it was first shown on a map. On an 1886 map, it is called "Vanderbeck's Mill Pond," thus indicating that it was used to power a sawmill.

Bernarr Macfadden, after whom it is now named, was born in Missouri in 1868. He was named Bernard Adolphus McFadden, but subsequently changed his name because he thought "Bernarr" sounded like the roar of a lion, and that "Macfadden" was a more "masculine" spelling of his name.

Macfadden founded Physical Culture magazine in 1899 and wrote over 100 books between 1900 and 1937. He has been described as "an eccentric millionaire who...built a publishing empire of body-building, physical culture and girlie magazines."

In 1927, Macfadden purchased an 18-acre estate at the corner of East Linden Avenue and South Woodland Street in Englewood. The mansion had 28 rooms, and Macfadden added a swimming pool, miniature golf course and basketball courts. The property included the millpond, which now served as an ornamental lake.

Bernarr Macfadden and his wife Mary separated in 1932, and Bernarr moved out of the Englewood estate. His wife, though, continued to live there until her death in 1969. The millpond (now a wetland) was purchased by the City of Englewood in the early 1970s and is part of the Flat Rock Brook Nature Center property.

Trail also joins. Soon, the Purple Trail and then the White Loop Trail leave to the right, but you should continue straight ahead on the Blue Loop Trail. Follow the Blue Loop Trail as it loops around, first to the east, then to the north. The trail runs close to the perimeter of the Nature Center property, with private residences visible through the trees.

At the top, a short side trail to the right leads to the eastern section of Van Nostrand Avenue. Just beyond, the Purple Trail joins briefly. Continue ahead on the Blue Loop Trail, which soon curves to the left and arrives at a T-intersection with the Red Loop Trail (at a sign for "Bridge Over Look"). Turn right and follow the Red Loop Trail, which begins a gentle descent. At the next Y-intersection, bear right onto the Yellow Trail, which continues to descend a little more steeply, then levels off.

Flat Rock Brook

When the Yellow Trail makes a sharp right turn, adjacent to a yellow "B.C.U.A." sign, continue straight ahead, now following the Green Trail. To the right is Flat Rock Brook, which soon widens into Macfadden's Wetland, named for the physical culturist Bernarr Macfadden (1868-1955), who lived nearby about 1930.

At the end of the wetland, you'll notice (to the right) a wooden bridge over a concrete dam. This bridge is known as the "Mystery Bridge" because it mysteriously appeared over one weekend. Just below the bridge, you may observe attractive cascades if the water level in the brook is high. This is a good place to take a break.

Continue ahead along the south side of the brook (do not cross the bridge), now following the Red Loop Trail. This is the most scenic portion of the hike, with the brook tumbling over rocks to your right. The trail descends on a moderate grade, with wooden steps provided along the steeper sections.

After a level stretch at the bottom of the hill, you'll come to a T-intersection. Turn left and follow the Red Loop Trail as it ascends steadily. When you reach the top of the climb, turn right onto the wide White Loop Trail, following the sign to the "Nature Center." Continue ahead to the paved road, with the Nature Center building directly in front of you. Turn left and return to the parking area where you began the hike.

43 Rockefeller State Park Preserve
Rockwood Hall

This loop hike follows carriage roads around the grounds of the former home of William Rockefeller, with gentle grades and panoramic views over the Hudson River.

Difficulty: Easy

Length and Time: About 2.1 miles; about one and one-half hours.

Map: Rockefeller State Park Preserve map
(available online at www.friendsrock.org/parkmap.html).

Directions: Take the New York State Thruway to Exit 9 (at the east side of the Tappan Zee Bridge). Turn right at the top of the ramp onto U.S. Route 9 (South Broadway), and continue north on Route 9 through the Village of Tarrytown. After 1.7 miles, you'll come to a complex intersection where you should bear left to continue on Route 9. In another 1.8 miles (3.5 miles from the Thruway exit), immediately after crossing under N.Y, Route 117, turn right at a sign for "Rockwood Road," and follow the ramp onto Route 117. After reaching a stop sign, continue ahead through an intersection, following the sign to "Kendal on Hudson," pass an exit from a parking area on the left, then turn left at the entrance to the parking area.

If approaching from the north, take the Taconic State Parkway or N.Y. Route 9A to N.Y. Route 117, proceed west on Route 117 past Rockwood Road, and follow the last sentence of the directions above.

Rockwood Hall is the site of the former summer home of William Rockefeller (1841-1922), brother of John D. Rockefeller. In 1886, he purchased Rockwood, a 200-acre estate, and built Rockwood Hall, a mansion with 204 rooms. Frederick Law Olmsted designed the landscape, which includes many ornamental trees. Following Rockefeller's death in 1922, the estate was converted into a country club, which soon went bankrupt.

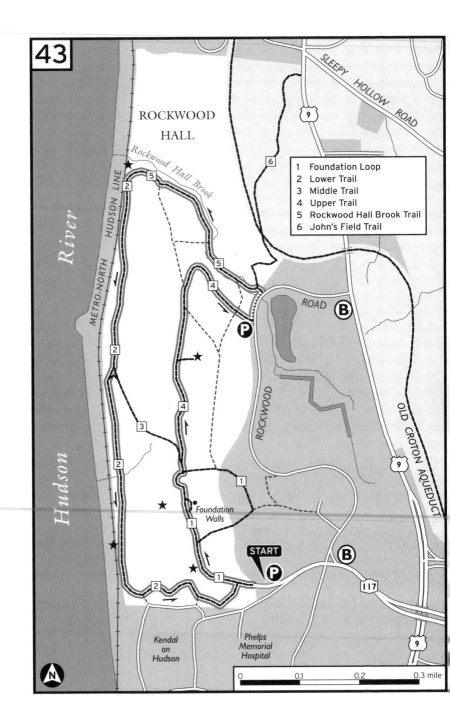

43

ROCKWOOD
HALL

Rockwood Hall Brook

River

Hudson

METRO-NORTH HUDSON LINE

1 Foundation Loop
2 Lower Trail
3 Middle Trail
4 Upper Trail
5 Rockwood Hall Brook Trail
6 John's Field Trail

SLEEPY HOLLOW ROAD

9

6

ROAD

B

ROCKWOOD

OLD CROTON AQUEDUCT

9

5

5

4

4

2

2

3

2

1

Foundation
Walls

1

START

P

B

117

9

Kendal
on
Hudson

Phelps
Memorial
Hospital

0   0.1   0.2   0.3 mile

N

In 1937, the property was acquired by John D. Rockefeller, Jr., William's nephew, who arranged for the mansion to be razed in 1941-42.

The Rockefeller family donated Rockwood Hall to New York State in 1999, and it now forms a part of Rockefeller State Park Preserve. Although the buildings are gone, the foundations remain, and the carriage roads that were constructed by the Rockefeller family offer an opportunity for a delightful stroll through the property, with panoramic views over the Hudson River. Bicycles are not allowed, and while equestrians are permitted (with a permit), the carriage roads are rarely used by horses. Although not blazed, the carriage roads in the park are easily followed.

ROCKEFELLER ARCHIVE CENTER

Rockwood Hall

From the western end of the parking area, follow the crosswalk across the paved entrance road, bear right onto a paved road (closed to traffic) and continue uphill on a gravel road. At the top of the climb, bear right onto another road, surfaced with paving stones, soon reaching a spectacular viewpoint over the Hudson River.

After passing a huge weeping beech tree, a path diverges to the right, but continue ahead, passing stone foundation walls to the right. These walls are all that remains of William Rockefeller's huge mansion. As you approach the highest point along the road, the views of the Hudson River broaden, and you can see the Tappan Zee Bridge to the left, beyond the Kendal on Hudson retirement community. For the best views, you'll want to walk across the grassy area to the low stone wall that overlooks the river.

View across the Hudson River from the grounds of Rockwood Hall

You may hear the sound of trains directly below you. Metro-North's Hudson Line runs along the east shore of the river, and you can clearly hear (but not see) the passing trains (you'll be able to see them later on in the hike).

After taking in the view, continue ahead along the road, which descends in a sweeping curve, bordered by stone walls. At the next intersection, turn left. Almost immediately, you'll reach a Y-intersection. Here, you should take the right fork. You're now following a gravel road that climbs very gently, soon coming out on a grassy field (to the right).

The road crosses another wooded area and emerges onto an open expanse, with grassy areas on both sides, and the Hudson River again visible through the trees on the left. Continue along the road, which curves sharply to the right at the end of the grassy area and reenters the woods.

When the gravel road ends at a locked gate, turn left onto the paved Rockwood Road and follow it downhill. Immediately after crossing a concrete bridge over Rockwood Hall Brook, turn left at a gate, then continue ahead on a gravel road, as another road departs to the right. The gravel road proceeds through a ravine studded with rhododendron, crossing five bridges over the brook in close succession. Continue to follow the road, which parallels the brook, until you approach the shore of the Hudson River.

A Grand Mansion

To construct Rockwood Hall, William Rockefeller imported stone masons from Scotland, master wood carvers from Switzerland, gardeners from England and horticulturists from Japan. He also employed the best American artists and craftsmen. Besides the main mansion, he built a three-story coach stable, a farm barn, a hennery, 17 greenhouses and a steel bridge spanning the New York Central Railroad (now Metro-North) tracks from the estate to a two-story boat house on the Hudson River. He arranged for a siding to be installed along the railroad and used it to store his private railroad car.

In an article that appeared in the *New York Times* on December 13, 1895, Rockwood Hall was stated to be, "in beauty and cost...second only to [the home] of George W. Vanderbilt, at Biltmore, near Asheville, N.C." The article described the fireplace in the main hall as being "about the size of an ordinary room," and it commented that the fireplace was equipped with an indicator, "regulated by a gilded weather-vane on the roof, which tells those sitting comfortably inside how the wind is blowing without."

After the death of William Rockefeller in 1922, his executors attempted to sell the property. They prepared an elaborate brochure which described the many features of the mansion in great detail, stating that "it is as good today as when it was built and, like the castles of England and Scotland after which it was patterned, it will endure for centuries." Unfortunately, the latter prediction did not come true, as the mansion was demolished about 20 years later.

A bench has been placed along the trail here, and this is a good place to take a break and enjoy the panoramic north-facing view, with Croton Point jutting out into the river. The railroad tracks are now visible below, and you may see a Metro-North or Amtrak train zoom by.

Continue along the gravel road, which now heads south, with a grassy slope to the left and the river to the right. As you proceed, you can see the river through the trees.

After passing a huge oak tree to the left, you'll come to a fork. Here, you should bear right and continue heading south along the river. Soon, you'll see stone walls above a grassy slope to the left. These walls mark the site of the Rockefeller mansion that you passed by earlier on the hike.

At the southern end of the Rockwood Hall property (marked by a number of evergreen trees), there are panoramic views up and down the Hudson River. Another bench has been placed here, and you may wish to pause once more to enjoy the views.

Continue along the gravel road, which bears left and begins to head east. At the next intersection, a path to the right leads into the Kendal on Hudson property, but you should continue ahead on the gravel road, which winds uphill. Upon reaching another path which heads into Kendal on Hudson, bear left and continue uphill on a gravel road bordered by stone walls. At the next intersection, bear right and head down to the parking area where the hike began.

Walking along the carriage roads of Rockwood Hall in the winter

44 Morristown National Historical Park

This loop hike, suitable for snowshoeing or cross-country skiing when the ground is covered with snow, follows rolling terrain around this historical park, passing several interpretive sites.

Difficulty: Easy to moderate (moderate to difficult for cross-country skiing)
Length and Time: About 5.5 miles; about three and one-half hours.
Map: Morristown National Historical Park trail map (available at visitor center).
Directions: Take I-287 to Exit 30B. At the first traffic light, turn right onto U.S. Route 202. Proceed north for 1.8 miles, and turn left onto Tempe Wick Road at a traffic light. Continue along Tempe Wick Road for 1.4 miles to the park entrance on the right side of the road. The visitor center parking area is just ahead.

From the parking area, proceed to the visitor center. After viewing the exhibits and obtaining a trail map, exit the back door, and continue ahead to a T-junction, opposite the Wick Farm. Turn left here, following a wide grassy road and passing the Wick farmhouse. Continue ahead downhill, cross a paved road, and proceed straight ahead along another paved road. Near the bottom of the hill, before reaching Tempe Wick Road, turn right at a sign to the Grand Loop Trail, which will be your route for the remainder of the hike.

Upon reaching the white-blazed Grand Loop Trail, turn right and proceed uphill for 0.2 mile. This is the steepest climb you will encounter and is not typical of the terrain on the remainder of the trail. The trail levels off and descends to reach a junction, marked by Signpost #3 (trail junctions in this park are marked by numbered signposts, which will be referred to in the hike description). Here, the trail bears left, passes

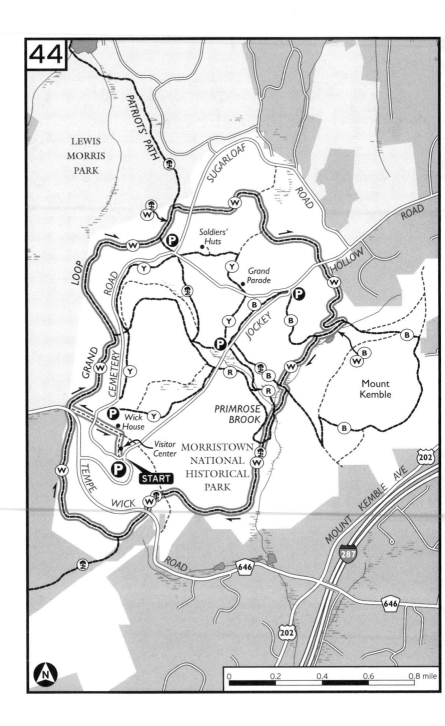

Wick House

a wire enclosure (part of a native plant restoration project), and climbs to the top of a hill, where it proceeds through thick barberry bushes and begins to closely parallel the park boundary. After a descent into a valley, it climbs to reach a junction (Signpost #4), where the Patriots' Path (blue tree-and-river logo on white) joins from the right. A sign points the way

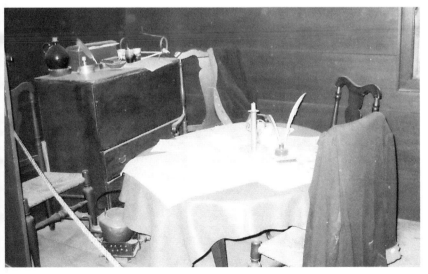

Inside the Wick House

A Winter of Suffering

Wrought into our national heritage is the image of Continental soldiers suffering at Valley Forge, Pennsylvania, during the winter of 1777-1778. Harsh as the conditions experienced by those soldiers were, they were not as severe as the misery they faced two years later, when the Continental Army wintered in Jockey Hollow, near Morristown. Valley Forge had been a refuge after the British drove the Continental Army from Philadelphia, but Morristown was chosen for its strategic location and natural defenses. It was within range of Philadelphia, New York City and the Hudson Highlands, yet it was tucked behind the Watchung Mountains – a formidable barrier to an attack. Washington had previously chosen this area – both in January 1777, when he brought his troops to Morristown after attacking the British forces at Trenton and Princeton, and two years later, when he wintered at Middlebrook (now Bridgewater), on the southern ridge of the Watchungs.

Snow was already falling as troops marched into Morristown in early December 1779, and it seemed to continue to fall into April. "The oldest people now living," Washington wrote, "do not remember so hard a winter." The rivers froze, including the Hudson and the Delaware. One observer recorded 28 snowfalls; the worst, a blizzard in the first week of January, left snow "four to six feet deep," reported James Thatcher, an army surgeon. Another two-day storm followed just three days later. When troops first arrived, they rushed to build log huts, but they didn't finish until February, leaving some soldiers in tents for over two months. In the end, over 1,000 soldiers' huts were erected on 600 acres of cleared forest.

Food, clothing, blankets and shoes were lacking, and some soldiers had not been paid in a year. "We have never experienced a like extremity at any period of the war," wrote Washington in desperation. An army private, Joseph Plumb Martin, wrote that, at one point,"I did not put a single morsel into my mouth for four days." He added: "I saw several men roast their old shoes and eat them." "But guard had to be mounted every day," Martin continued, and as soldiers marched to their posts, "they might be traced by the blood of their feet."

One brief mutiny was thwarted by appeals to loyalty, and with spring came relief from what may have been the harshest winter of the century.

-*Jim Simpson*

Soldiers' Huts

to the restored Soldiers' Huts (downhill on the right), which are worth a short side trip.

Follow the Grand Loop Trail as it continues ahead, now running concurrently with the Patriots' Path. When the Patriots' Path leaves to the left in another 900 feet (Signpost #5), turn right and continue to follow the Grand Loop Trail as it descends, passing Signpost #6 and continuing across an open field. After crossing paved Sugarloaf Road, the trail reenters the woods at Signpost #7. It ascends gradually, levels off, then bears right and descends across the side of a hill, with views through the trees to the left. At the next intersection, marked by Signpost #8 – about two miles from the start – the Grand Loop Trail turns left and soon levels off. It crosses paved Jockey Hollow Road, passes Signpost #9, and reenters the woods. The trail now runs close to the park boundary, with private homes visible just to the left.

After descending gradually and bending sharply to the left, the Grand Loop Trail turns right at Signpost #10, joining a blue-blazed trail. The joint white/blue trail follows a wide dirt road and passes a small pond on the left. A bench has been placed here, making it an attractive spot for a break. Just beyond, a Y-intersection is reached (Signpost #22). Here, the blue-blazed trail leaves to the right, but you should take the left fork, continuing along the white-blazed Grand Loop Trail, which descends gradually and begins to parallel a stream on the left. Then, about three miles from the start, the Grand Loop Trail arrives at a T-intersection (Signpost

#21), where it turns left. It is now joined by the Patriots' Path and a blue-blazed trail, both of which come in from the right. The joint trails cross a wooden bridge over a stream and soon arrive at Signpost #20. Turn sharply right here, following the Grand Loop Trail and the Patriots' Path (the blue-blazed trail continues straight ahead).

The joint Grand Loop Trail/Patriots' Path descends to cross the red-blazed Primrose Brook Trail at Signpost #30. Just beyond, the trail crosses Primrose Brook on a wooden bridge, crosses a feeder brook on another wooden bridge, and again crosses the Primrose Brook Trail at Signpost #31. As the trail continues ahead, Mt. Kemble is visible through the trees on the left. After a gradual ascent, the trail bears left and passes an interpretive sign with the story of the Connecticut Line. Then, just ahead, the Grand Loop Trail/Patriots' Path crosses the wide, unblazed Mendham Road Trail (Signpost #55).

Just before reaching paved Tempe Wick Road, the trail bears left and descends to cross the road (Signpost #56). It turns right, descends to cross a stream on a wooden bridge (Signpost #57), then climbs to a junction (Signpost #58). Here, the Patriots' Path (following the route of the New Jersey Brigade Trail) continues ahead, but you should turn right, following the white blazes. The Grand Loop Trail heads west and then north, roughly parallel to Tempe Wick Road. At Signpost #59, a dirt road joins from the left, and the Grand Loop Trail descends to end at Tempe Wick Road. To return to the parking area where you began the hike, turn right onto the road marked with a "Do Not Enter" sign and proceed ahead past the Wick Farm to the visitor center.

45 Westchester Wilderness Walk
Pound Ridge, N.Y.

This loop hike follows winding paths past interesting natural features through a 150-acre preserve in Pound Ridge, in the heart of Westchester County.

Difficulty: Easy to moderate.

Length and Time: About 6.0 miles; about four hours.

Map: Westchester Land Trust map (available online at www.westchesterlandtrust.org or from kiosk at trailhead).

Directions: From the George Washington Bridge, take I-95 to the Major Deegan Expressway North, which becomes the New York State Thruway. Take Exit 4 and proceed east on the Cross County Parkway to the Hutchinson River Parkway North. When the parkway ends, bear left and continue on I-684 to Exit 4 (Mount Kisco/Bedford). Turn right at the bottom of the ramp and follow N.Y. Route 172 for 3.5 miles. At a Mobil gas station, turn right onto Long Ridge Road. In 2.5 miles, turn left onto Upper Shad Road and continue for 0.3 mile to a small parking turnout on the left side of the road. The trailhead is marked by a small green sign for the Zofnass Family Preserve.

The Westchester Wilderness Walk might not fit the dictionary definition of "wilderness." The area is criss-crossed with stone walls – remnants of the early settlements in the area – and houses may occasionally be seen from the trails. But remarkably, for nearly the entire hike, one is entirely removed from the surrounding civilization of Westchester County. The trails have been routed – often, quite circuitously – to pass many unusual and interesting natural features, resulting in a hike that will probably seem longer than the map appears to indicate. The walk is a unique experience that is well worth the 40-mile drive from the George Washington Bridge!

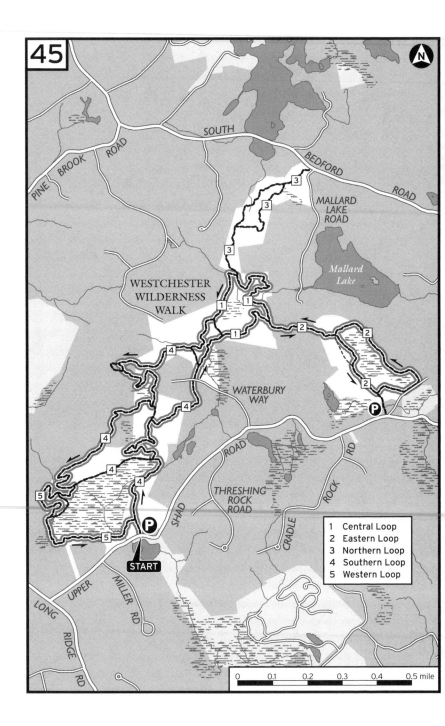

45

WESTCHESTER WILDERNESS WALK

SOUTH

PINE BROOK ROAD

BEDFORD ROAD

MALLARD LAKE ROAD

3

3

3

Mallard Lake

1

1

1

2

2

2

4

4

WATERBURY WAY

4

4

4

SHAD ROAD

4

5

THRESHING ROCK ROAD

CRADLE ROCK RD

5

P

P

START

UPPER MILLER RD

LONG RIDGE RD

1	Central Loop
2	Eastern Loop
3	Northern Loop
4	Southern Loop
5	Western Loop

N

0   0.1   0.2   0.3   0.4   0.5 mile

292 Hike of the Week

The trails in the preserve form five loops, four of which will be covered in this hike. They are blazed with green plastic markers and blue paint blazes on rocks. Many of the trails are bordered by logs. However, the hiker should be alert for sharp turns, some of which are easily missed, especially if the ground is covered with snow.

The trail begins at a kiosk just beyond the parking area, where a map of the preserve is posted. Take time to read the inspiring story of the assembly – over a period of 20 years – of various private lots into the preserve by Paul Zofnass, a Manhattan investment banker, without any public funding. The trail continues along a woods road, with a wetland on the left. It soon passes, on the left, the start of the West Loop. This will be your return route, but for now, continue straight ahead. A short distance beyond, a sign on the right marks the Princess Pine Grove – named for the tiny club moss found in the area. This is the first of many named natural features along the trail, most of which are marked by signs.

A stone wall along a trail in Westchester Wilderness Walk

Soon, the trail narrows to a footpath and crosses several streams on rocks. When you reach a T-intersection, with a wooden bridge on the right, turn left and cross a rock causeway, with a wooden handrail, over a stream. Just beyond, you'll come to a junction, where the South Loop begins. Turn right and follow the loop in a counter-clockwise direction. Upon reaching Becky's Brook, the trail turns sharply right and soon

Paul Zofnass' Vision

The many pleasures of the Westchester Wilderness Walk owe much to the passion, persistence and vision of one man, Paul Zofnass, and his wife, Renee Ring. Described by one writer as a "little Eden," the 150-acre preserve took some 20 years to assemble from donations of the couple's own property as well as acquisitions from neighboring landowners. Westchester Wilderness Walk is the result of its creator's enormous infusion of time, energy, money and fervor.

The Zofnass family bought their home in 1982 and enjoyed walking in nearby woods, which were trailless at the time. Alerted by the appearance of survey markers, they learned that a developer had divided an old farm between their land and the woods into six parcels. They purchased one of the parcels and a neighbor purchased two more, simply to hold them in an undeveloped state. From that beginning, the story of the preserve came to encompass many individual stories (detailed in a March 21, 2004 *New York Times* article).

As Mr. Zofnass started investigating properties on all sides of the core, he approached landowners with the concept of protecting the land as a unified preserve open to the public. Some were receptive to his conservation message, some were interested but unable to participate at the time, and some were unpersuaded. With the patience to wait years for opportunities and undertake painstaking negotiations, the willingness to purchase some properties himself for donation to the preserve, and abundant creativity – for example, in acquiring the parcel that would provide convenient public access to the preserve – Mr. Zofnass eventually prevailed.

The Westchester Land Trust has played a critical role throughout the process, accepting land grants, holding conservation easements on some of the parcels, and providing legal assistance. The entire preserve has been assembled without using any public funds.

With the help and support of family and friends, Paul Zofnass has laid out and constructed all the preserve's hiking trails, currently totaling 10 miles, and continues to maintain them. He has also established a trust fund to assist in taking care of the land, in the spirit of the stewardship that has marked this and his other environmental endeavors.

-Charlotte Fahn

Climbing the narrow passage between rocks that leads to Trudeau's Point of View

passes the ruins of Tom's Cabin. A short distance beyond, you'll climb rock steps in a narrow passage between two rocks and reach Trudeau's Point of View.

When you arrive at the South Loop Short Cut, turn right to continue on the main loop. After descending a little, you'll pass various plaques that recognize the dedicated efforts of the Zofnass family in protecting the preserve. You'll go by a wetland bordered by well-laid stone walls, then cross a paved private road and pass several more plaques. Just beyond, bear right at a junction, following a sign for the Main Trail.

After crossing a wet area on rocks, the trail climbs a rock stairway to reach Tulip Tree Heights. A short distance beyond, you'll arrive at Jessica's Junction, where you should turn right to follow the Roundabout in a counter-clockwise direction. Then, in about a quarter of a mile – after passing a stone bench at Mossy Knoll – you'll reach another intersection. Here, you should turn right onto the "lollipop stick" of the East Loop.

After a relatively level section, you'll reach the top of the Grand Stone Staircase. Two routes are provided to descend this interesting feature, with the left route designated as "easier" and the right route "harder." Neither route is particularly difficult, but you will be returning this way, so you may wish to select the "easier" route for the descent and the "harder" route for the ascent on the return.

After a short descent, you'll reach an intersection where the East Loop proper begins. Bear right to follow the loop in a counter-clockwise direction. You'll cross a wet area on large rocks, climb a little, then turn left onto a woods road, with a large wetland to the left. When you reach a sign "Out to Upper Shad .1 m," turn left to continue along the trail.

At the end of the wetland, you'll come to another paved private road. Turn left and follow the road for 250 feet, crossing the outlet of the wetland on the road bridge, then turn left, cross a small stream on a rock bridge, and reenter the woods. This is about the halfway point of the hike. The trail now follows a rather rugged footpath along the northeast shore of the wetland, with several cliffs looming above to the right.

Moss Falls

When you reach the end of the loop at the northwest corner of the wetland, turn right, following the sign for the Central Roundabout. You're now retracing your steps along the "lollipop stick" of the loop, going back up the Grand Stone Staircase and continuing to the junction with the Roundabout. Here you should turn right, following the sign "Roundabout (continued)."

The trail descends to cross a stream on large rocks. A short distance beyond, it climbs to Over the Top (a rock outcrop to the left of the trail) and descends to Moss Falls, a huge boulder covered with moss. It then climbs to Razor Ridge Rock. After paralleling a stone wall, the trail turns left, making a sharp U-turn, and descends. Be alert for this turn, which is easily missed.

The trail circles the interesting Roundabout Rock and soon arrives at another junction. Here, you should turn left, following the sign "Roundabout to South Loop." Immediately, you'll cross a stream on rocks. After briefly paralleling the stream, the trail bears left and begins to head south.

At the next junction, you should turn right at a sign "South Loop – to Kiosk" and go through Wedge Walk Rock, a narrow passage between two boulders. You'll soon pass the aptly named TV Antenna Rock and descend to a stream. The trail turns right and follows along the stream on large rocks, with the stream directly below (this section of the trail is marked with blue paint blazes). After a short distance, the trail turns left and climbs rock steps to the left of a large boulder. It passes Fowler's Rock and Pauley's Point Rock and then runs near the edge of an escarpment, with views over a wetland below.

After curving to the left and descending, the trail passes Jurassic Rock and soon begins to run along the wetland. It loops around to cross one end of the wetland on rocks and passes the Triple Red Oak. Then, at the next junction, turn right, following the sign for "Quest" (don't follow the South Loop Shortcut).

The trail makes a long loop to the southwest, passing Layer Cake Rock, Lichen Ledge, Tulip Tree Squeeze and Cantilever Rock. After paralleling a long, slanted rock, it makes a sharp U-turn and begins to descend on switchbacks. Near the base of the descent, it follows stone steps along an attractive cascade. It continues on a level path alongside a wetland.

In a short distance, you'll notice a sign for the West Loop Trail on the right. Turn right and follow this trail, which parallels several rather tall

Layer Cake Rock

and thick stone walls, then climbs a little and winds through stands of cedar. After passing Mayo Fort, the trail descends on switchbacks to a T-intersection by a stone wall, where you should turn right.

The trail now heads along the Western Wetland Walk, with a wetland on the left and a stone wall on the right. For much of the way, you follow stepping stones over wet areas. At the end of the wetland, the trail turns left, crosses the outlet of the wetland on a rock bridge, and soon reaches a T-intersection just north of the main entrance. Turn right to return to the kiosk where the hike began.

46 Sterling Forest State Park

This hike follows the Indian Hill Loop Trail, which offers several viewpoints of the surrounding countryside and traverses abandoned farmlands with numerous old stone walls.

Difficulty: Moderate

Length and Time: About 3.6 miles; about two and one-half hours.

Map: New York-New Jersey Trail Conference Sterling Forest Trails Map #100.

Directions: Take N.Y. Route 17 North through Sloatsburg and Tuxedo, and continue on Route 17 past the intersection with N.Y. Route 17A into Southfields. About 1.3 miles beyond the intersection with Route 17A, turn left onto Orange Turnpike (County Route 19) and continue for 1.3 miles to the park entrance on the right (marked by a sign for "Indian Hill"). Turn right and follow the dirt road ahead for 0.2 mile, then turn right into the parking area.

This hike follows the yellow-blazed Indian Hill Loop Trail, described here in a counter-clockwise direction. From the information kiosk in the parking area, the trail proceeds through a hemlock grove, turns right and climbs to the crest of a rise. After descending a little, it climbs through mountain laurel to reach a open granite ledge, with south-facing views over Sterling Forest, Harriman State Park and the Ramapo Valley.

A short distance beyond, the red-blazed Furnace Loop Trail joins from the right. Continue ahead, now following both yellow and red blazes, as the joint trails climb to the ridgetop and descend into a valley, crossing several stone walls. After climbing to another rock ledge, with views to the south and east, they descend to a junction with a woods road. The trails turn right onto the road, but you may wish to detour to the left on this

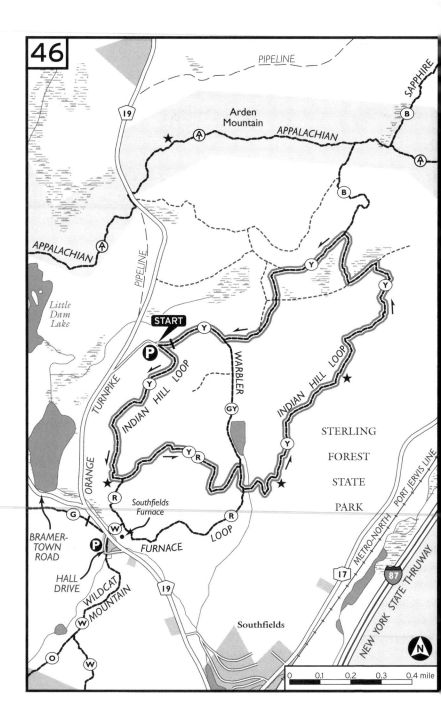

46

PIPELINE

SAPPHIRE

B

19

Arden
Mountain

APPALACHIAN

A

A

B

APPALACHIAN

A

PIPELINE

Y

Y

Little
Dam
Lake

START

P

Y

WARBLER

INDIAN HILL LOOP

Y

Y

INDIAN HILL LOOP

GY

STERLING

Y

R

FOREST

Y

R

STATE

R

Southfields
Furnace

PARK

R

FURNACE LOOP

G

W

METRO-NORTH PORT JERVIS LINE

BRAMER-
TOWN
ROAD

P

HALL
DRIVE

19

17

87

WILDCAT

W

MOUNTAIN

Southfields

NEW YORK STATE THRUWAY

O

W

N

0   0.1   0.2   0.3   0.4 mile

The Indian Hill Tract

Although now part of Sterling Forest State Park, the Indian Hill tract never was owned by the Sterling Forest Corporation. In the 19th century, it was owned by the Townsend family and used primarily for the harvesting of timber.

The southern part of the Indian Hill tract contains the historic Southfields Furnace. Between 1804 and 1806, a charcoal furnace for smelting iron ore was constructed here by Peter Townsend, whose family also owned and operated the nearby Sterling Furnaces in Sterling Forest. In 1839, the first Southfields Furnace was dismantled and rebuilt to accommodate the use of Pennsylvania coal as fuel.

At the height of its operation (in the 1860s), Southfields Furnace included a complex of 28 homes for workers, a general store, a weigh station, and associated outbuildings. The furnace closed in 1887. Today, all that is left is the ruins of the furnace and its charging bridge.

Recognizing its historic and scenic value, Scenic Hudson acquired the Indian Hill tract in 1997 from a golf course developer and partially stabilized the furnace ruins. Before conveying the property to the State of New York in 2002, Scenic Hudson invited the New York–New Jersey Trail Conference to construct the Indian Hill Loop Trail, which was opened on National Trails Day in June 1999. This trail was the first new hiking trail to be built in Sterling Forest State Park, and it remains one of the few foot trails in the park that does not follow pre-existing woods roads for most of its length.

road (marked with the yellow-bird-on-green blazes of the Warbler Trail), which leads in 200 feet to a dam and a picturesque pond.

The joint yellow and red trails soon turn left, leaving the woods road. Just beyond, the red-blazed Furnace Loop Trail leaves to the right. For the remainder of the hike, you'll be following only the yellow blazes of the Indian Hill Loop Trail. The trail now crosses a stream on rocks and climbs to a panoramic south-facing viewpoint from a rock ledge. It then ascends to the ridgetop, which it follows north.

After a relatively level stretch, the trail climbs to the highest point on the ridge (1,047 feet). Just beyond, rock ledges to the right of the trail offer unobstructed views across the Ramapo Valley to Harriman State Park.

An unusually wide stone wall along the Indian Hill Loop Trail

Green Pond Mountain dominates the view, with the grassy Elk Pen in the foreground and the New York State Thruway below in the valley.

From the ridge, the trail descends gradually on switchbacks. Near the bottom, it briefly follows a stone wall, then turns right onto a woods road. At the base of the descent, it turns left onto a woods road between unusually wide stone walls. Soon, the trail turns right, goes through a gap in a massive stone wall, and continues on a footpath, passing a huge oak tree.

After crossing a stone wall, the Indian Hill Loop Trail reaches a junction with a blue-blazed trail that begins on the right and heads north to connect, in 0.4 mile, with the white-blazed Appalachian Trail. Here, the Indian Hill Loop Trail turns left and begins to parallel the stone wall. It soon crosses two more stone walls, as well as a woods road lined on both sides with wide stone walls.

After passing through a wide gap in yet another stone wall, the trail turns left onto a grassy woods road. At a T-intersection, it turns right onto another woods road, which it follows for about a quarter mile to the barrier gate just beyond the parking area. Turn left and climb to the parking area, where the hike began.

47 Mahlon Dickerson Reservation

This loop hike passes the Headley Overlook, goes over the highest point in Morris County, runs along the unusual Pine Swamp and follows the railbed of the historic Ogden Mine Railroad.

Difficulty: Moderate

Length and Time: About 6.7 miles; about four and one-half hours.

Map: New York-New Jersey Trail Conference Jersey Highlands Trails (Central North Region) Map #125; Morris County Park Commission map (available from kiosk at trailhead or online at www.morrisparks.net).

Directions: Take I-80 to Exit 34B. Proceed north for 4.3 miles on N.J. Route 15, and get off at the exit for Weldon Road/Oak Ridge/Milton. After 1.3 miles on Weldon Road, you will pass a sign marking the entrance to the Saffin-Rock Rill area of Mahlon Dickerson Reservation. Continue for another 1.5 miles (2.8 miles from Route 15) and turn right into the Saffin Pond parking area.

On the southeast side of the parking area, you will notice a triple black-diamond-on-teal blaze, marking the start of a connector trail to the Highlands Trail. Follow the black-diamond-on-teal blazes, which head east along the pond, cross a footbridge over a stream and proceed south along the eastern shore of Saffin Pond. You may notice a number of trees that have been felled by beaver activity in the area.

At the southeast corner of the pond, you'll reach an open area with a bench and approach a bridge over the dam of the pond. Turn left here onto a gravel road, the route of the teal-blazed Highlands Trail, which soon begins a gradual ascent. At the top of the climb, bear right at a T-intersection with a bench and continue to follow the teal diamond blazes as they descend along an eroded woods road. At the base of the descent, bear left

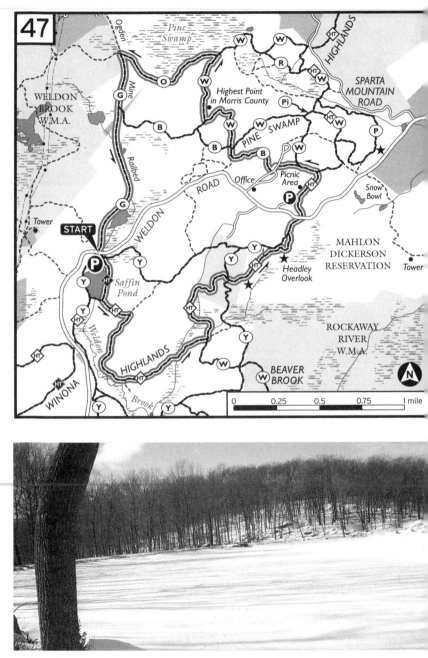

Saffin Pond

The Ogden Mine Railroad

The Ogden Mines, located on the hill southeast of Ogdensburg, N.J., were opened in 1772 by Abram Ogden. Initially, the ore was transported by wagon to Lake Hopatcong. In 1831, the completion of the Morris Canal, which connected to Lake Hopatcong, facilitated the transportation of the ore to furnaces in eastern Pennsylvania.

When demand for the iron ore increased during the Civil War, the mine owners and other prominent businessmen chartered the Ogden Mine Railroad Co. in 1864. The 10-mile-long railroad was completed from the mines to Nolan's Point on Lake Hopatcong in 1866, but it did not connect to any other railroad for the next 16 years. The ore was transferred onto canal boats and shipped to its destination via the Morris Canal.

In 1882 – the peak year of the New Jersey iron industry – the Central Railroad of New Jersey leased the Ogden Mine Railroad and built a five-mile branch connecting it to its High Bridge Branch near Wharton. The line, now known as the Ogden Mine Branch of the Central Railroad of New Jersey, provided both freight and passenger service. Passenger excursion trains often were operated to Nolan's Point on Lake Hopatcong.

Although the mines along the route began to decline in the 1880s, traffic on the railroad increased in 1889, when Thomas Edison constructed a large ore separating and concentrating plant near the Ogden Mine. Edison himself often traveled on the Ogden Mine Branch to visit his plant, and a town constructed for the workers was named Edison. But the plant was not commercially successful, and it was abandoned about 1900.

Regular passenger service on the Ogden Mine Branch ended in 1923. By the 1930s, the automobile had superseded the excursion trains, and with the closures of the iron mines along the line, the railroad had little traffic. The Central Railroad obtained permission to abandon operations north of Nolan's Point in 1935, and the rails were removed from the entire branch in 1941. But much of the right-of-way north of Route 15 – the original route of the 1866 Ogden Mine Railroad – can still be followed today, and this hike incorporates a section of this historic railroad.

A stream along the Highlands Trail

and continue along a relatively level stretch of the Highlands Trail, with Weldon Brook – the outlet of Saffin Pond – to your right. When you reach a Y-intersection, bear left, continuing to follow the teal diamond blazes.

After another level stretch, the trail crosses a stream on a wide wooden footbridge and bears left. Soon, it bears right and climbs to reach a high point marked by a large boulder to the left of the trail. Just beyond, you'll reach a T-intersection. The white-blazed Beaver Brook Trail begins on the right, but you should turn left to continue on the teal-diamond-blazed Highlands Trail. The trail descends to cross a tributary stream, climbs over a knoll, then descends to recross the main stream on rocks. The trail

View to the southeast from the Highlands Trail

now climbs, passing interesting rock formations on the left. After proceeding through a rocky area, the trail descends to cross the main stream (for the third time) on rocks.

The Highlands Trail now begins to climb – steeply in places – coming out on several exposed rock outcrops along the way. After crossing a yellow-blazed woods road in a large clearing, the grade moderates. Soon, you'll reach a broad overlook to the east and southeast from a rock outcrop to the right of the trail. Hardly any civilization is visible from here; you see only forested hillsides, with Lake Hopatcong visible in the distance to the right. After a slight dip, the trail climbs through a canopy of mountain laurel to reach another viewpoint. This viewpoint, marked by a bench and designated on the map as the Headley Overlook, is more popular because it is nearer the road, but the first overlook provides a less obstructed view.

Continue ahead on the Highlands Trail, which now descends on a woods road, and bear right at the next T-intersection. As the trail approaches Weldon Road, it bears right at a fork, then crosses the paved road and soon emerges onto a parking area. A nearby open pavilion with picnic tables is a good spot to take a break.

Follow the teal diamond blazes of the Highlands Trail as they continue along a paved service road from the end of the parking area, passing a fitness center on the right. The pavement ends in about 500 feet, and you will begin to follow white blazes, in addition to the teal diamond blazes of the Highlands Trail. Soon, you'll reach a junction with the white-blazed Pine Swamp Circular Trail. Turn left, leaving the Highlands Trail, and follow the white blazes along a woods road. When you reach a Y-intersection, a short distance ahead, bear left, leaving the white-blazed trail, and proceed ahead on a blue-blazed trail.

Continue along the blue-blazed trail as it bears left and follows the edge of an open field, then turns right and passes in front of a restroom building. Immediately bear left at a fork and follow the road for about 100 feet. Opposite Campsite #4, you'll notice a sign pointing to the Pine Swamp Trail. Turn right and follow the blue blazes into the woods.

In about a third of a mile, you'll reach a complex intersection. First, turn right at a T-intersection, joining a yellow-blazed bike trail. Just ahead, bear left, continuing to follow the blue-blazed trail, then turn right onto the white-blazed Pine Swamp Circular Trail, which ascends on a winding woods road also marked occasionally with blue horse trail markers.

Near the top of the climb, a black-dot-on-blue trail begins on the left. Continue ahead on the white-blazed trail, passing a bench on the left, and you'll soon reach the highest point in Morris County (1,395 feet), marked by a sign to the right of the trail. The trail now descends to reach a junction in a hemlock forest. Bear sharply left here, leaving the white-blazed trail, and follow an orange-blazed woods road. To your right is the unusual Pine Swamp, with its tall spruce, hemlock, rhododendron and mountain laurel.

In another two-thirds of a mile – after a short but rather steep descent – you'll reach a junction with the green-blazed railbed of the Ogden Mine Railroad. Built in 1866 to transport the ore from local mines, it was abandoned in 1935. Turn left and follow this nearly-level railbed through rock cuts and over embankments. In about a third of a mile, you'll reach the western end of the blue-blazed trail on the left. Soon afterwards, you'll pass two wetlands – first on the right, then on the left. The hill visible beyond the wetland on the left is the one you climbed earlier in the hike to reach the highest point in Morris County. Continuing ahead, the railbed begins to parallel Weldon Brook on the left. After passing another large wetlands area, you'll reach Weldon Road. The parking area where you began the hike is across the road on the left.

48 Minnewaska State Park Preserve

This loop hike, suitable for cross-country skiing, runs along dramatic cliffs of Shawangunk conglomerate, with many fine views.

Difficulty: Moderate (moderate to strenuous for cross-country skiing).

Length and Time: About 8.5 miles; about five hours.

Dogs: Not permitted on groomed ski trails.

Map: New York-New Jersey Trail Conference Shawangunk Trails Map #104; Minnewaska State Park Preserve map.

Directions: Take the New York State Thruway to Exit 18 (New Paltz). Beyond the toll booths, turn left onto N.Y. Route 299 and continue west through the Village of New Paltz. When you cross the bridge over the Wallkill River at the west end of the village, continue ahead on Route 299 (do not turn right towards the Mohonk Mountain House). In another 5.5 miles (from the Wallkill River bridge), Route 299 ends at a T-intersection with Route 44/55. Turn right here and follow Route 44/55 as it negotiates a very sharp hairpin turn and climbs to pass under the Trapps Bridge (a steel overpass). Continue for about three miles past the Trapps Bridge to the entrance to Minnewaska State Park Preserve, on the left side of the road. A per-person trail fee is charged at the gatehouse when cross-country skiing is available; at other times, a parking fee is charged. Continue uphill for 0.4 mile to the parking area at Lake Minnewaska.

Information: For information on snow conditions, call Minnewaska State Park Preserve at (845) 255-0752. Hiking on the carriage roads in Minnewaska is not permitted when they are covered with snow and groomed for cross-country skiing.

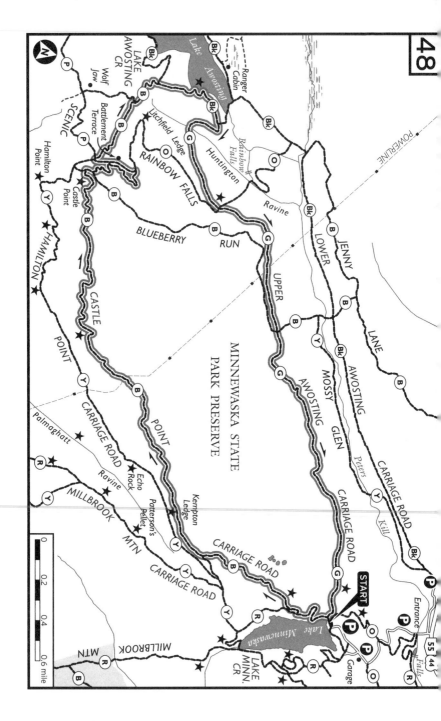

48

Lakes Minnewaska and Awosting

Originally known as Coxing Pond, Lake Minnewaska was acquired in 1875 by Alfred H. Smiley, twin brother of Albert K. Smiley, the owner of the neighboring Mohonk property. Alfred proceeded to build two hotels overlooking the lake – Cliff House, opened in 1879, and Wildmere, opened in 1887 – and to acquire Lake Awosting and its surrounding lands. The Minnewaska estate remained in Smiley family ownership until 1955, when it was sold to Kenneth B. Phillips, Sr., who had served as general manager of the property. In 1971, the State of New York and The Nature Conservancy acquired a 6,725-acre parcel centered on Lake Awosting and dedicated it as Minnewaska State Park. Phillips remained the owner of the remainder of the Minnewaska estate, but the two historic hotels on Lake Minnewaska closed during the 1970s. About 1980, the Marriott Corporation unveiled plans for a new 450-room hotel and conference center, 300 condominiums, and an 18-hole golf course around Lake Minnewaska. A broad coalition of conservation groups, led by the local Friends of the Shawangunks and including the New York-New Jersey Trail Conference, strongly opposed the proposal. Finally, in 1987, the 1,200 acres surrounding Lake Minnewaska were purchased by the State and added to the park. Minnewaska State Park Preserve now includes over 21,000 acres.

From the end of the parking area, descend on the red-blazed Lake Minnewaska Carriage Road that encircles Lake Minnewaska. This descent is rather steep for cross-country skiing, but it is not typical of the grades you'll encounter the rest of the way. After a short descent, you'll reach a junction with the green-blazed Upper Awosting Carriage Road (a swimming area is to the left, and restrooms are to the right). Bear left, continuing to follow the Lake Minnewaska Carriage Road, which now begins to climb. About 0.4 mile from the start, you'll reach a junction with the blue-blazed Castle Point Carriage Road.

Turn right and follow the Castle Point Carriage Road, which continues to climb gradually. Soon, you'll reach an open area, the site of a former golf course, with views of the Catskills to the north. After passing a side trail on the left, which leads to the Hamilton Point Carriage Road, there are views to the left over the Palmaghatt Ravine. Soon, you'll reach Kempton Ledge, with excellent views across the ravine and over the Wallkill Valley beyond. The large boulder visible on the other side of the ravine is known as Patterson's Pellet.

The carriage road continues generally uphill, with some short descents and one twisting curve. About two miles from the start, you'll pass under a power line. A short distance beyond, you'll reach a series of open ledges that afford broad views over Palmaghatt Ravine, with the rocky face of Gertrude's Nose – the tip of the escarpment across the ravine – clearly visible.

View over the Palmaghatt Ravine towards Gertrude's Nose from the Castle Point Carriage Road

After some more twists and turns, the carriage road comes out at Castle Point, a steep promontory with panoramic views to the south and east. Lake Awosting is below to the west, and Sam's Point may be seen directly ahead to the south (near the communications towers visible in the distance). The elevation of Castle Point is 2,200 feet, and you've climbed over 500 vertical feet from Lake Minnewaska. If it's not too windy, this is a good place to take a break.

The carriage road turns right and begins a steady descent, immediately passing the southern end of the Blueberry Run Trail (marked by a sign). In the next three-quarters of a mile, the carriage road makes several sharp turns (skiers should exercise care). At a hairpin turn to the left, the orange-blazed Rainbow Falls Trail leaves to the right. After passing under the dra matic ledges of the overhanging Battlement Terrace, the Castle Point Carriage Road arrives at a junction with the Hamilton Point Carriage Road. Bear right, continuing to follow the Castle Point Carriage Road.

Battlement Terrace along the Castle Point Carriage Road

Soon, the unmarked Slate Bank Carriage Road leaves to the left and, a short distance beyond, you'll reach a junction with the Lake Awosting Carriage Road. Continue straight ahead, now following black blazes instead of the blue blazes that have marked the route up to this point. You'll soon reach a beautiful viewpoint to the left over Lake Awosting – another good spot for a break.

At the next junction, the black blazes turn left, but you should continue straight ahead, now following the green blazes of the Upper Awosting

Carriage Road. As the carriage road bends to the right ahead, you'll see the impressive cliffs of Lichtfield Ledge. The carriage road soon begins to follow along the base of these cliffs, which often feature hanging icicles in the winter.

The carriage road crosses the orange-blazed Rainbow Falls Trail near the end of the cliffs, and it continues ahead, soon recrossing the power line and the blue-blazed Blueberry Run Trail. From here to the end of the carriage road at Lake Minnewaska, the route is less interesting, but the carriage road passes through pleasant woods and follows a gently descending grade – a good way to end a cross-country ski trip.

A little over a mile from the power line, you'll reach an open area known as the Orchard (some old fruit trees from the former orchard may still be seen). Then, after a short, gentle climb, you'll pass an excellent north-facing viewpoint to the left, with the Catskill Mountains visible in the distance. Just beyond, the Upper Awosting Carriage Road ends at the Lake Minnewaska Carriage Road, near the swimming area on Lake Minnewaska. Turn sharply left and follow the Lake Minnewaska Carriage Road uphill, back to the parking area where the hike began.

View of snow-covered Lake Awosting from the Lake Awosting Carriage Road

49 Ward Pound Ridge Reservation

This loop hike traverses the hills of this Westchester County park, climbing to a panoramic lookout over the Cross River Reservoir and the interesting Leatherman's Cave, and passing a number of other features of interest.

Difficulty: Moderate

Length and Time: About 6.5 miles; about four and one-half hours.

Map: Ward Pound Ridge Reservation map (available at trailhead kiosk or online at www.trailsidemuseum.org).

Directions: From the George Washington Bridge, proceed north on the Henry Hudson Parkway, which becomes the Saw Mill River Parkway. Take Exit 4 and continue on the Cross County Parkway, which becomes the Hutchinson River Parkway. Just beyond Exit 26 (the exit for I-287) bear left and continue on I-684 towards Brewster. Take Exit 6 (Cross River), which briefly joins the Saw Mill River Parkway, then exits to N.Y. Route 35. Turn right and follow Route 35 east for 3.7 miles to N.Y. Route 121. Turn right onto Route 121, cross a bridge over the Cross River, then immediately turn left and enter Ward Pound Ridge Reservation. Continue for 0.7 mile to the tollbooth (a parking fee is charged on weekends, daily in the summer). Make the first right beyond the tollbooth onto Michigan Road, and continue for 0.7 mile to a parking area just before a turnaround circle at the end of the road (if this parking area is full, additional parking is available uphill to the left).

Ward Pound Ridge Reservation, the largest park in Westchester County, was opened in 1938. Over thirty farms were acquired for the park, and old stone walls, which once marked the boundaries between the various farms, criss-cross the reservation. The trails – most of which are woods

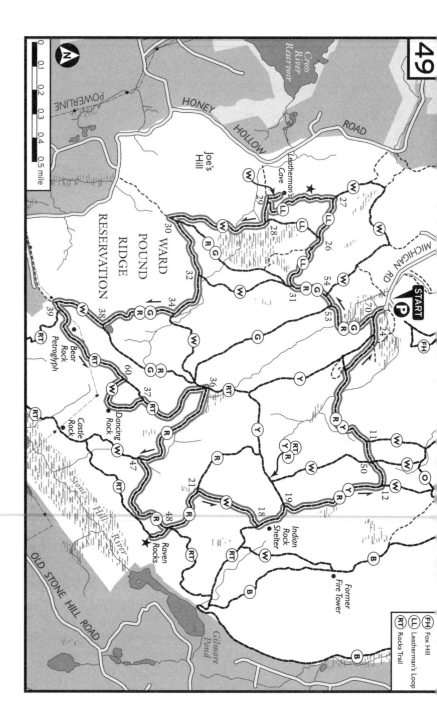

49

WARD POUND RIDGE RESERVATION

Joe's Hill

Cross River Reservoir

HONEY HOLLOW ROAD

Leatherman's Cave

POWERLINE

Bear Rock Petroglyph

Castle Rock

Dancing Rock

Stone Hill River

Raven Rocks

Indian Rock Shelter

Former Fire Tower

Gilmore Pond

OLD STONE HILL ROAD

MICHIGAN RD

START

N

0 0.1 0.2 0.3 0.4 0.5 mile

(FH) Fox Hill
(L) Leatherman's Loop
(RT) Rocks Trail

oads – are open to hikers and equestrians, but bicycles are not permitted. Most trail intersections are marked by numbered brown signs posted on trees. These numbers are shown on the park map and referred to in the description below. Since the trail system in the park is complex, hikers should obtain a copy of the free park map before beginning the hike. This hike will generally follow the Red Trail, but with several detours to include a number of interesting features.

From the circle at the end of the road, bear right and follow a road blocked by a wooden gate. Just beyond, you'll pass a kiosk on the right (trail maps are available here) and come to a fork at intersection #70. Bear right, following the red and green arrows, then bear right again at the next intersection (#53), as one leg of the Green Trail leaves to the left.

Proceed ahead on the Red and Green Trails, passing intersection #54 on the right. At intersection #31, turn right onto the Leatherman's Loop Trail (marked by "LL"-on-white blazes). When you reach the next intersection (#26), proceed straight ahead, but turn left at the following T-intersection (#27) and continue to follow the "LL" blazes, which proceed along a winding route to the top of a hill. Here, just to the right of the trail, rock ledges afford a panoramic west-facing view over the Cross River Reservoir. A wooden bench has been placed here, and this is a good point to rest and take a short break.

The panoramic west-facing view over the Cross River Reservoir

Continue ahead along the Leatherman's Loop Trail, which descends rather steeply on a footpath. After passing under an interesting over-hanging rock, you'll reach intersection #29. Turn around, and you'll see a small sign on a tree for the "Leatherman's Cave." Bear left and follow

The Leather Man – An Intriguing Character

Because his 60-pound clothes were made of old leather, he was dubbed the Leather Man – a mysterious hermit who wandered on a circuit through parts of Westchester, Putnam and Dutchess Counties, as well as western Connecticut, from 1883 until his death on March 20, 1889 near Ossining, New York. Sleeping in caves or shelters, rarely speaking, accepting food, and then walking on, he followed a regular 34-day, 365-mile path through the many small towns in the area. He regularly visited certain families, but would not stop at a household which had made him feel unwelcome.

What is known about the Leather Man is limited to what was reported in many local newspapers of the time and some photographs. Everything else is a mystery. Although his headstone read Jules Bourglay, that was not his real name. Hearsay suggests that he was born in Lyon, France, the son of a wealthy wool merchant, but because of economic ruin or an unhappy love affair, he left for America. Others reported that he was French Canadian. Since he did not speak, many unproven rumors abound: he had considerable real estate holdings; he was a Poughkeepsie businessman; he was Portuguese and a devout Catholic (carrying a prayer book and crucifix); he was a fugitive from justice.

Upon his death in 1889, he was given a pauper's burial at the Sparta Cemetery in Ossining; in 1953, a bronze plaque was added. However, as a result of research by Dan W. DeLuca in *The Old Leather Man* (2008), it became clear that the name on the headstone was not correct. The Ossining Historical Society, which maintains the cemetery, sought professional expertise to see if the body could provide further information. In spring 2011, the burial site was excavated. However, no bones were found – only coffin nails – and thus no DNA evidence was obtained. In May 2011, the nails and some dirt from the original site were set into a new coffin and buried at a more prominent location at the Sparta Cemetery, with a new headstone and commemorative plaque added. The mysterious nomad, still silent, rests.

-Ruth Rosenthal

the white blazes uphill to the cave, which was one of the regular camp sites of the "Leather Man," who wandered along a circular 365-mile route n the 1880s, staying in each of 34 campsites or shelters along the way. The cave provides shelter from the elements but must have been rather ɪncomfortable to sleep in! After exploring this interesting feature, retrace ʏour steps to intersection #29 and turn left (east), now following the "LL" ɒlazes along a wide woods road.

ɪeatherman's Cave

When you reach intersection #28, the Leatherman's Loop Trail turns ɪeft, but you should bear right and continue on a white-blazed trail. After ɪrossing a bridge across a stream, the trail begins a gentle climb. At the top ɒf the rise, the white-blazed trail turns left at a fork and almost immedi-ɪtely reaches intersection #30, where it ends at a junction with the Red and ɪreen Trails. Bear right at the fork, now following red and green blazes. ɪfter continuing past intersection #32, you'll parallel a stream on the left ɪnd climb gradually on a winding woods road. When you reach intersec-ɪion #34, bear right to continue on the Red and Green Trails.

After descending a little and passing a wetland on the left, you'll reach ɪntersection #38. Here, the Red and Green Trails turn left, but you should ɪurn right onto a white-blazed trail. At the next fork, the trail bears left ɪnd crosses under a power line to reach intersection #39. Turn left onto ɪhe Rocks Trail (marked with "RT"-on-white blazes) and climb to the ɪear Rock Petroglyph (on the left side of the trail), which features a carv-ɪng by Native Americans in the shape of a bear.

Continue along the Rocks Trail, which crosses under the power line ɒnce more and descends to reach intersection #60. Turn right at this

Bear Rock Petroglyph

junction and follow a white-blazed trail up to Dancing Rock — a flat rock where farmers used to dance to celebrate the completion of the harvest — then continue along the white-blazed trail, which loops around and descends to end at another junction with the Rocks Trail (intersection #37).

Turn right onto the Rocks Trail, which passes a small pond on the left and descends steadily to the next (unnumbered) junction, where the Red Trail joins from the left. Just ahead, you'll come to intersection #36. Turn right here, leaving the Rocks Trail, and continue along the Red Trail, which heads southeast, following a wide woods road through a valley. At intersection #47, a white-blazed trail begins on the right, but you should bear left to continue along the Red Trail. After climbing a little, the trail bears left around a curve, with seasonal views to the right through the trees across the Stone Hill River valley.

When you reach intersection #48, turn sharply right onto the Rocks Trail and follow it for about 500 feet to Raven Rocks — a spectacular unobstructed overlook over the Stone Hill River valley from a cliff (use caution, as there is a sharp drop here!) After taking in the view, retrace your steps to intersection #48 and turn right onto the Red Trail.

At the base of a descent, you'll come to intersection #21. Turn right, leaving the Red Trail, and follow a white-blazed trail, passing jagged, moss-covered cliffs on the left. After crossing a stream, you'll reach intersection #18. Here, the white-blazed trail ends, and you should turn left onto the Rocks Trail, almost immediately passing the Indian Rock Shelter on the right. Native Americans frequented this spot because the overhanging rocks offered protection from the rain.

Continue ahead on the Rocks Trail, which crosses two streams on wooden bridges. After crossing the second bridge, bear left, uphill, to reach intersection #19, where the Rocks Trail ends at a junction with the Red and Yellow Trails. Turn right, soon passing dramatic cliffs to the left. Continue to follow the Red and Yellow Trails along a wide woods road for about a mile, returning to the parking area where the hike began.

50 Harriman State Park
Iron Mines

This hike leads to interesting remnants of old iron mines and climbs to several panoramic viewpoints from open rocks.

Difficulty: Moderate

Length and Time: About 5.5 miles; about three and one-half hours.

Map: New York-New Jersey Trail Conference Harriman-Bear Mountain Trails Map #119.

Directions: Take N.J. Route 17 North to the New York State Thruway and take the first exit, Exit 15A (Sloatsburg). Turn left at the bottom of the ramp onto N.Y. Route 17 North, and continue through the village of Sloatsburg. Just past the village, turn right at the traffic light, following the sign for "Seven Lakes Drive/Harriman State Park." Follow Seven Lakes Drive for about 7.8 miles to the parking area for Lake Skannatati, on the left side of the road. The turnoff to the parking area is 0.7 mile beyond the Kanawauke Circle.

At the northwest corner of the parking area, find the aqua-blazed Long Path, marked at the trailhead with a distinctive circular disk featuring the Long Path logo. Follow the Long Path along the north shore of the lake on a rocky footpath through a mountain laurel thicket. About half a mile from the start, the trail bends away from the lake, crosses Pine Swamp Brook, and soon passes by a huge rock ledge to the right. A little over a mile from the start, you'll climb to a junction with the yellow-blazed Dunning Trail (laid out in 1933 by Dr. James M. Dunning, a volunteer with the Appalachian Mountain Club).

Bear left and follow the joint Long Path and Dunning Trail, which briefly run together. When the trails split at a fork, take the left branch and continue to follow the yellow blazes of the Dunning Trail, which descends through laurel along a wide woods road.

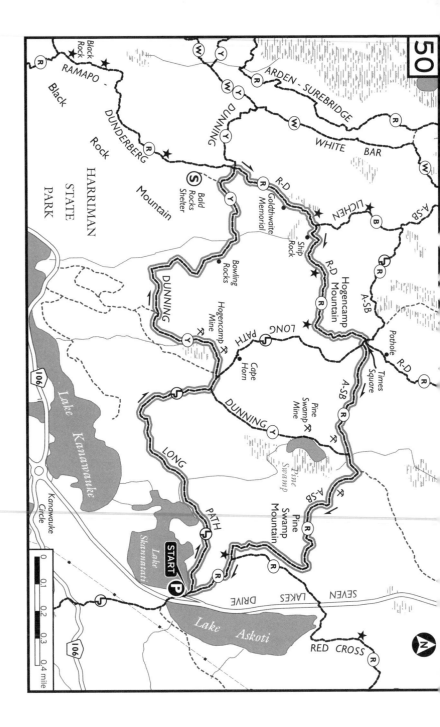

50

When you reach the base of the descent, you'll notice stone foundations on both sides of the trail. These are remnants of the village built in the late 1800s to house workers at the adjacent Hogencamp Mine. According to the late historian James M. Ransom, there were once 20 houses, several barns, a school and a store in this location. Iron ore was mined at this site from 1870 to 1885.

After crossing a brook, you will observe a stone platform to the left. It was built out of tailings – the technical term for the pieces of rock discarded during the mining process. Piles of tailings may be found throughout this mining site. A short distance beyond, you will come to a vertical mine shaft, about 25 feet in diameter, on the right side of the trail. The shaft is filled with water, and a seven-inch cast-iron pipe (once used to dewater the mine) protrudes from it. Use extreme caution when approaching this open shaft! On the opposite side of the trail, iron rods may be seen protruding from a crumbling concrete base (now covered with grass), with a stone-lined well, three feet in diameter, beyond.

Continue south along the Dunning Trail, passing the Pine Swamp to the left. The trail soon curves to the right. One section of the old grassy road followed by the trail has been extensively built up using mine tailings. A section of this road was once known as the "Crooked Road," as it follows many curves around the hills in an attempt to keep the road as level as possible. The lake visible to the left is Little Long Pond.

After a mile on the Dunning Trail, you will come to a very large bare, rocky area, known as "Bowling Rocks" for the boulders that dot the bare rock. The trail continues through a rather open area, with views to the left over the ridge to the south.

About 0.4 mile from Bowling Rocks, after a short climb, you'll reach a junction with the red-dot-on-white-blazed Ramapo-Dunderberg (R-D) Trail. (This junction, which is on the crest of a ridge, is marked by a cairn, but it is easily missed. If you find yourself beginning a long, steady descent, you've gone too far and should return to the highest point, where the junction is located.) Turn right and follow the red-dot-on-white blazes northward. You are now at about the halfway point of the hike.

The R-D Trail passes through an area where the scars of a forest fire are quite noticeable. It crosses a huge open rock surface, known as the Whaleback. Just beyond, look for a plaque on a boulder to the right of the trail. It was placed in memory of George E. Goldthwaite, a member of the Fresh Air Club of New York, who was reputed to have hiked the

Iron Mining in Harriman

The Highlands of northern New Jersey and southern New York contain large quantities of high-quality iron ore, which is buried deeply beneath the ground. Cornelius Board first discovered these iron ore deposits in 1730, and from the middle of the eighteenth century until the end of the nineteenth century, many iron mines were established in the Highlands region – including over 20 mines in the area that now forms Harriman-Bear Mountain State Parks.

The mines were worked by miners who used hand drills, sledge hammers and black powder (later dynamite) to remove the ore from the surrounding rock. The life of a miner was a difficult one. As explained by Edward J. Lenik in his book *Iron Mine Trails* (published by the Trail Conference but now out-of-print), "a miner's workday consisted of exposure to bad air, inhaling rock dust, standing in water and a constant fear of explosion, cave-in or suffocation."

The discovery of iron ore in the Mesabi Range in Minnesota towards the end of the nineteenth century spelled the end of mining in Harriman. The Minnesota iron ore was not of as high a quality as the ore in Harriman, but it was much more accessible and easy to extract from the ground. Even transportation was no longer a problem, as railroads provided an economical and efficient method of transporting the iron ore and its products. By the 1890s, nearly all of the iron mines in Harriman had closed down, but their remnants are still visible today.

---

entire 21-mile R-D Trail in less than five hours – quite a feat for hiking this steep, rocky trail! The trail now steeply descends a rock face to cross a stream on a log bridge, and it climbs to a junction with the blue-blazed Lichen Trail (which leaves to the left). A short distance beyond, the R-D Trail passes beneath a large overhanging rock, known as "Ship Rock" for its resemblance to the prow of a ship.

The trail continues ahead to climb Hogencamp Mountain. The bare rock summit of this 1,353-foot mountain – one of the highest spots in Harriman State Park – affords a wide panorama of the surrounding area. The tower visible straight ahead in the distance is a microwave relay tower for AT&T, located near Gate Hill Road. The trail makes a sharp left turn here and begins a steady descent, soon entering a deep evergreen forest

This is a welcome change from the open rocky expanses that you've followed for the last mile and a half.

At the base of the descent, you'll reach "Times Square," marked by a fireplace next to a huge boulder. It was so named because it is located at the junction of three trails and serves as a popular meeting place for hikers. Turn right here and follow the Arden-Surebridge (A-SB) Trail, marked by inverted-red-triangle-on-white blazes (to be distinguished from the red-dot-on-white blazes of the Ramapo-Dunderberg Trail). The A-SB Trail briefly runs together with the Long Path, but almost immediately bears left and begins a steady descent on an old mining road. In half a mile, it reaches the northern end of the yellow-blazed Dunning Trail, where it crosses a stream below an attractive cascade.

An excavation of the Pine Swamp Mine along the Arden-Surebridge Trail

Just beyond the stream crossing, you will notice a large rectangular cut in the hillside to the left of the trail. This excavation is part of the Pine Swamp Mine, another mining venture in the area, which was opened about 1830 and was worked intermittently until 1880. As you continue along the trail, several other excavations and open pits (now filled with water) may also be seen. One interesting feature, visible in the second excavation, is a long, round depression in the rock – the mark left by the drill bit used to excavate the mine.

After passing these mine openings, the trail bears right and descends into the woods. Soon, you will pass a stone wall and several stone foundations to the left of the trail. These are remnants of the village that once housed the workers at the nearby mine. The A-SB Trail now passes by the northern end of the Pine Swamp and soon begins a steady ascent of Pine Swamp Mountain. Just beyond the summit, a viewpoint affords a broad panorama to the south over Lakes Skannatati and Kanawauke. After passing a junction with the Red Cross Trail, the A-SB Trail descends steeply to the parking area at Lake Skannatati, where the hike began.

Lakes Skannatati and Kanawauke from Pine Swamp Mountain

51 Abram S. Hewitt State Forest
Bearfort Ridge/Quail Trail Loop
from Warwick Turnpike

This loop hike traverses the Bearfort Ridge, with its unusual puddingstone conglomerate rock and pitch pines growing out of bedrock, passes through a rhododendron tunnel, and comes out on the shore of Surprise Lake.

Difficulty: Moderate to strenuous
Length and Time: About 6.0 miles; about four and one-half hours.
Map: New York-New Jersey Trail Conference North Jersey Trails Map #116.
Directions: Take I-287 to Exit 57 and continue on Skyline Drive to its western end at Greenwood Lake Turnpike in Ringwood. Turn right and proceed for 8.4 miles to a Y-intersection with Union Valley Road. Take the right fork and continue ahead for 0.3 mile on Warwick Turnpike. Park in a turnout on the right, just beyond a short concrete bridge.

From the parking turnout, walk east on Warwick Turnpike, going back over the concrete road bridge. Just east of the bridge, you'll see three white blazes that mark the start of the Bearfort Ridge Trail. This will be your route for the first half of the hike. Follow the white blazes uphill through rhododendrons and hemlocks. In about 500 feet, the trail joins a woods road that comes in from the right. Just beyond, follow the white blazes as the trail turns left, leaving the road. (The orange-blazed Quail Trail, which continues ahead along the road, will be your return route.) The white-blazed trail continues to ascend on a wide footpath. After crossing a stream, it levels off through mountain laurel. A little over half a mile from the start, the trail descends briefly to cross a wider stream and continues through a rhododendron grove. At the end of the rhododendrons,

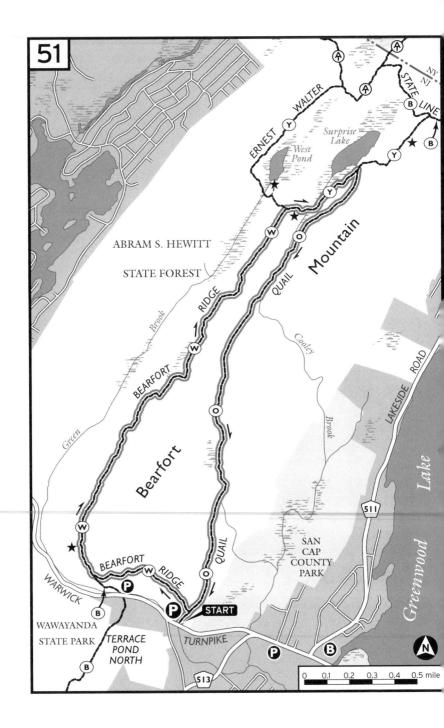

51

ERNEST WALTER

West Pond

Surprise Lake

ABRAM S. HEWITT

STATE FOREST

Mountain

RIDGE

QUAIL

Brook

Cooley

Brook

BEARFORT

LAKESIDE ROAD

Green

Bearfort

Lake

Greenwood

511

511

QUAIL

SAN
CAP
COUNTY
PARK

BEARFORT   RIDGE

WARWICK

P

P

START

WAWAYANDA

STATE PARK   TERRACE
POND
NORTH

TURNPIKE

P

B

N

0   0.1   0.2   0.3   0.4   0.5 mile

513

a blue-blazed trail which leads to Warwick Turnpike goes off to the left. Continue ahead on the white-blazed trail.

The Bearfort Ridge Trail now begins a steady, rather steep climb. About a mile from the start, it passes a large, lichen-covered outcrop to the right. It continues to climb until it reaches the crest of the ridge, marked by pitch pines. Here, a large conglomerate rock outcrop to the left offers an expansive view to the south. Upper Greenwood Lake is visible through the trees to the west and, on a clear day, the New York City skyline may be seen in the distance to the east.

After taking in the view and resting from the steep climb, continue ahead, following the Bearfort Ridge Trail north along the puddingstone conglomerate ridge, through pitch pines. You'll make a brief but steep climb, and the vegetation will change to hemlocks and laurels. The trail continues at an elevation of about 1,300 feet, having climbed about 600 feet from the trailhead. After about half a mile of walking along the ridge, the trail crosses an open rock outcrop, with several large glacial erratics, passes more pitch pines, and descends to cross a wet area.

The trail continues to wind through a hemlock forest, passing a limited viewpoint through the trees to the right. About two miles from the start, it comes out on a rock ledge overlooking a swamp to the west. Here, a narrow wedge of the bedrock has split away from the main ledge, forming a deep crevice. This is a good place to take a break.

DAN BALOGH

This narrow wedge of bedrock has split away from the main ledge

Abram S. Hewitt: A Man of Mettle

His brusque, no-nonsense manner had earned Abram S. Hewitt the nickname "growler" from reporters: it was said that saloon keepers couldn't find an epithet too harsh. And in his two-year term as Mayor of New York City, his unyielding devotion to reform had angered, variously, his own party, the police, immigrants and even some labor groups.

So, when he lost his bid for reelection in 1888, it was no surprise. As mayor, many of his reforms had been stifled by Albany; home rule did not come into force until a new state constitution was enacted in 1894. But the plans he put forward – for the first subways, for small parks in crowded neighborhoods and for controlling a forest of utility poles choking the city – were all eventually adopted.

Hewitt's loss of the 1888 mayoralty race marked the end of his role as a public official – which had included a role in ousting the Tweed Ring, five terms in the U.S. House of Representatives and the chairmanship of the Democratic Party as it was returning to national prominence.

During the Civil War, his intrigues helped to ease a shortage of rifled muskets for Union soldiers. Domestic iron was not of sufficient quality for gun metal, with the result that the iron had to be imported from England. Hewitt, in a bit of industrial espionage, learned the process, and by 1863 he was producing superior quality metal. Later he was among the first to implement new steel-making technology.

Hewitt had entered politics as a civic duty and brought to it the same qualities of efficiency and progressiveness that had made him one of the most innovative industrialists of his time. He had come from a humble background and became a protégé of and, later, son-in-law to Peter Cooper, the inventor, industrialist and philanthropist. With Cooper's son Edward, he established the Trenton Iron Works as well as the Long Pond Ironworks along the Wanaque River. Vast forested tracts in the Jersey Highlands were needed to support these ironworks. This 2,000-acre state forest, acquired by the state in the early 1950s, formed a part of the lands purchased by Hewitt to supply charcoal for the furnaces at the ironworks.

Upon Hewitt's death in 1903, President Theodore Roosevelt, an opponent in the 1886 mayoralty race, called him "an inspiration to the decent performance of duty by all who wish well of the state."

-Jim Simpson

When you're ready to continue, proceed north along the trail, which climbs to a rock outcrop with a huge boulder. It continues along a whaleback rock, through pitch pines, and reaches a limited viewpoint to the east. The trail now descends steeply, through hemlocks and laurels. After crossing a stream amid jumbled rocks at the base of the descent, the trail climbs to a rock outcrop studded with pitch pines, which offers a limited east-facing view through the trees.

From the outcrop, the trail descends gently, levels off, and then climbs to another rock outcrop – marked by several cedar trees – with a magnificent view to the north and east. Surprise Lake is visible to the north, and Sterling Forest and the Wyanokies may be seen to the east, with an arm of the Monksville Reservoir visible in the distance. You've now gone three miles from the start of the hike.

View of Surprise Lake from the junction of the Bearfort Ridge and Ernest Walter Trails

The white-blazed Bearfort Ridge Trail ends here, at a junction with the yellow-blazed Ernest Walter Trail. Turn right and follow the yellow-blazed trail as it heads downhill through a rocky area and soon crosses a stream. The trail continues through a dense rhododendron grove, with the thick rhododendrons forming a canopy over the trail in places. About half a mile from the end of the Bearfort Ridge Trail, you'll notice an orange-blazed trail coming in from the right. Continue ahead on the yellow trail

Surprise Lake

for about 100 feet to an open area which overlooks Surprise Lake – a pristine, spring-fed lake. This is another good spot to take a break.

Now retrace your steps along the yellow trail, but when you come to the junction of the orange trail, bear left and follow the orange blazes. You're now on the Quail Trail, a woods road that will lead you back to the start of the hike. Follow the orange blazes as they climb gently for a short distance and then begin a steady descent. In three-quarters of a mile, you'll cross a stream on rocks. This crossing can be a little tricky if the water is high. In 500 feet, the trail crosses another stream and then climbs briefly, soon resuming its descent.

A third stream is crossed in another mile. A third of a mile beyond, be sure to bear right, as another woods road goes off to the left. When the orange-blazed trail ends at a junction with the white-blazed trail, continue ahead along the road and then bear right, following the white blazes downhill, back to the trailhead.

52 Harriman State Park
Dunderberg Spiral Railway and Bald Mountain

This loop hike follows portions of the never-completed Dunderberg Spiral Railway, climbs to the summit of Bald Mountain, and passes several expansive viewpoints over the Hudson River.

Difficulty: Strenuous
Length and Time: About 7.0 miles; about five and one-half hours.
Map: New York-New Jersey Trail Conference Harriman-Bear Mountain Trails Map #119.
Directions: Take the Palisades Interstate Parkway to its northern terminus at the Bear Mountain Circle and proceed south on U.S. Route 9W for about four miles. At the base of a downhill section of the road, as the road reaches the river level, you'll notice a large parking area on the right side of the road. (A side road, Old Ayers Road to Jones Point, leaves sharply to the left here.) Park in this gravel parking area.

From the parking area, walk south on Route 9W for a few hundred feet. Just beyond road signs for Routes 9W and 202, you'll see three blue blazes and three red-dot-on-white blazes on a tree adjacent to the road. These blazes mark the start of the Timp-Torne (blue) and Ramapo-Dunderberg (red-dot-on-white) trails. You'll be following the Timp-Torne Trail for the first part of the hike and returning on the Ramapo-Dunderberg Trail.

Follow the blue and red-dot-on-white blazes into the woods along a level footpath through an area of tangled vines. Soon, the trail will bear left and climb stone steps, and you'll reach a stone-arch tunnel to the left. This tunnel is a remnant of the Dunderberg Spiral Railway, the construction of which commenced in 1890. The plan was to have the rail cars pulled up the mountain on a cable incline by a stationary steam engine,

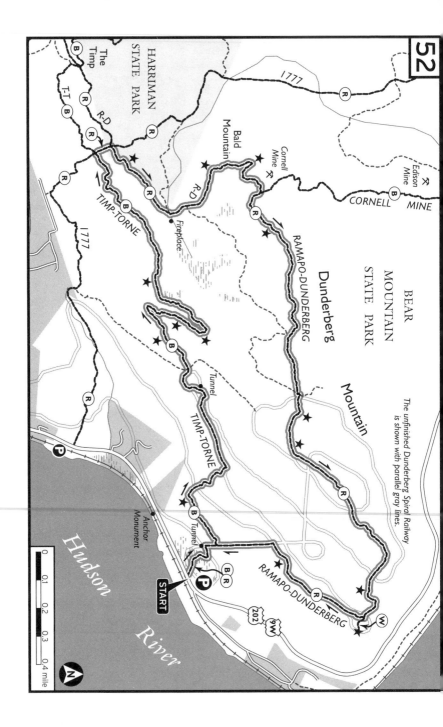

The unfinished Dunderberg Spiral Railway is shown with parallel gray lines.

START

Anchor Monument

Hudson River

HARRIMAN STATE PARK

BEAR MOUNTAIN STATE PARK

Dunderberg Mountain

The Timp

Bald Mountain

Cornell Mine

Edison Mine

CORNELL MINE

Fireplace

Tunnel

Tunnel

TIMP-TORNE

RAMAPO-DUNDERBERG

RAMAPO-DUNDERBERG

52

1777

0   0.1   0.2   0.3   0.4 mile

N

The lower tunnel of the Dunderberg Spiral Railway

with the downhill journey being made by gravity. Large sums were spent on the project, two tunnels were partially completed, and much of the line was graded, but the promoters ran out of funds, and the railway was never finished. The tunnel you see to the left was designed to allow the ascending trains to pass over the route of the descending trains.

The trail now bears right and ascends more steeply on switchbacks and stone steps. At the top of the climb, you'll reach a junction. Here, the red-dot-on-white blazes continue ahead, while the blue blazes turn left. Follow the blue blazes of the Timp-Torne Trail, which head southwest,

The Dunderberg Spiral Railway

The Dunderberg Spiral Railway project, conceived in 1889 by entrepreneurs from New York City, was inspired by the Mauch Chunk Summit Hill and Switchback Railroad of Mauch Chunk (now Jim Thorpe), Pa. Henry J. Mumford – who was to become treasurer of the Dunderberg Spiral Railway – and his brother leased that abandoned coal mine railroad in 1870 and operated it successfully as a pleasure ride. The passenger cars were pulled by cable up the mountain and returned to the base by gravity.

Realizing that Dunderberg Mountain was easily accessible from New York City by the Hudson River steamships and the recently completed West Shore Railroad, the entrepreneurs engaged Mumford to build a similar spiral railway on Dunderberg. On November 9, 1889 a corporation was organized to construct the railway. The prospectus estimated that there would be at least 300,000 passengers per year!

The plan was to have the cars pulled by a stationary steam engine up two inclined planes to the summit, about 900 feet above the Hudson River, where the passengers would disembark. After taking in the scenery, they would reboard the cars, which would coast by gravity down a nine-mile route, with several switchbacks and spiral curves. The average grade was to be about 1.9%, and the prospectus stated that the railway was designed to offer "a surprise at every turn" and "a constantly changing view." It was also planned to erect a hotel at the summit of the mountain.

Work on the railway started in the spring of 1890, but after a year the enterprise faltered. The precise reason for its collapse is not known. However, a series of questionable deals by the Holland Trust Company – which was financing the Spiral Railway – came to light in 1890, and this may have made the investors reluctant to commit additional funds. In any event, after about $1,000,000 had been spent, work ended by the spring of 1891, and the project was abandoned.

The railway was never completed, but about two-thirds of the route was graded, and two tunnels were built (although the upper tunnel was not finished). Today, over a century later, the graded portions of the railway are still evident, and the Timp-Torne and Ramapo-Dunderberg Trails have been routed to follow several graded sections, passing both of the tunnels. This hike includes these graded sections of the railway.

parallel to the river. The trail continues to climb, but on a more moderate grade. Soon, views of the river appear through the trees.

In another ten minutes, the trail turns right and heads away from the river. After going through a rocky area on switchbacks, you'll arrive at a graded section of the railway. Follow the blue blazes as they turn left and continue along this level, graded embankment for the next quarter of a mile. With the railbed ahead blocked off by fallen trees, the trail turns right and climbs to the next higher level, where it turns left. Just ahead you'll come to the portal of an unfinished tunnel, intended for use by the descending trains.

A hiker along a graded section of the Dunderberg Spiral Railway

The trail now returns to the lower level of the graded railway, which it follows around a curved embankment, with views over the Hudson River. The curved roadbed ends at the opposite end of the uncompleted tunnel, but the trail bears left, crosses a stream and then a woods road, and climbs to another viewpoint, looking south along the river. Beyond the viewpoint, the trail is relatively level, and even descends a little.

Watch for a very sharp right turn in the trail, which reverses direction and heads northeast on a switchback, uphill at first. After another level stretch, the trail reaches a panoramic viewpoint, looking both north and south along the Hudson. Peekskill is visible at a bend in the river to the north, and the New York City skyline may be seen in the distance to the south.

From the viewpoint, the trail again reverses direction and heads southwest on a relatively level footpath. After passing another panoramic viewpoint that looks south along the Hudson, the trail climbs gradually, with cairns (piles of rocks) marking the way in places. From the crest of the rise, there are views of the ridge to the north, which will be your return route. The trail now begins a steady descent, with rock steps provided along one steep section. At the base of the descent, the trail intersects a woods road, with the junction marked by a small cairn.

Turn right here, leaving the blue-blazed Timp-Torne Trail, and follow the woods road, which is blazed with white "1777" blazes, commemorating the use of this road by the British in their attack on Fort Montgomery during the Revolutionary War. You'll be following this road for only about two or three minutes. When you see the red-dot-on-white blazes of the Ramapo-Dunderberg Trail crossing the road, turn right and follow these blazes. You'll be following the red-dot-on-white blazes for the remainder of the hike.

The Ramapo-Dunderberg Trail climbs to a viewpoint from open rocks, with Bear Mountain (identified by the stone tower on its summit) visible ahead (through the trees), and Bald Mountain to the right. The trail continues over a rise through dense mountain laurel thickets, then descends to briefly join a woods road that crosses a stream at a fireplace. Just beyond, follow the red-dot-on-white blazes as the trail bears left and begins to climb Bald Mountain.

After a level section, the trail climbs to the summit ridge, which it reaches at a south-facing viewpoint. The trail continues along the relatively level ridge, then makes its final climb to the summit. Just before reaching the 1,115-foot summit of Bald Mountain, the trail makes a very sharp right turn. Continue ahead on a white-blazed side trail to the summit, and proceed to a rock outcrop just north of the summit that offers a panoramic view to the north over the Hudson River, Iona Island and the Bear Mountain Bridge. You've now gone a little more than halfway (and have finished nearly all of the climbing), so this is a good place to take a break.

When you're ready to continue, return to the trail, and be sure to take the left fork. The trail begins to descend, passing an opening of the Cornell Mine on the right. At the base of the descent, the blue-blazed Cornell Mine Trail leaves to the left. Continue ahead on the Ramapo-Dunderberg

Bear Mountain Bridge and Anthony's Nose from the summit of Bald Mountain

Trail, which follows the ridge of Dunderberg Mountain, with several ups and downs.

About a mile from the junction with the Cornell Mine Trail, the Ramapo-Dunderberg Trail briefly joins a woods road and then climbs to a high point with a view. After a slight descent, it climbs steeply to reach an even better viewpoint. You can see the Hudson River to the right (south), with Bear Mountain and the Bear Mountain Bridge to the left (north). Continue along the ridge of Dunderberg Mountain, passing through thickets of dense birch saplings.

After descending from the ridge, steeply in places, you'll notice a viewpoint from a rock outcrop just to the right of the trail, with Peekskill directly across the river. A short distance beyond, as the trail curves to the right, a short white-blazed trail leads ahead to another viewpoint. The trail soon joins another graded section of the railbed, with several gaps where the grading was never finished, and passes more views over the Hudson River.

At a stone abutment (built to carry the cars going up the mountain), the trail turns sharply left and descends steadily along the right-of-way

Stone abutment of the Dunderberg Spiral Railway

excavated for the cable incline. After about ten minutes, you'll reach a junction with the blue-blazed Timp-Torne Trail. Continue ahead, following both blue and red-dot-on-white blazes back to the parking area where the hike began.

Index

We invite you to join

the organization of hikers, environmentalists, and volunteers whose skilled efforts have produced this edition of *Harriman Trails: A Guide and History*.

The **New York-New Jersey Trail Conference**, founded in 1920, is a federation of member clubs and individuals dedicated to providing recreational hiking opportunities in the New York-New Jersey region, and to representing the interests and concerns of the hiking community. The Trail Conference is a volunteer-directed public service organization committed to:

- Developing, building, and maintaining hiking trails.

- Protecting hiking trail lands through support and advocacy.

- Educating the public in the responsible use of trails and the natural environment.

Join now and as a member:

- You will receive the *Trail Walker*, a quarterly source of news, information, and events concerning area trails and hiking. The *Trail Walker* lists many hikes in the New York-New Jersey metropolitan area, led by some of our more than 100 member hiking clubs.

- You are entitled to purchase our authoritative maps and books at significant discounts. These highly accurate, up-to-date trail maps, printed on durable Tyvek, and our informative guidebooks enable you to hike with assurance throughout the region.

- You are also entitled to discounts of 10% (and sometimes more!) at most local outdoor stores and at many mountain inns and lodges.

- Most importantly, you will become part of a community of volunteer activists with similar passions and ideas.

Your membership helps give us the clout to protect and maintain more trails. As a member of the **New York-New Jersey Trail Conference**, you will be helping to ensure that public access to nature will continue to expand.

NEW YORK-NEW JERSEY TRAIL CONFERENCE
156 Ramapo Valley Road ◆ Mahwah, NJ 07430 ◆ (201) 512-9348
www.nynjtc.org ◆ info@nynjtc.org

Other Hiking Books Available From the Trail Conference!

Authoritative Hiking Maps and Books
by the Volunteers Who Maintain the Trails

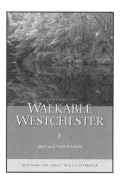

WALKABLE WESTCHESTER

Second Edition (2014), Jane and Walt Daniels

A comprehensive guide to trails throughout Westchester County, this second edition mentions over 200 places to walk with over 600 miles of trails. It includes historical information and maps for most parks, and indicates which parks are suitable for the handicapped, bikes, horses, dogs and cross-country skiing. The parks are arranged by size, and a locator map is provided. Information on public transportation is also included.

sc. 448 p. 6 x 9, B&W photos and maps

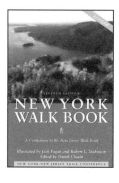

NEW YORK WALK BOOK

Seventh Edition, Revised (2005), Edited by Daniel Chazin

The hikers' "bible" since 1923, it is still the same indispensable regional reference book. Full trail descriptions with maps, sections on geology, history, hiking tips, and much more. The magnificent sketches include many new ones by Jack Fagan. This last printing h updated trail descriptions and completely revised chapters for Black Rock Forest, Storm King, and Sterling Forest.

sc. 484 p. 5 3/8 x 8 1/8, B&W illustrations, full color maps

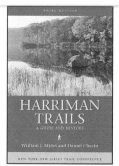

HARRIMAN TRAILS

Third Edition (2010), William J. Myles and Daniel Chazin

Bill Myles' original guidebook to the trails in Harriman/Be Mountain State Parks has been completely revised by Dan Chazin. It is much more than a guide. Years of research ha produced a fine history as well. Marked and unmarked trai lakes, roads and mines are all covered in depth. A comple reference work, with many historical photos.

sc. 421 p. 5 3/8 x 8 1/8, B&W photos

Visit www.nynjtc.org—for more information and newest products